Michael Bernard Buckley

Diary of a Tour in America

Michael Bernard Buckley

Diary of a Tour in America

ISBN/EAN: 9783337014957

Printed in Europe, USA, Canada, Australia, Japan

Cover: Foto ©ninafisch / pixelio.de

More available books at **www.hansebooks.com**

DIARY

OF A

TOUR IN AMERICA.

"In a new circle every character is a study, and every incident an adventure."
DISRAELI's *Lothair*, ch. iv.

BY

REV. M. B. BUCKLEY,

OF CORK, IRELAND.

A Special Missionary in North America and Canada in 1870 and 1871.

EDITED BY HIS SISTER KATE BUCKLEY.

Dedicated to the Irish People at Home and Abroad.

PUBLISHED FOR THE EDITRESS IN GREAT BRITAIN, IRELAND, AMERICA AND CANADA.

DUBLIN:
SEALY, BRYERS & WALKER,
94, 95 & 96 MIDDLE ABBEY STREET.
1889.

(ALL RIGHTS RESERVED.)

A WORD TO THE READER.

At the instance—indeed I might say the urgent request—of many friends of my deceased brother, the following pages are, after many years, given to the public. There is no pretence at book-making in this "Diary of an American Tour," written by an Irish Missionary Priest in the United States and Canada. The jottings in his journal were evidently the impulsive impressions of the moment; and it is a matter of question with me whether they were ever designed for publication, or only meant as pleasant reminders of interesting circumstances and events.

Yielding, however, to the oft-repeated suggestions of friends, lay and cleric, on both sides of the Atlantic, I commit the Diary to the Press, and to the indulgent consideration of the Irish people the world over — " indulgent consideration," advisedly. There may be found, here and there, thoughts and opinions savouring of a too free criticism of persons, parties and principles; and perhaps had the writer been spared, and induced to supervise publication, some angularities would have been filed down, and a few personal animadversions omitted. I cannot undertake to edit the work out of its original character ; besides, many of Father Buckley's best friends have urged that, as his character and capacity as a Patriot and a Priest are disclosed in these casual notes, it would be unfair to his memory to take from their point and piquancy by a too punctilious pruning.

With this apologetic explanation I send forth Father Buckley's experiences of a Tour on the American Continent.

KATE BUCKLEY.

CONTENTS.

CHAPTER.	PAGE.
I. THE VOYAGE FROM IRELAND,	1
II. ASHORE,	14
III. NIAGARA,	28
IV. THE BRITISH FLAG AGAIN,	37
V. QUEBEC AND THE SAGUENAY,	66
VI. THE LAND OF THE BLUE NOSES,	87
VII. ST. JOHN. GOOD-BYE TO CANADA,	104
VIII. THE "ATHENS OF AMERICA," AND SOME OF THE ATHENIANS,	136
IX. THE EMPIRE CITY,	210
X. "A PRIESTLY FENIAN,"	229
XI. NEW YORK IN SUMMER,	252
XII. A TRIP IN LEATHERSTOCKING'S LAND,	309
XIII. CONCLUSION,	328

APPENDIX.

FUGITIVE PIECES IN VERSE AND PROSE,	345
FACETIÆ.	381

DIARY

OF A

TOUR IN NORTH AMERICA.

CHAPTER I.

THE VOYAGE FROM IRELAND.

May 22nd, 1870.—A clergyman and myself were appointed by our Bishop to make a tour through America for the purpose of raising funds for the completion of the Catholic Cathedral of Cork. We arranged to sail by the Cunard Royal Mail steamer "China," which was to leave Queenstown on Sunday, May the 22nd. The day at length arrived, and, accompanied by an immense concourse of friends, we proceeded by the 2 o'clock train to Queenstown direct. On arriving there we found a still larger gathering of our fellow-citizens, who had come to bid us farewell. The "Jackall" (tender) was soon filled, and, when it could hold no more, slipped its moorings and proceeded to the "China," which lay within the harbour's mouth. The hundreds who could not come on board saluted us with waving hats and handkerchiefs from the pier. We reached the "China," and, much to the surprise of the passengers who had come from Liverpool, the "Jackall" discharged its whole living freight on board. There was frequent shaking of hands with us, last words of hope and encouragement, words of love and promised remembrance, parting sighs and tears; this lasted for more than half-an-hour, the big ship examined in every nook and corner by the curious visitors, and the whole spectacle brilliant and gay with decent citizens and comely women, from the lady of rank to the kitchen-maid, for all love the priest alike. Then the whistle sounded a retreat, parting words and hand-shaking were renewed and redoubled, and the "Jackall" became filled once more with its gay freightage; she accompanied us out until we got fairly to sea; then she was loosed, and our distance became greater and greater every moment. Suddenly our parting friends raised a shout, a cheer, such as can be given only in Ireland; it was again and again repeated, hats and handkerchiefs waving from every hand, every eye turned towards us, while we, standing on the bridge, returned the adieux of our friends with all the vigour and earnestness which can be expressed in the gyration of a hat.

Soon the tender was lost to sight, and we stood out to sea. We then proceeded to the saloon, where dinner was prepared. Our cabin passengers numbered 86; steerage, 350. We had a table to ourselves. With us were Mr. John Morgan Smith and his wife, married only the Thursday before. After dinner we proceeded to the deck, where we viewed with pleasure the waning beauties of the Southern coast. I see far off the hills to whose tops I had often climbed, and nearer, the bays and creeks where I had bathed and boated in the days of old lang syne. Shall I ever return to behold them again? God only knows. This Atlantic is a very wide expanse of water, and big ships go down into the sea, and are never heard of more.

We sing as twilight falls, and Mrs. Smith, a handsome young American lady, who has a splendid voice, attracts a good deal of attention by her part of the performance.

Thus, in a half-dreamy state of feeling, with a curious mingling of pleasure and sadness, we spend our first evening on the broad Atlantic.

Monday, May 23rd.—I am the only one of my party, numbering six, that appears at breakfast; all are confined to their berths with sea-sickness. I pace the deck from 6 till the breakfast hour; the birds that last evening followed in our wake have all disappeared, and we are now apparently the sole inhabitants of the vasty deep. No craft appears in sight the whole live-long day; we are as much alone as if the Western country had never been discovered; the wind blows freshly and the ship pitches pleasantly, and I enjoy the whole scene.

I now begin to look about me, and to view the passengers. We often hear of the fraternal feeling that grows up at sea among those who travel together for any length of time; I wait to see when this feeling is to spring up, but the process is slow; no more than three people have spoken to me to-day, a Mr. Springer, of Springfield, Ill., a Mr. Moorehead, of Philadelphia, a Dr. Strong, of Cleveland, Ohio. The first of these gentlemen is a pure American, a lawyer, and of most agreeable manners. Mr. Moorehead is an elderly gentleman, tall and active; he is accompanied by his wife, her daughter, Miss Badger, his son, a fine young gentleman, and Miss Bradbury, a friend; they are returning after a tour through Europe, Egypt and the Holy Land. Mr. Moorhead opens a conversation with me. He is of American birth, but of North of Ireland parents; is a member of the celebrated New York Banking firm, J. Cook and Co. Dr. Strong is an Irishman, over twenty years in America, thoroughly Hibernian, with the unmistakable accent, and a fund of quiet humour; he has made his fortune; and is returning with his wife and son, after a year's stay in Ireland.

Up to noon to-day we have made from Queenstown 241 miles.

Tuesday, May 24th.—This day is fine, and the wind falls to our stern; so we hoist sails and the vessel looks more important in her full dress. At breakfast only two of our party besides myself appear, and even they fly precipitately at the bare sight of edibles which only stimulate the appetites of myself and my equally fortunate fellow-voyagers.

By a chasm created at the dinner table owing to the absence of two young ladies, I am thrown into immediate proximity with a young gentleman, who I find is a Frenchman. He is studying a French-English conversation book, while I am engaged at Ollendorff's French method. A happy thought strikes me—to enter into a compact with him that during the voyage I should teach him English while he taught me French. He is delighted with the proposal. "Je ne demands pas mieux," he says. So we proceed to business at once. We exchange cards, and he learns to pronounce my name though not without an effort. Strange, however, as my name was to him, his was more extraordinary to me. He was named "Jules Osuchowski,"—born in Paris of a Polish father. He can translate English very well, but can scarcely speak a word; while his whole ambition is to speak it as well as I speak French. After every meal—and there are four each day—we translate and converse, and make very rapid progress.

Up to noon to-day we have made 303 miles, but we feel very lonely, having seen no signs of life anywhere beyond the ship—no birds, no fish, no passing sail all round the horizon.

To-day I make new acquaintances, and am compensated for the absence of my sick friends.

Wednesday, May 25th.—The day is very wild and stormy; the ship rolls and pitches and the wind makes a tremendous noise through the cordage and canvas over our heads; it is impossible to walk a yard in a straight line, and I am quite sore from constant leaning against tables and railings in the saloon. I am deprived of all control of my power of movement, and rush frantically into the arms of a gentleman who has his back fixed for safety against the wall. I join with a few gentlemen in a game of whist to kill time; but the cards are tossed about and get mixed, and we must give up.

Outside the saloon door, at the head of the staircase, a number of us gather and we sing, sometimes solos and sometimes in concert. This gives great satisfaction to ourselves, but much more, it appears, to people lying in their berths who have nothing to do but to listen. They afterwards declared they were delighted.

I go on deck with some difficulty, as the wind sternly opposes my progress. It is a magnificent spectacle—the huge waves rushing by at a furious pace; great seas rolling into the ship at the bow and filling the air with spray; the sailors clad in shapeless garments of oil cloths, hoisting or reefing sails; the boatswain's whistle or his loud voice directing their movements, and the great ship riding on in its toilsome course with all the grace and majesty of a high-mettled charger. I and a few others stand near the funnel which shelters us by its bulk, and warms by its heat.

The wind rises higher and higher; it roars louder and louder, and I begin to fear a hurricane, when the captain (Macaulay) appears amongst us, looking cool and whiffing a cigar with the nonchalance of a paterfamilias in the midst of his penates. "Good morning, gentlemen!" he says in a gruff basso. "Good morning, captain," we reply. "Fine weather this!" he cries in the same tone, but apparently with a keen sensation of pleasure. We all burst out laughing at the captain's notion of fine weather, but we felt relieved nevertheless. I had intended to ask the captain whether this was a hurricane, but felt ashamed after his remark; but at length a squall came that made the ship lurch and halt in her course like a frighted steed; it whistled like a tortured spirit, and roared though the rigging in a hideous discord of agony. "Captain," I asked, with affected coolness, "I suppose this is what you would call——' I was still ashamed to say hurricane—"at least half a gale?" "Half a gale!" cried the skipper, contemptuously. "No; this is what we sailors call a *stormy wind*," and he turned on his heel, chuckling at the landsman's notion of a gale. *Stormy wind*, thought I. Good gracious, what must a hurricane be!

I go into the saloon, and my French friend and I do a big lesson of French and English. The difficulty of going outside throws us very much together, and we have all got thoroughly into the fraternizing spirit. I find one of the passengers has got himself into a warm controversy with an Indiana gentleman who contends that the utmost latitude should be allowed for obtaining divorce between man and wife. He would look upon the slightest inequality of temper as a sufficient ground. The other gentleman has the support of the general moral sense of the passengers, and carries his point. The Indianian is shunned for the rest of the voyage, especially as he subsequently proclaimed himself an Atheist.

To-day we made 330 miles up to noon. The clock is put back half-an-hour every day at 12. We discover two ships to-day in the offing, and we are pleased with the additional sight of Mother Carey's chickens.

Thursday, May 26th.—The wind has abated and the sea is calm, the sun shines, and the air is balmy. Almost all the passengers come on deck, and we now see many faces for the first time—faces of those who had been sick. There is a general feeling of pleasure all around; the steerage passengers too are all up and seem to enjoy the happy change. Two large ships are in view—one passes us at right angles almost half a mile ahead. We speak her. She is the "Mary Carson," bound from England to New York. She salutes us by a flag raised above the stern, and we return it in the same way. "A rather stern salutation!" I say to a few bystanders. "One would expect it to have been made at the *bow*," said Mr. Springer, and he receives the applause due to his superior wit.

After dinner a large party of us sit on deck—the Moorehead party—including the Misses Badger and Bradbury forming the nucleus of it. We have a series of songs all round. My friend and I have to do the most of the singing. Miss Badger is very smart, lively, and pretty. She throws out a vast collection of conundrums, but I answer them easily, having heard them all before. Her memory for events is equally good, so we are all very pleasant and happy, and the voyage loses the tedium of monotony. Dr. Strong and I spend the evening with the purser—a very agreeable man.

From noon of yesterday up to noon to-day we only made 244 miles owing to the strong wind. My Frenchman speaks English much better, and I am becoming quite *au fait*.

Friday, May 27th.—The sea is very calm to-day but the air is bitterly cold—cold as winter. I don't mind it as I have a grand frieze coat which excites the envy of some American gentlemen, one of whom vainly offers twice its value for it. Nearly every one is on deck to-day. The great cold, we are told, indicates that we are not far from icebergs—an unpleasant discovery—but fortunately there is no fog, so that should we encounter those terrors of the deep we would not be wholly unprepared for the event. But no iceberg appears; we see, however, two or three ships, but they are far away, and a huge whale is seen near us, spouting up columns of water from the smooth surface of the sea.

The gentlemen of our company, amongst all of whom, with few exceptions, a warm spirit of friendship seems to have started up, amuse themselves by betting on the number of miles we will have run up to noon; this they do every day; we make 309, and several pounds are won and lost on the event.

After lunch we have a great gathering on deck, the Mooreheads, Mr. Springer and ourselves. Mr. Springer is a general favourite, and laughs so heartily at everything and is so natural and genial. We all have great singing and punning. The whole body of cabin passengers flock to hear the songs and jokes. I tell my Frenchman story and we produce quite a sensational effect.

At four o'clock we proceed to dinner, and just as we are in the middle of that important portion of the day's business, the cry rings through the cabin, "An iceberg, an iceberg." The passion of hunger fiercely rules the human breast, but curiosity appears to hold over mankind a still more exciting influence. There was a grand rush from the dinner-table to see the iceberg. I gazed through the window above me and saw it at a great distance ahead, so I resolved to finish my dinner and view the wonder afterwards, which I did. The deck was crowded, even ladies who had not left their berths from the beginning flocked up to see the iceberg—there it was, when we were nearest to it, almost a quarter of a mile distant, a huge mountain of ice standing a hundred feet out of the water and about eight hundred feet in length, solitary, white and formidable, slowly floating away from its arctic home and seeking involuntarily the latitudes where it must melt and perish. It was a novel and magnificent spectacle.

All the passengers are on the most familiar terms; we sing and tell stories together on deck, the ladies reclining in easy and rocking chairs, the gentlemen in all kinds of attitudes; and there is great laughing and merriment

Miss Badger, who is very clever and interesting, goes in for amusement in a business-like manner; she organizes concerts for the saloon every evening, in which her friend, Miss Bradbury and I are to be the principal performers; these concerts are duly advertised to come off at half-past nine, after supper, and we use the phraseology of full-dress and reserved seats, and carriages ordered at eleven, and a good deal more that amuses us by its very innocence; indeed it struck me forcibly that a sea voyage has a tendency to develop all the good qualities of human nature and to keep the bad in abeyance.

Saturday, May 28th.—Very cold, winterish, biting weather. We are on the banks of Newfoundland; it is always cold here we are told. Cape Race is the nearest land, but it is a distance of 195 miles. All passengers come on deck. There are fishing boats all around us. We see whales and shoals of porpoises and ships enough now. There is great betting on the distance since yesterday; we make 331 miles. A Jew named Soboloski is nearly always successful; he is a pearl fisher, and one who has travelled the world. I should not like to bet with him upon anything. We have among the passengers men and women from all parts of the world— a strange gathering—but almost all speak the English language.

Sunday, May 29th.—Tremendous fog, the steam-whistle sounding all the time, a very unpleasant sound, for it warns of the danger of collision, and a collision on the high seas is a fearful thing. I find out a young Irishman, Dr. O'Brien, who had been either too modest or too sick to make himself known until now. He has an awful Irish accent and manner of speaking. "Good morrow, Doctor," I begin. "Good morrow, Father B.," he replies; "foggy weather, this—very." "I trust," said I, "there is no danger of a collision." "Well," said he, in a tone and with an accent impossible to put to paper, "if we meet any of them small crafts, we'd be bully enough for 'em! but if we meet our match—begor, that would be a horse of another colour."

Prayers are announced for $10\frac{1}{2}$ in the saloon. The doctor (of the ship) is to read the Service. With a delicate attention which I appreciated highly, the Captain, of his own impulse, placed his own cabin at my disposal, where I could give prayers for such Catholics as I might find on board. I could only find a Mr. Loving, a Spanish gentleman, and Doctor O'Brien. The ladies were indisposed, and the young Frenchman would not come, although solicited. I recited the rosary. After the saloon service was over, a deputation waited on me, with a request that I would deliver a sermon for the whole congregation; but I was deterred by the novelty and difficulty of the task, and respectfully declined. There was no singing, nor betting, nor indeed anything *profane*, in the mildest sense of the word; but we consoled ourselves by talking over the concert of the previous evening. A volunteer, a young gentleman from America, amused us very much by his imitation of the mocking bird. Even the Frenchman came out spontaneously with some French ditties.

This was a stupid day; we registered 332 miles since yesterday. After dinner fog came on, and the steam-whistle shed a gloom over us all.

Monday, May 30th.—The whistle went on all night and

all morning. Everything dull and uninteresting. We see nothing, and fear everything. The Frenchman and I spend half the day at the languages, and have both made wonderful progress. All crowd into the saloon, and the day and night are spent in chat, and anecdote, song, and other amusements.

Tuesday, May 31*st.*—One of the passengers teaches Miss Badger and Miss Bradbury the "Bells of Shandon," to which they have taken an extraordinary fancy. The ship stops for the first time since we left Ireland to take soundings, for the fog still continues.

There is great betting on the pilot-boat which will first meet us; there are 24 entries, and a pool of £6 is made at 5s. per head. I invest. The fog clears off, and we anxiously look for the pilot-boat. My number is Nine. At length the boat is seen a long way ahead. The purser, through a glass, discovers the number to be One. The Jew who overheard the observation went to the saloon, and found out the gentleman who had drawn number One. He offers him four pounds for his chance; the gentleman, a Spaniard, consents, and thus the Jew, by a stratagem scarcely moral, makes two pounds profit.

The pilot comes aboard; he brings some American papers, which are eagerly seized and read. We hear, for the first time, of the frustrated Fenian raid on Canada, of the deaths of Mark Lemon and Sir John Siemen.

We soon sight land—Long Island on the right, and by-and-by Long Branch on the left. Nearer and nearer we approach to land; we pass Sandy Hook, and about seven p.m. are anchored in quarantine outside Staten Island. The sea is soft and calm, and all is still around; night falls balmy, and the lamps from the houses and streets are reflected in the sleepy tide ; steamboats, with red and blue lights, glide like visions above the quiet water.

Our voyage is at an end, but we must have one pleasant night yet. Charley Strong, the doctor's son, for the first time produces his violin, and there is dancing on deck which is kept up to a late hour. We then have some songs, and the effect on the Staten Islanders must need have been agreeable. We retire to our berths, and feel sad that the pleasures (modified by steam-whistle) of the last nine days will soon be past for ever.

Wednesday, June 1st.—All up at 5 o'clock—morning lovely—I converse with a man to whom I had not spoken from the beginning of the voyage. I said we had a pleasant passage, to which he assented. Our singing, I said, was agreeable. "Yes," he replied, "but I'll tell you a curious thing. It is astonishing how easily you amateurs amuse people. Now, if I went about making free among the passengers any night during the voyage I should have made them laugh until they could laugh no more—either that or they would have been so disgusted that they could not have laughed at all." This was all a puzzle to me ; I could not understand it. He opened his coat and pointed to several medals hung on his vest. I inspected the first that came to hand and found it was a presentation of the citizens of Geneva to Tony Denver, the *clown*, for his talent in that character on the stage. The other medals were presentations from the citizens of other places. A clown may be amusing on the stage, but a very uninteresting character on a sea voyage.

All on deck at half-past six, and we scarcely recognise each other in our various costumes, every one being dressed to meet again the outer world. After breakfast we prepare to land. There is a general handshaking, and many interchanges of mutual remembrances are made. The captain seems quite affected at our parting from him. We all hope to meet each other again, though we know that we shall never ALL meet till summoned together by the last trumpet.

CHAPTER II.

ASHORE.

IT is past. Four of us enter a carriage belonging to the Metropolitan Hotel into which our luggage also is stowed. We proceed; soon we find our carriage gets stopped in a narrow passage; we appear to be blocked up; there are carriages before and behind us; at either side of us is a wooden wall. There is a sound of a steam engine somewhere in the neighbourhood. Every moment we expect the way to be cleared so that we may pass, but we remain at a standstill. "Well," I exclaimed, "if this be what they call American progress, it is the slowest I ever saw." "Oh!" said my friend, "it is ridiculous. I will speak to the driver." And, putting his head out of the window, he cried, "Driver!" but there was no response. At length he jumped out of the carriage, determined to push matters forward. I then put my head out of the window, and, looking ahead, I saw that the horses, carriages, people, wooden walls, steam engine, floor and all were moving at a rapid pace across the water, and that, in fact, we were simply in a monster ferryboat, steaming from Jersey City to New York.

We reach the Metropolitan, a vast hotel in Broadway. We enter an immense hall, with marble pavement and Corinthian pillars. A number of negro servants take down our luggage. At a large counter we write down our names in the Visitors' Book, and are billeted off to our several rooms, which are on the third floor, whither we are quickly transported by a vertical railway or lift. Our luggage follows, and in a few minutes we are in our room, with all our baggage around us. Charley, a dark servant, is most attentive. He points out all the conveniences of the house, brings us ice water, the newspapers, pen and ink. We have only to ring for Charley, and Charley will be with us in an instant. We write home at once to our friends, and thus acquit ourselves, first of all, of what we consider a sacred duty.

We dine at 5—sumptuous dinner, served by negroes There are none but black servants here. The saloon is immense in proportion and rich in decorations, and the darkies lounge and move about in a very free and easy manner. Father Mooney comes and meets me for the second time. I had met him in Ireland two years ago, when he was making a tour through Europe. He is pastor of St Brigid's here. He is kind and good-natured, and very generously invites us to stay at his house while we are in New York, or as long as we please. Next day we pay our bill at the Metropolitan. At 10 the waggon comes to fetch our luggage and the carriage to convey us to the Chateau Mooney.

Soon another carriage and pair are at the door. We

are to go off with him to the races on Long Island. We are curious to see American racing, and readily comply. We reach Brooklyn, pass through Prospect Park—a young park yet, but one of great promise. The "races" are very different from ours at home and rather disappointing. There is to be sure a good course, and a grand stand, and quite a number of carriages, and ladies and gentlemen; but the people are not here—there is no crowd, no excitement, no bustle or noise; tents there are none; the thimble-rigger and trick-o'-loop man are nowhere to be found, and even "Aunt Sally" is a *non-est* woman once in her life. It is to be a trotting match; no horseback business, but a lot of men are mounted on what we call gigs at home—gigs of the slightest conceivable structure made of hickory, and these are to do the trotting match. We get on the grand stand; the race is about to come off, and the horsemen strive to get themselves into position. A false start, the bell rings and calls them back. Again they try it. Another false start, and another bell. This goes on for at least a dozen times, till it becomes quite disgusting, and the horses are worried and tired, and the race is, in fact, spoiled. When it does come off there is no excitement about it; the course is rounded once, a mile heat, and all is over. This repeated several times, constitutes the whole.

We reach Brooklyn rather late, and sup at the house of a Mr. Levi, one of the gentlemen who accompanied us. We then get home at a seasonable hour, chat over the events of the day, and retire.

Friday, June 3rd.—We commence business to-day, and make 525 dols. We drive through the Central Park, which is indeed magnificent, and which may fairly compete with the " Bois de Boulogne," both in its park-like splendour and in the gay and brilliant style of its equipages, which roll through it in quick succession and in multitudinous array all through the afternoon. A splendid band played for the amusement of the people, who listened with great attention, and displayed a praiseworthy decorum as well in their costume as in their conduct.

We dined to day at Brooklyn. We had a very agreeable evening, especially as almost all the guests, numbering about twenty, were from the " beautiful city." Before dinner we drove out to Greenwood Cemetery, which is the most beautiful I have ever seen. Why do people speak so much of Pere la Chaise? Greenwood is a paradise. You enter by a magnificent gate of brown stone, with carvings representing appropriate passages from the Life of Christ. This gateway is of great magnitude as well as of beauty. The grounds, which form a very large area, are undulating, with lovely sloping lawns, hedges, and borders, and paths running along in every direction. Trees abound, especially willows ; and there are some charming lakes, into which those willows droop. The paths and avenues have romantic names—such as Violet Path, Vision Path, Fountain Hill, Amaranth Glade, Rose-dew Bower, &c., &c. The tombs and monuments charm by their splendour and variety ; some are of enormous magnitude. On the whole, it is impossible to conceive a cemetery more beautiful.

In the evening we went to hear the Rev. Henry Ward Beecher in his tabernacle. The building was filled, and it was curious to observe the number of means employed to temper the excessive heat. The preacher stood without

C

any peculiar costume on a platform. There were an armchair, a table, and flowers all round ; there was nothing remarkable in his style or delivery.

Coming home to night by Fulton Ferry saw three distinct fires amongst the shipping ; the engines were hard at work. My friend and I having received an invitation to an evening party, we attired ourselves in full dress, and ordered a carriage. We drive to Park Avenue, and the splendid mansion of our host was strikingly manifest to our admiring vision by a vast array of gorgeous equipages disgorging their fashionable occupants at its door. A verandah extemporized for the occasion against the chance of rain, led to the main entrance where a grave darkey, in white gloves and stiff shirt collar, received us. He pointed upstairs, whither we went, and finding a cloak-room deposited our hats and overcoats ; we then descended the staircase amidst a throng of ascending and descending ladies and gentlemen, until we reached the grand drawing-room which was illuminated and decorated in very elegant and brilliant style ; it was filled with what the newspapers call the "gay votaries of Terpsichore," amongst whom our host himself was conspicuous on the "light fantastic" with the ever radiant smile—in a word, we find ourselves at a grand ball where some two hundred persons were present, and I confess with my grave attire I felt I was out of place, so I resolved to keep as much as possible among the gentlemen.

After the set of quadrilles was finished we turned towards our host, who stood on the hearthrug as on a conspicuous place where he might give audience to the guests who had recently arrived. He appeared charmed to meet us and led us away, introducing us to every one as he passed. I must say every one was kind and affable, and unaffected; gentlemen seemed anxious to converse with us, and several young ladies did us the honour of soliciting for an introduction. There was little, if indeed anything, to distinguish the whole scene from a gathering in an Irish home. To me, who am unaccustomed to circles of fashion, it certainly did appear that the ladies were very extravagantly dressed, and painted, powdered, and dyed, but I dare say the same custom prevails with us. It is to me simply abominable, and I always argue that when a lady resorts to so much artificial beautifying, she has little beauty of her own to go upon.

The gentlemen very agreeable, but they appear to me to be all bitten with the mania of self-laudation that characterises Americans; they seem to think "New York is the greatest city in the world—yes, sir." It may be the greatest city in the world, I do not know, but why should they so constantly proclaim it? And not only is New York the greatest city in the world, but every thing in the city is the greatest of its kind to be found anywhere. A great city no doubt, it is, very great, and will assuredly increase before long to incalculable dimensions in size, importance, and commercial activity. It is, so to speak, a young city; but where are its great buildings? Where is its Westminster Abbey, its Thames Embankment, its St. Paul's, its Tuilleries, its Madeline's, its St. Peter's, its Underground Railway?

I join the gentlemen in a quiet room where there is some agreeable refreshment. Here I am introduced to Dr. C—— the greatest surgeon in America, a man whose fame has reached every country, even in Europe. "Of course you have heard of him?" I am quite ashamed to say in his presence that I have not heard of him up to this, which causes surprise. We get home, and before retiring I ask Father Mooney's assistant, "who is Dr. C——?" "Never heard of the man in my life," was the reply. "The greatest surgeon in America," I add. "Nonsense," said the gentleman I questioned.

The public institutions of New York are mostly built on islands situated in the Bay. Of these islands the largest is called Blackwell's Island, and to-day, in company with some friends, we proceed thither by steamer. The day is fearfully hot on this island, which is two miles long. There are four admirably conducted Institutions—viz., a charity alms house, corresponding with our notion of a workhouse, a penitentiary for criminals, a lunatic asylum, and an hospital of incurables. We pass through them all and are much pleased by their condition. In the penitentiary we meet the chaplain, an Italian priest named Gelasis, who receives us very kindly and conducts us through the whole island.

The penitentiary, which is a prison, is a very long building, consisting of an immense corridor with cells at either side, and around all is a gallery with other cells opening off it. He takes us into the Horror Ward for females; here are two females in *delirium tremens;* he tells one that she is getting better, but she does not understand him, for she is a German. I tell her the same in her own language, and she smiles and says "*Ya.*" Here is the lunatic asylum, the women's side—what a Bedlam! They are all in a large yard with the hot sun raging down on them. They all flock about us, each preferring some complaint against somebody and trying to cry each other down in vociferousness. Such becomes their violence that we begin to get afraid, but the keepers assures us there is no danger.

The men somehow were more interesting, and excited more pity. One black man pleaded hard to get only a hat and a pair of boots, he wanted no more, and he would go immediately and stop the passing steamer which would come and fetch us all away from this accursed island. Another, a very good looking, intellectual faced man, with a merry twinkle in his eye, put a piece of wood into his mouth saying, "do not be afraid, I'll not bite you," as if he put the wood there to prevent the possibility of his biting us. He then asked if we would wish to hear him sing. We signified our desire, and he sang a plaintive ditty, in which there was mention of flowers, and rivers, and sunshine, and happy days gone by. A tear stole to my eye, and I could not restrain it. He sang beautifully and with fresh pathos as if he felt the full charm of the sentiment. When he had finished he said, flourishing his arms and smiling, "Now what do you say to something operatic?" We said, "Very good," and he said, "Well, then, here I am, Don Cæsar de Bazan," and he paced the stage with the air of an hidalgo. He then sang, in a deep baritone, and acted as he sang. The affectation of dramatic vocalization and gesture was admirable and we applauded to the echo, at which he seemed delighted. He then prepared for another performance, when a lunatic stepped forward and whispered in my ear, "Don't mind that poor fellow, he is mad." This was too ludicrous. We left the asylum with a strange feeling of sadness, not easily chased away.

In the hospital we found a woman from Kerry, who spoke no language but Irish. I conversed with her; she was content with her lot, therefore needed no consolation. Almost all the inmates of the island, excepting the lunatics, were Irish.

A friend drove us out in his carriage and pair to the "Catholic Protectory," an institution some miles away, and intended for the purpose of what we call a reformatory. The Americans have adopted a name of milder import. There are two large houses, one for boys (800) and the other for girls (500); both are under the charge of members of religious orders, and in all points, with very few exceptions, are well conducted. The late Dr. Ives, the converted Protestant Bishop, took a wonderful interest in them. They are really admirable in all their arrangements, and seem to be in charge of most efficient protectors.

Coming home through the Park this evening I see fireflies for the first time; the Park is almost on fire with them; they present the appearance of innumerable small stars twinkling for a second, and suddenly becoming extinguished, just a few feet over the earth. The effect is novel and delightful. The moon is up and develops the beauties of the Park. It is indeed a magnificent drive, and justifies the praises of the New Yorkers.

I learn that Mr. Eugene Shine has arrived, and is staying at the Nicholas Hotel, Broadway. Mr. Shine is a Cork gentleman who realized a large fortune in America, and purchased an estate near Killarney, where he resides. He left Ireland last January for St. Louis, and has now arrived from the latter place *en route* for home. He is a great friend of mine, and I am delighted at all times to meet friends, but especially now in a strange land. I visit Mr. Shine at the hotel, and he seems very glad to see me. We go across to Brooklyn to see a mutual friend, with whom we spend the whole of the evening.

To-day we pay a round of visits; they are all out. We find Mrs. Sadlier in, to whom I had a letter of introduction from Mr. John Francis Maguire, M.P. She has obtained fame as a writer of fiction—a nice, good lady, kind and gentle. This afternoon, accompanied by my young friend Mr. Attridge, I go to Manhattanville, some ten miles from the centre of the city, to visit Madame Gallwey at the Convent of Sacre Cœur, a splendid convent and grounds— more like a baronial castle than a convent. Madame Gallwey is a sister of Mrs. Thomas Waters, of Cork, but the sisters parted and have never met since they were children. The nun appears; she is a fine old lady—gay and lively in her manners. The convent contains a large number of Sisters, and they chiefly devote themselves to the education of young ladies, numbering about three hundred. Strange to say, about one-third of these young ladies are not Roman Catholic, but of every variety of religious persuasion, and yet they are bound to go through all the religious exercises of the convent, such as morning and evening prayer, Mass, Benediction, Rosary—in a word, all, save Confession and Communion. This is the result of an express understanding between the nuns and the parents of the children.

The Sisters make it a rule never to leave the young ladies alone. No boarder walks alone, and no two boarders or more ever walk without a nun accompanying them. Consequently, it is necessary that all the boarders should go through all the exercises of the convent together simultaneously, because there would not be nuns enough to accompany them if they divide into detachments. Many Protestant young ladies thus become Catholics; and though, as a matter of course, this must give satisfaction to the Sisters, they do not seek to effect the change nor is their system destined for the purposes of conversion.

I was led to the chapel by Madame Gallwey during the Benediction, for it was within the Octave of Corpus Christi. There were all the Sisters and the three hundred young ladies, the latter dressed in white and with white veils. The chapel was a very pretty one, and the whole spectacle charming. After the devotion the Sisters had supper prepared for us. I was introduced to Madame White, a niece of the celebrated Gerald Griffin—an elderly lady and a person of elegant manners and appearance. I remarked that her hatred to England was intense, and she used very forcible expressions, which I now forget, expressive of her antipathy. We walked out and surveyed the grounds, which were very pretty. I went with a young friend to Elizabeth, a village in New Jersey, about fifteen miles from New York, to see a woman whose daughter in Cork wished me to call on her. Elizabeth is an extremely pretty village, and well worthy of a visit. This afternoon, in New York, and at other times, I was amused by people coming up to me in the streets and asking me was I Father Buckley, of Cork.

Sunday, June 19*th.*— This was a most agreeable day surely; it was hot, very hot, but it was very pleasant, for my dear friend, Mrs. Attridge, gave me a beautiful drive in a carriage and pair to Long Island. There is Calvary Cemetery, where her brother, John MacAuliffe is buried—a name familiar in New York, and dear to me. This visit was the only melancholy episode in our drive. Poor John MacAuliffe, the good, the great-hearted, the unthinkingly generous and high-spirited—he is buried here! I had spent a pleasant month in his company seven years ago; we had been to Killarney together, and elsewhere; he is now dead and buried, and I stand over his grave in Long Island. This cemetery cannot be compared to Greenwood in any way whatsoever. One characteristic it had for me, and that was that almost every tombstone bore an Irish name.

We drive to Flatbush. Here I call on Father Paul Ahearn, a Cork priest, who receives us with great kindness. We go on to Coney Island, and see crowds of people of both sexes bathing; their costumes are neither elegant or graceful, but I envy them the luxury of being in the cool water this burning weather. Yet the breeze along the sea shore is delicious. We sit in a small nook and have a nice little pic-nic of our own, with a beautiful view of the surrounding sea. On our way home we call at Bath, a little bathing place with a few houses, in one of which our friends are lodging. They are at home before us; we take tea with them. We spent a pleasant few hours, and got home about midnight.

Monday, June 20*th.*—At 6 o'clock this evening we prepare to leave in a carriage for Delmonico's, to dine with Mr. Charles O'Connor. Father Mooney was to accompany us. He was loud in his praise of the first lawyer in all America, and flattered me on the great honour which was being paid me. I endeavoured to look humble. A little before 7 we arrived at the hotel, and were shown upstairs into a very elegant room, where there was quite a number of gentlemen. I had never seen Mr. O'Connor, but, having once seen his photograph, I was able to single him out from the rest. He was a tall, thin, straight old gentleman, with grey hair and white whiskers, and beard cut very short—gentlemanly in appearance, with bright eyes and very good teeth. He welcomed me, and introduced me to the other gentlemen, who were all very distinguished citizens of New York, fifteen in number (there were three judges).

At 7 dinner was announced. We proceeded to the next apartment, and there took our places. Every gentleman had his place at table indicated by a very ornamental card, with his name inscribed, and each one had, besides, a very pretty bill of fare, got up specially for the occasion. Indeed I may say that the banquet —for the repast wanted nothing to deserve the title— was quite worthy of Delmonico's celebrated name. I, of course, had the post of honour next the host. At my right hand was Judge Daly, a very scholarly man, and at the other side of my host was Father Hecker, perhaps the most distinguished ecclesiastic in New York. Everything was superb, from the egg to the apple; it appeared to me to be a paragon of dinners.

I found that Mr. O'Connor is great-grandson of a very distinguished namesake of his, Charles O'Connor, of Balangar, who lived in the last century, and was one of a prominent trio, including Mr. Curry and Mr. Wyse, who were mainly instrumental in forming what was known as the "Catholic Association," which had a great deal to do in procuring a remission of the Penal Laws. Judge Daly also is the great-grandson of Denis Daly, a very remarkable name in the old Irish Parliament. I thought it strange that I should be just then sitting between the great-grandsons of two men of whom I had so often read with pleasure and admiration. I regret that my memory is so bad; otherwise

I should be able to record some good things that were said this evening.

Thursday, June 23rd.—We drive to Wall-street by appointment to meet Mr. Eugene O'Sullivan. He has been many years in America, and has amassed a large fortune. He gave us 250 dols., and invited us to spend the evening at Long Branch, a fashionable watering-place, some thirty miles from the city. We took, with him, the steamer from some wharf not far from Broadway, and proceeded on our way. The steamer is one of the so-called "floating palaces." No hotel was ever so magnificently furnished or decorated. Luxury was studied in everything—not simple comfort, but luxury. The afternoon was lovely, and the sea breeze delightful to us coming from the broiling streets. Crowds of people were on board; but there was no crushing—there was room for all.

Mr. O'Sullivan introduced us to the pastor of Long Branch, a Frenchman. He accepted an invitation to come and dine with us. We landed not far from Sandy Hook, and took the train, which brought us in half-an-hour to our destination. Mr. O'Sullivan's house was not far from the station—a large frame-house, with piazzas on every floor, and not a quarter of a mile from the sea shore. The Atlantic stretched away before us, with many ships and steamers and fishing-boats dotting its surface. We were introduced to Mrs. O'Sullivan, a fine handsome lady.

The season has not yet commenced in Long Branch, but when it does it is very gay; it is one of the most fashionable watering-places in America. A great number of hotels are here, all frame buildings. We go to see them after dinner. One is 700 feet long. The apartments are magnificent. Space is the grand feature of all. In one immense drawingroom a gentleman sat reading a newspaper. He seemed as lonely as Adam in Paradise before the creation of Eve, but enjoyed the advantage of his progenitor, inasmuch as the latter had not the luxury of reading the papers. These hotels hang almost over the sea, and must have a pleasant time when the place is full. We loitered about the shore almost till midnight, enjoying the cool air, and listening to the ocean breaking its swelling waves.

Next morning we return to town by the steamer, and bade Mr. O'Sullivan farewell, with many thanks for his kindness. The heat of the day was insufferable, so we leave New York to-morrow.

CHAPTER III.

NIAGARA.

Saturday, June 25th.—It was our intention to go up the Hudson to Albany, by steamer, a distance of 145 miles. The scenery of this river is praised beyond measure, and we were naturally curious to see it. We left by carriage for the wharf, whence the steamer was to start; but what with the bad streets and the great traffic, the horses did little more than crawl, so we lost the steamer by ten minutes. This annoyed us exceedingly, but we had to bear it with patience. We drove to the Railway Terminus—a considerable distance—and took our tickets for the train which would start at half-past ten, so that we had only an hour and a-half to wait. The time we beguiled as best we could, and that was difficult enough.

At length the bell rings, and we proceed to the train. Now, I wish to mention here that in American railway trains there is no distinction of classes — the country is democratic and all the people travel on the same footing. A ticket-holder can walk from one end of the train to the other and please himself with a seat. The seats are all upholstered sumptuously, fit for the great as well as the humble. We step into one carriage—it is full—so we pass into another. This has plenty of room, and is got up far more luxuriously than the one we left. The walls are decorated beautifully; there are not seats, but armchairs and lounges, all upholstered in scarlet velvet; a magnificent carpet under foot, and tables, on which the travellers may place their books or papers, while at the foot of the carriage is a large and gorgeously ornamented fountain, containing ice-water, of which, in American trains during hot weather, there is a large consumption. This I thought, is very fine, and the Americans after all are a great people; they study comfort in everything, and they are right. What a grand thing this equality is, in a State : any man, no matter what his rank, has only to pay his six dollars and enjoy this splendid room, and travel his 145 miles in four hours and a-half, express. Yes; I regret having thought anything hard of America. I see things improve and my views, no doubt will change. "Tickets!" shouts the conductor, entering our carriage, as soon as the train had moved off. I show mine. "Another dollar," he says. "What!" I cried, "another dollar ?—for what ?" "This," said he, "*is a drawingroom car !*" Now, what a drawingroom car was I had no notion, but I clearly saw that, let Americans say what they will, there is a distinction of classes in their trains, so they need not brag so much of their Equality. A parlour car would have suited me just as well, but of course I kept my position, paid my dollar, and sought refuge for my vexed spirit in the pages of " Lothair."

A great nuisance in those trains is caused by boys passing through and flinging a book, or a bottle of perfume, or some other article into your lap, and passing down the length of the train, doing the same to everyone else. You are supposed to look over the book, or perfume, or whatever it is, and make up your mind to buy it or not. The boy returns, and should you buy, he takes your money, and should you not buy, he takes his wares. I never saw anyone buy. This is repeated very often, and, to a stranger, is rather startling, especially if he is rapt in thought, or buried in a book.

Albany is a pretty city, with the Hudson running through and one side rather elevated. The streets good, with trees in many places on both sides; remarkably quiet after New York; clean, with good pavements; neatness and elegance. This is the capital, and here the Senate, for the State of New York, holds its sittings. We found the thermometer at 105° in the shade. Stopped at the Delavan House—a branch of the Metropolitan in New York—and conducted the same way. Called on Father Wadhaues, V.G., a kind and gentlemanly man, He asked us to dine to-morrow. We agreed. Called on a few other persons to whom I had letters.

Sunday, June 26*th.*—Dined with Father Wadhaues; in the evening called on a Captain O'Neill, from Cork, of the Police

He was not in and I left word to have him call at our hotel. He called at 10 o'clock, a fine young man. He said he was to be married next Wednesday, and would have us to go see his future wife. We went and saw the young lady at the house of her father; there was a small festive gathering and the Captain seemed to speed very well in his wooing.

Monday, June 27th.—Leave Albany 7.45 a.m. for Niagara, 316 miles by rail. A lovely day, and splendid country, hill, valley, river, woodland, smiling plains, in many places the primeval forest, in many the stumps only of felled trees, not yet grubbed out, marking where the forest had been. Several cities of modern growth, but of ancient name, on our way— Troy and Rome, Utica, Syracuse, and Palmyra.

Three of our fellow-travellers were remarkable—two men and a young woman—dressed as if of middle rank in life. They spoke German; one man of coarse and rugged features, such as a novelist might take for his villain. When the train stopped at Syracuse the police entered and arrested the trio, who offered no resistance, and were marched off immediately. A telegram from Albany or elsewhere had notified that the criminals were *en route* for Syracuse. I could not learn what was the charge against them.

We did not reach Niagara until 9.45 at night, fourteen hours of railway travelling. We arrived in the midst of fearful thunder, lightning, and rain; put up at the Monteagle House, some two miles and a-half from the Falls; heard the roar of the falling water through my open window all night like—like what?—like the snoring of an Icthyosaurus!!

Tuesday, June 28th.—Had expected to find on the hotel book the names of Mr. and Mrs. Swayne, and Mr. and Mrs. Smyth who had promised to arrive here this day, on their way from Chicago; they are making a tour, but we were disappointed. We hired a carriage and drove to the "Falls." I shall not describe them; they are immense and awful, and thus sublime. I shall leave the description for to-morrow.

On returning to our hotel we found that our friends had arrived meanwhile, and were now in their rooms brushing off the dust. They did not exactly expect to see us here; they had given us their programme, and we had said it was just possible we might meet them here. I passed away the time in the billiard room, playing with myself but left the door half open, so that I might command a view of any one coming down stairs. After about a quarter of an hour Mr. Smyth appears; when he sees me his astonishment is intense, he falls back as if it were my *fetch*. He soon understands the whole thing. He promises not to tell any one. So when they come down by-and-by and see us, their surprise and pleasure are boundless.

We spend a very pleasant and quiet evening together; there is some good playing in the drawingroom, a piano and a small band of hired musicians. The thunderstorm of the previous evening is repeated and the effect is marvellously grand. We go out on the piazza to admire it; the whole air is lit up every few seconds by a vivid light; the trees and fields start into view, and their green colour is quite perceptible. The graceful lineaments of the suspension bridge shine out and we see dimly, even at the distance of a few miles, the misty vapour rising from the "Falls," while we distinctly hear the noise the waters make. Then comes the loud crashing thunder, and now the terrific rain, the lightning all the while calling into fitful life the slumbering charms of the scenery. It is a sublime and terrible spectacle. But now the rain sweeps around us in strong gusts, and soon the piazza is flooded. We re-enter the drawingroom, where ladies sit and children play, and the sweet sounds of music are heard, while the occasional flashes of lightning dart into our midst, light up for a second the tall mirrors and almost blind us by their dazzling brilliancy.

Wednesday, June 29th.—St. Peter's and Paul's Day. I think of my parish, called after these saints, and my church, and my fellow-priests. It is no holiday here. It is observed on the following Sunday. A very, very hot day. A gentleman of our party goes off to a college, two miles distant, to see what is called the "Commencement." This is nothing more nor less than an examination or exhibition and distribution of prizes at the end of the collegiate year, and the commencement of vacation. There are to be a great number of priests there and a large gathering of lay folks, friends of the students. In this small place (for Niagara is a small place) a thing of this kind produces quite a sensation, and is, besides, a pleasing spectacle.

I prefer remaining with my friends and "shooting Niagara" again. There are two suspension bridges, one over which the railroad passes (there is a passage for the people under the railroad), and the other adapted for foot and carriage passengers. We reach the latter. It is a slight and graceful structure, 1,300 feet long and 196 over the river, the Niagara River below the Falls. As carriages are compelled to walk slowly for fear of creating too great a vibration, we are able to have an excellent view of

D

the Falls. The American Falls rush into the river at a perpendicular height of 180 feet, and at the side of the river, the Horse Shoe, a little above, so called from the shape of the river's bed at the point of descent, they come with such force as to make a curve, which they retain until they strike the rocks below. Thus it is possible for persons to descend and stand under the curve of the falling water without getting wet, and it is done every day. Millions of tons of water fall here every day, and so great is the spray caused by concussion with the rocks below that it rises in white clouds to a great height over the point of descent, and falls like rain even on the land adjacent. The river for miles below the Falls is streaked with white, like the sweat on the flanks of a courser after a hard race. Yes, the Niagara Falls are the essence of the sublime. There is something awful in the thought that those waters have been flowing thus through the long centuries that have passed since Nature's last upheaving. While thrones and dynasties have risen and fallen, while nations have passed from the impotence of infancy to the vigour of mature existence, and thence downward to the imbecility of decay and decrepitude, the Niagara Falls have fallen with the same monotonous thunder-sound—unchanged by the will of the Deity, defiant of the arts of man, playing for ever the same majestic tune—falling for centuries unseen by human eye, discovered at last by some red man, Iroquois or Huron, perhaps, on the war-path, who called it in his native tongue " Niagara," or " the Thunder of Waters"—come upon some few centuries ago by the first white man, a French Jesuit missionary, who spread their fame through the old Continent, whence millions since come to visit them—but falling, falling, falling, still the same, groaning in the same sad conflict with the hard rocks below, and emerging weary and slow from the mysterious battle-ground, where reigns eternal strife and noise.

We arrive at a house which is called the "Museum," but which, besides the curiosities it contains, and which may be all seen for a dollar, seems to be a refreshment place, a photographic establishment, and a dressing-room for those who wish to view the falls from beneath. Several tourists pass, and stay at the "Museum," and dress to see the Falls *ab infra*. The costume for a gentleman consists of yellow oil-cloth trousers, coat, and headgear of the same. He looks, when fully equipped, something like an Esquimaux Indian. Ladies wear the oil-cloth head-dress like a nun's cowl, and a long robe also like a nun's, and gutta-percha shoes. Several ascend and descend under the guidance of a black man. They go as far as the rocks on which the waters fall, and where they form the curve I have described. We did not descend; we stand on the road and get ourselves photographed in a group, with the American Fall for a background; the picture is finished and framed in a quarter of an hour. As usual, no number of the group is satisfied with his or her appearance. Mrs. Smith, who is very good-looking, is very much annoyed with her likeness, for a small vixen of a sunbeam would seem to have cut her across the nose.

We indulge in some hurried luxury peculiar to America; it was well iced and that was enough for me. Everything is iced in America, indeed without ice I do not see how liquors of any kind could be kept in a state fit for use.

We return in our carriages by the suspension bridge, and proceed to "do" the river above the Falls. We cross into an island called Goat Island, and walk thence to points directly over the Falls. One feels a horrible inclination to fling oneself down and commit suicide amongst the boiling surf. I keep at a respectful distance. We then cross by bridges, on foot, to three islands, called the "Three Sisters." Here the river is one formidable spectacle of rapids, as the waters madly rush down an inclined plane over huge jutting rocks towards the Falls, and foam and roar like some huge monster undergoing excruciating torture. The bridges connecting the "Three Sisters" are flung over rapids, and the effect is peculiar, as you stand on the bridge and see within two feet under you the raging, rushing water, and think what would be your fate in the grasp of such a liquid avalanche—only for the bridge. It is like looking at a hungry tiger through the bars of his cage.

After various stoppages at little picturesque taverns, and various refreshments of ice-cream, or other coolers, we reach our hotel, and are somewhat startled by the announcement that we cannot have dinner. I must observe that this hotel was the worst I was ever in; but we made it very clear that we should pack up and go to an hotel where we could get dinner, and then they prepared something. After dinner we walked to the second suspension bridge—the railway one. We meet a huge waggon filled with trunks, and then a huge waggonette filled with boys singing. These are a contingent of lads from the College going home after their "Commencement." We pass through the foot-passengers' bridge; the railway is overhead. The view along the passage is very beautiful—800 feet long, 196 high; the river below, and the Falls beyond. We continue our walk along the other bank of the river—the banks are awfully high and precipitous and nicely wooded—the whole scenery very pretty.

This evening, while cooling ourselves sitting on the piazza, the lightning and thunder and rain of the previous evening are repeated, and on a grander scale. An old lady sits with us; she is very old, and her hair is milk white; she says that she is 87 years old; that she is Welsh, and came to New York in the year 1801! Her reminiscences of that city are strange—in fact, it must have been little more than a thriving town then. What a change! But the old lady happens to be a Protestant, and cannot conceal her bigotry, which takes almost a form of hatred towards me. She speaks very insultingly of the Catholic ceremonies of religion—of priests, with their "bibs and tuckers," and assures Mr. Smyth that I am secretly plotting his conversion to the errors of the Romish Church. As she is so old, we listen in silence, and when she has finished we quietly disperse. She then discovers her mistake, and tries to explain it by pleading "garrulity" of old age; but it is too late, and we avoid her for the rest of the evening.

CHAPTER IV.

THE BRITISH FLAG AGAIN.

Thursday, June 30th.—This morning we prepare to leave for Montreal, a distance of, I suppose, more than 400 miles. While my friends are getting ready, I sit on the piazza, and am soon accosted by a lady whose appearance it would not be easy to forget; she is tall, bony, masculine, hard-featured, with long black ringlets, no cap, very large teeth, high cheek bones, and generally formidable aspect; her age might be fifty-five, her accent is very American, and so is her phraseology, which I regret I cannot accurately report. She began, "You're a minister, I bet?" I replied in the affirmative. "Yes," she said, "I guessed you were; religion is a thing to be looked to. You have seen the Falls?" "Yes." "I should like to see them, but I don't kinder like to go alone. A lady oughtn't to go alone to these places—ought she? You're a good-looking kind o' man—do you know I am a phrenologist? Yes, sir; I can make out any kind o' character. That suspension bridge is a pretty thing, eh? It must have cost a pretty good deal of money to build that bridge. You'll go to Saratoga, I bet?" And so she ran on, stringing together a lot of short sentences on subjects the most remote from each other. The visitors from the hotel gathered around us; she examined all their bumps, and pronounced on every one's character in terms rather amusing. I am quite sure that if we had not come away suddenly she never would have stopped talking.

We took the train for Lewiston. The line runs along the bank of the Niagara River for about five miles, just at the edge, and at a height of nearly two hundred feet. In most places the fall to the river is quite precipitous, and the whole is hard to look at. The trains travel very slowly, which, while it diminishes the danger, prolongs the fear and suspense. I should not like to travel the same line again, and I fear very much some fine day it will come to grief. Arrived at Lewiston, the river, we find, is very broad. Nearly opposite is a village called Queenstown, and on the heights behind is a very splendid

THE BRITISH FLAG AGAIN.   39

monument to General Brock—a general who, in some battle of which I am entirely ignorant, was killed on the spot. Happy thought! read up about General Brock!

We take a steamer which bears us away down the river. Here the banks are high and well wooded, and the spectacle is very beautiful. Suddenly the river widens, and becomes an immense lake (Ontario)—an inland sea. We lose sight of land altogether in front, and, after an hour, on every side. It would require no stretch of imagination to conceive that you were on the Atlantic. About half-past one o'clock we reach the city of Toronto, which is built on the lake. The view of the city from the water is very pretty. My friend, Father Flannery, had been stationed for some years in Toronto, but is now in Amhestberg, some 300 miles to the west. I wish we could see him, but that, I fear, is impossible.

At Toronto we change steamers. The one we embark on is larger and more beautiful than the one from Lewiston; it is not quite a "floating palace," but to me it is quite palatial in its style. We dine under the British Flag, and there is a remarkable improvement in the diet. John Bull feeds well. The weather is very warm. I take up a copy of the *New York Herald*, and the heat of the great city is described in curious headings. For example—"Melting Weather in New York—Mercurial Antics among the Nineties."

Apropos of the *New York Herald*, its flippant way of telling terrible things attracts my observation. Thus in this very number I find:—"Yesterday John Barry met Thomas Carter in Thirtieth-street, and said he was going to drown himself. He kept his word." Again:—"In Delaware-street, near the Ferry, lies a defunct equine"—nothing terrible about this, however, except the vulgarity of the style. And again:—" In Fiftieth-street, yesterday, a man shot a canine which had bitten a boy named White."

Lake Ontario, still an inland sea. We are several miles out when we discover a butterfly accompanying us; he keeps always about the head of the vessel, and flies with it as if for a wager — sometimes he approaches the water so nearly that we are sure he is lost, but he invariably turns up fresh and vigorous—cuts a few gratuitous capers in the air, and then continues his steady course. This continued for more than an hour, and every one was surprised to find so small a creature as a butterfly pursuing so long a journey, and at so great a rate of speed. We all knew and felt with a pang of pity that drowning was his inevitable doom, but there was no help for it.

Here we had a striking illustration of the viscissitudes of weather in these parts. A dark cloud sprang up before us—huge and dense—every moment it thundered and grew blacker and more terrible. Behind us were sunshine and summer; before us the blackness and horror of winter. Suddenly a flash of forked lightning ran along the whole length of the frowning mass, and now we saw the rain steadily approaching us; the "big drops fell heavy one by one" on the deck. All rushed into the saloon, and in a twinkling we stood in the midst of blackness, cloud, lightning and rain, while the thunder pealed over our heads with all the veritable ring of Heaven's own artillery. I stood at the door of the saloon with some other gentlemen to view the wild scene, and to admire its grandeur to the full. We were protected over head by a canopy. A young man of respectable appearance emerges from the saloon and accosts me, "I beg your pardon, sir," he said, "but may I take the liberty of asking whether you are a Catholic priest." I assured him that I was. "Well sir," he said, and there was a tone in his voice indicating shyness and fear, " I may tell you that I have just been married only two days. My wife and I are on our honeymoon. She is sitting on a sofa in the saloon, and is horribly afraid of lightning. Would you kindly come and sit by her? It may give her courage. She told me to ask you. We are both Catholics, and love the priesthood." I of course assented, though by no means proof myself against the fear of lightning. I found the lady to be very young and very charming; and by all the arts I could employ, I had not much difficulty in dissipating her fears. The gentleman's name was Meagher, from Albany.

Montreal is over 300 miles from Toronto, so we shall have to sleep on board to-night, and all the while we shall be ploughing the deep waters of Lake Ontario.

July 1st.—About 6 o'clock this morning I put my head through my cabin window and find that our vessel is just stopping at one of the wharfs of a very beautiful city, which, on inquiry, I learn is Kingston ; like Toronto it is prettily situated on the water. Here the lake terminates, and from it emerges the river on which we now find ourselves— namely, the St. Lawrence. I dress and go out in front, but the weather is *bitterly cold*. To me, who had been so long the victim of heat, a cool sensation is delightful, but this is not cool but cold. I am forced to seek out my portmanteau and take a big coat, whose acquaintance I had not made for weeks, and don it, and even then it is cool enough. All my friends feel as cold as I do ; the ladies are obliged to put on heavy shawls, and the gentlemen feel a strong inclination not only to walk but to tramp along the deck.

The river St. Lawrence with its thousand islands is a broad and in some places very broad river—the islands which I believe number not only a thousand, but eighteen hundred, are of all shapes and sizes, from the uninhabited and cultivated one of a thousand acres, to the one whose nose only peeps above the water; on some grows nought but the primeval forest, and lives nought but the wild cat, and the wild cat's prey; on others a solitary tree nods at us as we pass. Another peculiarity of this great river are its "rapids," which are numerous; that is, a sudden change of water from glassy smoothness to a wild conflict of waves, rushing against each other in eternal noise and confusion, such as I have already described when telling of Niagara. In one place called Lachine these rapids are considered dangerous, for the vessel has to pass at the rate of thirty miles an hour through two sharp projecting rocks, placed at a distance not much wider than the vessel itself. The greatest care is necessary on the part of the captain and helmsmen, who number four for this purpose—to prevent a catastrophe. We reach the first of the rapids, and descend at a headlong pace, and at a considerable incline; it is pleasant and exciting. We are again in smooth water, wending our way through the lone and wooded islands, with an occasional village on either bank, and the church spire for the most part covered with tin, glittering perhaps too vividly in the sun; and now we meet parties of pleasure, boating and seeking some good spot for a picnic, and waving their handkerchiefs at us as we pass. It is a festive day in Canada—" Dominion Day," the third anniversary of the declaration of Canadian Independence.

The rapids again, the same rush and conflict and roar and confusion; waves dashing into spray by contact with projecting rocks, and here is a sad reminder of the fate which we must avoid—the skeleton of a steamer in the midst of the rapids—a steamer named the "Grecian," that rushed here upon ruin some twelve months ago.

The weather is now warm again as behoves it in July, and we fling off our heavy clothes and bedeck ourselves in lighter and more graceful costumes. We are in lake St. Francis, a vast expansion of the St. Lawrence, forty miles in length. Shall we have light to pass the rapids of Lachine? The captain cannot say; should we be too late we must only diverge into a canal made for the purpose of avoiding the rapids, and arrive very late at Montreal, but should we have light enough we may reach our destination about half-past 9 o'clock.

Here is a lady with a very smiling face going amongst the passengers collecting money for those who suffered by the fire at the Saguenay below Quebec; she reaches us in due time, and is very gracious and winning in her manners; she rejoices in the high-sounding title of Madame Morel de la Durayutaye; she is French Canadian, and scarcely speaks English. I sympathise with her as a fellow beggar, we all subscribe, and she never ceases in her importunities until she has succeeded in her demands on board, from the captain to the fireman. When she has done, she attaches herself to our party, and plies her French and her smiles with increasing assiduity.

The sun is now red in the heavens, and as may well be supposed the spectacle is lovely; the smooth broad surface of the water, the balmy air, the wooded islands, the pretty villages on the banks, and beyond the "mountains robed in their azure hue." The captain has announced that he will have light enough to do the Lachine Rapids; this causes a general commotion. All flock in front, the sun has gone down, and we know how short is an American twilight. A quarter after eight and it begins to grow dark—but here are the rapids. We are in them, steering right for an island until you think we shall inevitably rush into it. Steam is shut off, and nevertheless we go at enormous speed; diverging from the line towards the island, the helmsmen with fixed gaze, and steady hands, under the guiding finger of the alert captain, make for a large projecting rock—you would think you were on it. No! a lurch of the vessel and we only graze it. Another rock at the other side—but another lurch, and we are off it—free! only that the conflicting waves make the vessel groan beneath. She labours on and on, steadily and gracefully, until we emerge from the *strages* of waves, and enjoy smoothness and silence once more. Before us stretches through the dim twilight a bridge about two miles long, supported on enormous pillars—Victoria Bridge. Beyond is a black mountain (Mont Royal, corrupted into Montreal); we shoot the bridge, and sky-rockets and other pyrotechnic "notions," got up in honour of Dominion Day, indicate beneath the mountains the position of the city of Montreal, and reveal by the fitful light the church spires and the tall masts of ships. We reach the wharf at half-past 9, and at 10 o'clock are seated at supper in the saloon of the first hotel in the City, the St. Laurence Hall.

July 2nd, 1870.—Our stay in Montreal extended to three weeks, and as the work of many days was of the same description, I gave up keeping a diary. I shall then sum up all that happened to us while in this city without particularizing the dates of the events. Our friends remained with us for three days, and we had a good deal of dining about. We visited several of the churches, of which there is an abundance in Montreal. Brooklyn is called the "City of Churches," but it appears to me that, for its size, there are more in Montreal. I have observed four churches, each of a different religion, within a few acres of ground; and there is one place where two streets cross each other, and at three corners out of the four there are churches. It appears the people here are very church-going, and on Sunday it was easy to observe that this was true, for the streets were utterly deserted up to two o'clock in the afternoon. The largest church is what is known as the "French Church," in Notre Dame Street, a fine building with two high towers, and immense bells; a pretty green square railed round stands in front of it. St. Patrick's Church, where the Irish most do congregate, is a splendid Gothic structure, quite finished, and well situated. The spire, however, is too small in proportion to the tower, and does not look well, being covered with tin instead of slate; and here I may remark that tin roofing is very general in Canada. It keeps the colour well and is lasting. I fancy this must have been an idea of the English commercial mind, as there are in England large tin mines, and it was deemed advisable to ship it in large quantities to some colony where the people were previously persuaded that it was useful for roofing.

We visit the convent of *Villa Maria* in the country, a few miles outside the city. This is a very fine convent, where, as at Manhattanville, young ladies are educated as boarders. It was here Mrs. Smythe received her education, and she was anxious to visit the old scenes after nine years' absence. Few of the sisters were able to recognise in the very stout Mrs. Smythe the active Irene Tomkins of nine years ago. The house is a magnificent one, and is called Monklands.

The drives around Montreal are very beautiful. The mountain is wooded to the top, and here and there, as you pass, splendid mansions, all of cut stone, and many of elegant design, peep out from the foliage, or stand in bold relief with the mountain for a background. In no place have I seen finer suburban residences. To drive "around the mountain" is considered indispensable for all tourists, and we conformed to the local obligation. The streets of Montreal are very fine, the West end (and by the way, how is it that the West end is always the most fashionable part of cities?) is very elegant. The great thing to be admired is the solidity of the buildings, and next, their great beauty of design. Almost all are of cut stone, and the Grecian style of architecture seems to be the favourite. The Bank of Montreal, the Courthouse, the Bonsecours Market, and the Hotel Dieu—buildings which I just put down at random—are worthy of any city in the world. The population of Montreal is over 30,000 of whom 24,000 are Irish Catholics.* I was surprised to find that with so large a Catholic population, there is not a single Catholic daily paper. There is a Catholic weekly called the *True Witnsss*, to distinguish it, I daresay, from a very

---

*Montreal has now over 142,000 inhabitants, with about 28,000 Irish Catholics. The *True Witness* still exists, and besides various French Papers, is still the only representative of Catholic journalism there. New York has still no Catholic daily paper.—ED.

Protestant daily called simply the *Witness*. But my surprise was lessened when I was reminded that even in New York, with a population of half-a-million Catholics, there is not a Catholic daily paper. The reasons of this are, that the leading papers have no special religious platform; and that the people are too intent on commerce to think about reading religious papers.

The young bride and bridegroom who were so apprehensive of the effects of lightning are stopping at our hotel. I have introduced them to our friends, and we form one party. On Sunday evening at their invitation I spend an hour in their room. Our friends left on the evening of Monday, the 4th, for Quebec, by steamer. We were all very sorry at the parting, one of the ladies shed tears, and there was great waving of handkerchiefs on both sides as the vessel rode away.

On Tuesday morning we thought it time to commence business. Accordingly we called on a Mr. N. S. Whitney, a gentleman who had impressed us favourably. We found him all that could be desired, though not a Roman Catholic. No co-religionist of ours could have taken us up more warmly. He regretted that as his wife and family were in the country, some 50 miles away, he could not ask us to his house; but he volunteered to come and introduce us to the Vicar-General, with whom he was very well acquainted. We accepted the offer. He introduced us, and we received a very cordial reception. The Vicar-General, in the absence of the Bishop, who is in Rome, accorded us every privilege in his power to bestow, on condition, however, that we should receive the sanction of Father Dowd, the pastor of St. Patrick's, and the chief of the Irish clergy in Montreal. We called on Father Dowd, who was even more gracious than the Vicar-General. He insisted on our leaving our hotel, and coming to live with him, as long as we remained in Montreal. I must here mention that all of the priests in Montreal are "Sulpicians,"—that is to say, clergy of the order of St. Sulpice, whose chief house is in Paris; that they are established here since the foundation of the colony, and are owners in fee of almost all the property of the city. The clergy attached to each church live in community, and practice in a very special manner the virtue of hospitality to all their brethren in the ministry. We accordingly remove our baggage from one hotel and take up our quarters with Father Dowd, whom we find to be the type of all that is excellent in a priest. The other clergy in the house were French Canadian by birth, viz.: Fathers Toupin, Le Claire, and Singer—the latter of German descent, but speaking the French language from childhood. The rules of the house are new to us. They rise at $4\frac{1}{2}$, breakfast *ad libitum*, dine at $11\frac{1}{2}$ A.M., and sup at seven. Night prayer at $8\frac{1}{2}$, and after that bed. I agree to conform in all, save the early rising, but I learn that I am not bound to observe any part of the rule; but that I am perfectly free to act as I please; I do conform, however, through respect for the rule.

There is another parish where the Irish abound—the parish of St. Anne's. A fine type of a Tipperary man, named Father Hogan is pastor—he is apprised of our arrival and our mission. Father Egan bespeaks his kindness in our favour. He holds a conference with Father Dowd on the subject, and they agree to permit us to preach next Sunday, and to announce that he would preach the

Sunday after, and take up a collection in the two churches after the sermon. Now there is a third Irish parish, called St. Brigid's, of which the pastor is a Frenchman named Campion, a clergyman of strong Hibernian sympathies, and we manage that as follows: There is in that parish a man named Mr. Donovan, who I was told by one of the Hegarty Brothers, tanners, Cork, was apprenticed to them some five and twenty years ago, and who has now made a fortune by the same business in Montreal. We go to visit him; he proves to be an excellent man, and places himself unreservedly at our disposal. He takes us to the house of Father Campion, to whom he introduces us. Mr. Donovan is the most important man in Father Campion's congregation. He is a teetotaler, and is President of a Temperance Association of men, numbering 200. Mr. Maguire, in his " Irish in America," makes special allusion to Mr. Donovan, as an illustration of what a young Irish emigrant may do in America who brings nothing with him but a Christian Brothers' School education, honesty, industry, and general good conduct. We found in Mr. Donovan a true and steadfast friend, who spared no exertion to promote the object we had in view, and in which he, as a Corkman, took a special interest. Father Campion, on Mr. Donovan's recommendation, permits me to preach on Sunday evening in his church, and to make a collection immediately after.

Accordingly on Sunday, in St. Patrick's, at High Mass, Father Dowd announces that I am to preach, and to solicit aid towards the erection of a Cathedral in Cork. I appear the moment he descends and preach. It would appear that my sermon gave great satisfaction, for I receive many congratulations through the day, and for the whole week after. I preached

E

the same evening at St. Brigid's, and collected 40 dollars. In the course of the day I was conducted from house to house by two Corkmen, and thus raised 140 dollars. I was struck by the polite and cheerful manner in which I was everywhere received. When I was introduced into a house the people were not embarrassed or displeased, but welcomed me heartily, were glad to see me, had hoped I would call, for they had heard of the object of my mission, regretted they had not more to give, but gave their little cheerfully. I was taken a little into the country to two holders, farmers named King. A tall labourer saw me enter, and overheard what I wanted. He waited till we came out, and stood at a considerable distance from the house. As I was passing, he called me and slipped half-a-dollar into my hand, regretting he could not give more. I was astonished at the generosity of the man, whom I would not think of soliciting. He was Irish, of course, and only one year from "the old country." During the week we collected a good deal in this manner.

I met several people from Cork, and they were overjoyed to meet me, who could tell them the history of the beautiful citie for the last generation. To some I spoke the Irish language, and their delight was inconceivable. I may here remark that wherever I go I find the love of Ireland amongst the Irish to be the most intense feeling of their souls—an all-absorbing passion, running like a silver thread through all their thoughts and emotions. They think forever of the old land, and sigh to behold it once more before they die. One man who drove us one day for an hour refused to take any payment. He was from Ireland, and we were two Irish priests, and that was enough for him! "What part of Ireland do you come from?" I asked. "From Wicklow, sir; I am 32 years in the country." "And do you ever think of the old country?" "Think," he exclaimed, "Oh! yes, sir, I do think of the old country, not so much by day as by night. In my dreams at night I see as distinctly as ever the lanes and alleys where I played when a boy. I fancy I am at home once more, but I wake and find that I am in Montreal, and am likely never to see my native land again." This dreaming of Ireland I found to be quite common; many people would give all they have in the world to get back again and live in Ireland steeped in poverty, rather than flourish wealthy in this strange land. And what is stranger still is, that amongst the young people, those love Ireland most who are born here of Irish parents. Their love is far more intense than the love of those who were born in Ireland. Philosophers must account for this; it appears to me to be a transmitted passion; they hear their parents constantly speak in terms of affection of the land of their birth. It is a land ever appealing to the sympathies of mankind—a land that has suffered in the great and noble cause of religion. The imagination of the young heightens the colours of the picture and awakes all the fire of patriotic passion. Attached to St. Patrick's Church is St. Patrick's Orphanage. The boys have a band, and they play no airs but Irish. My ears were so constantly regaled with "Patrick's Day" and "The Sprig of Shillelagh" that I could hardly persuade myself that I was in Canada. Wherever I have gone I have been assured of this passion of the Irish—whether Irish by birth or by descent—this ardent love of their native land. No doubt something will come of it some day. I am aware that in many parts of America there are persons who studiously conceal that they are Irish—who don't think it respectable; but they are recreants, and of no account; they are units in thousands.

But to return. In the course of the Sunday after I had preached, I found two cards on my table—"Messrs. Michael and John Burke." They had called to pay their respects. I returned their visit the following day. They proved to be the greatest friends we had encountered yet. Both are from Kanturk, in the County of Cork. They came 18 years ago, and are now independent. They have each a large grocery store; were unmarried, and had two sisters, each sister living with a brother. They are ardently attached to each other, and are Irish in every respect. During our stay in Montreal these people did for us, unsolicited, all that they could have done for their nearest relation, their dearest friends. They took us around amongst their friends, and got us a deal of money. They would have us to dinner and supper. They drove us out in a magnificent carriage and pair to Lachine, on the St. Lawrence; in a word, they spared no exertion on our behalf, and were most respectful in their manner, proving, if proof were wanting, to me that the Irish are naturally ladies and gentlemen. No lady or gentleman in all the world, no matter of what lineage or rank, could have treated us more courteously. *Honour to them and prosperity!*

Another great friend was Doctor Kirwin, a gentleman to whom we had a letter of introduction from an Irish officer. Dr. Kirwin is Irish, but is here for the last 25 years. His business had made him intimate with the officers of the British army here and out in Quebec for many years. He is passionately fond of horses, and keeps many. He came one day with a drag and a splendid pair of horses, and drove us round the Mountain. A fine, dashing fellow, full of genuine Irish feeling, reminding me much of my dear deceased friend, Denny O'Leary, of Coolmountain. One day we lunched at his house, and met his wife, a very charming lady. He was obliged to go off to the races at Saratoga, and, as he will be going again on the 12th August, we agreed to meet him there.

I may conclude the history of our collection at Montreal by stating that, between all we received in the churches, and from private individuals, we realized 1000 dollars! which we converted into a draft, and sent the bishop £200! This was magnificent. So pleased were we with the people, that we promised to come back in winter for a few days, "just to see what kind of thing a Canadian winter is," but in reality that I may deliver a lecture in St. Patrick's Hall, where we hope to raise another, 1000 dollars. Several gentlemen, besides those already mentioned, came to pay their respects, and to ask us to dinner. Indeed, I must say, once for all, that I never received so much kindness anywhere as I did in Montreal, and I doubt very much if people elsewhere are capable of being so obliging and polite.

It was no use for us to sound the generosity of the French-Canadians. A great antipathy seems to exist between them and the Irish, clearly not on religious grounds, inasmuch as both are Catholics; but the feeling illustrates the truth that men's minds are embittered as much, if not more, by political and national prejudices as by difference of religious faith. In many places efforts have been made by the ecclesiastical authorities to blend the two nationalities, but oil and water are not more dissociable. Not only here but elsewhere I have remarked that there is a decided prejudice against the Irish Catholic, and that it is only by some fortunate combination of circumstances, or by the force of rare talent, that such a one can attain in the States or in Canada any prominent position. D'Arcy McGee attained a pitch of popularity, perhaps unequalled for its heartiness in America, and the honours paid to him after his death will never be forgotten in the history of Montreal. All classes combined to honour the victim of the assassin; and no less than sixty Protestant clergymen assisted at the Requiem High Mass celebrated over his remains in the Church of St. Patrick. But on analysing this singular tribute of respect to the memory of this Irish Catholic, I find that although a great deal of it was owing to the extraordinary talents of the man, especially to his rare eloquence, yet much more was due to the fact that he was what is known in public life as a "trimmer," one who aspired to please all parties at the sacrifice of his inward sympathies and convictions; and more again to the circumstance that he fell a victim to a murderer, employed by the Fenians—the Fenians who would wantonly invade the Dominion and disturb the peace of Canada. This is the solution of the honours paid to D'Arcy Magee before and after his death, as I have it from those who knew him and prized him most. I visited his widow's house, and had the pleasure of making the acquaintance of his daughter, a very interesting young lady. Mr. M. P. Ryan, an Irishman, is now M.P. for Montreal, a Catholic, and another Mr. Ryan represents Montreal in the Upper House, also a Catholic, so that it is possible to get on, but very difficult under the pressing weight of Irish Catholicism.

The national game of Canada is called lacrosse. It is an Indian game, and is so called from the name which the Indians give the instrument with which it is played. The game somewhat resembles our game of "hurling," and is played in this manner. There are twelve at each side, each armed with a weapon somewhat resembling a "racket," only that the net-work is much larger and looser. At each end of the field are two poles, separated by a distance of 8 feet, and a flag flies from each pole. The contending parties defend their own poles, and the game consists of driving the ball through the poles of the enemy. This is extremely difficult, as the poles are so well guarded on both sides, and the excitement of the spectators is very great, for the victory appears every moment about to be won or lost; and just as it seems inevitable, some happy stroke drives the ball into the centre of the field where some splendid manœuvring is displayed in the effort to push it to either side. Now, I have said that this lacrosse is an Indian game, and for playing it the Indians are well adapted by nature, being endowed with considerable activity and proverbial fleetness. But in emulation of them a club was started in Montreal of young gentlemen, sons of respectable residents, some Protestants, and some Canadian Catholics, called the Montreal Lacrosse Club. Those contended frequently with the Indians, but the latter always procured the championship.

I may mention that in the neighbourhood of Montreal are some Indian villages, and there aboriginal families still reside, speak their own language, and conform to all their ancient usages, except as far as Christianity tempers their savage propensities, for they are nearly all Catholics, and have their priests and churches like civilized men. They dress like their neighbours, and are peaceful and tractable. The chief village where these descendants of the fierce Iroquois dwell is on the St. Lawrence, some 8 miles up from Montreal, and is as well as I can write it spelt Changanawagh (pronounced Kaw-a-na-wau-ga). This is the head-quarters of the "Indian Lacrosse Club."

Now, there is, as we have seen, a strong Irish element in Montreal, and some active young Hibernians—a few born in the old country, but the majority merely of Irish parentage—associated themselves together with a view of contending for the championship of the game of lacrosse. They called themselves the "Shamrock Lacrosse Club." Having studied the game they played again and again, and were beaten, but they persevered, and some few months before my arrival in Montreal, they beat the Indians, and became the champions much to the delight of all the Irish, and to the extreme mortification of their opponents, and the third association, namely, the "Montreal Lacrosse Club." Though covered with glory, they did not relax their efforts, but practised with as much assiduity as their business would allow, for they were all artisans and had little time for so laborious an amusement as lacrosse. They were all parishioners of Father Hogan, and dwelt in a quarter of the city known as Griffinstown, in name sufficiently indicative of Hibernian origin. The Tipperary priest stimulated them in their athletic pursuits, for he knew the strong prejudice existing against his countrymen, and was glad to discover at least one new means by which they could crown themselves with honour.

It was now a question whether the Shamrocks could preserve the dignity of championship which they had won with so much difficulty. There are in Montreal a great number of orphans under the care of the priests of St. Patrick's; they live in a large asylum not far from the church, and the domestic management of the institution is conducted by the Sisters of the "Grey Nunnery," a Canadian convent formation. Once a year the boys and girls get what is called a pic-nic, but which conveys a different meaning in Canada from that attached to it in these countries. With us a pic-nic is associated with a long journey, a romantic spot, a green sward, and costly viands of all descriptions. In Montreal it sometimes is that, but on the present occasion it meant that the children are marched to a certain field where there is a large gallery erected for them to sit, and eat and view the game of lacrosse played by the "Shamrocks" and the Indians of Changanawagh. Thousands are to assemble, and having paid fifty cents a head, are to enjoy a similar privilege, and by paying other cents may indulge in the cooling luxury of "ginger beer," or soda water, the proceeds of the whole to go to the orphans; the spectacle is to be varied by running and football, and during the interval the band of the orphan boys are to play Irish national airs. The day is fixed— Thursday, the 14th of July — the public expectation is on the *qui vive*, and the Hibernian's mind is tremulous lest the Shamrocks preserve their honour; the game is to commence at three in the afternoon. Accordingly I go to Father Hogan on Thursday, and we dine at 12 o'clock; he is to drive me to the grounds. There are other clergymen who wish to see the game as well as I. The weather is beautiful, the sun shining if anything too brightly, and all promises well. Three o'clock is approaching, and we begin to prepare for starting, when suddenly comes another of those atmospheric changes so peculiar to hot climates. The sun darkens, a thick black cloud covers the mountain (Mount Royal), at the foot of which the game is to be played; soon the lightning flashes, the thunder rolls, the rain falls, but strangest of all, a fierce hurricane arises and rushes over the city with the well-known shriek of the tempest. Father Hogan is in despair lest the game may not come off. "It will clear up," he says, "it will clear up." But, no; it does not clear up, but comes down in savage and more savage fury every moment.

At length, about half-past three, there is a partial cessation, and we drive to the ground. The Shamrocks and Indians are there, and a goodly gathering of the sons and daughters of Erin, but it is too evident that the game cannot be played, for the ground is too sloppy, and it is raining still. A postponement until Monday is announced, and there is a general dispersion, and a strong repining against the capriciousness of the clouds. It was well the game was given over, for we had no sooner arrived at home than the tempest arose in a form to which its previous conduct was but as child's play. The thunder, lightning, rain, and wind were blended together in one mad medley, and while the eye was bewildered by watching the drifting ocean of descending water and almost blinded by the frequent flashes, the ear was appalled by the howling voice of the hurricane, tearing huge trees, unroofing houses, destroying chimneys, and cutting up the streets as if it were a ploughshare. One church spire was toppled over, and one boy was killed; the shipping had enough to do, and, in a word, a storm passed over Montreal, the like of which "the oldest inhabitant" had never witnessed.

But it cannot be raining always. Monday came and was fine. We were on the lacrosse grounds; seven thousand spectators are present, almost all Irish boys and girls, all well and tastefully clad, all smiling and happy. The ground is roped off for the contending parties, and the spectators are seated on a gallery extending the whole length of the field, presenting a charming aspect, with the wooded mountain for a background. A small stand is erected where the clergy sit under a canopy, Father Hogan being most conspicuous by his large handsome form, and trembling all over with the excitement of fear and suspense for the success of his protegees. The orphans' band plays the melodies of Ireland. The gingerbeer corks are popping out every moment, and the whole scene is as bright and as brisk as it could be. It appears we have had a great miss. Moffit, one of the crack "Shamrocks," has just won a foot-race against an English runner of great note. Father Hogan denounces it as imprudent, considering that Moffit must have puffed himself for the game of lacrosse, for Moffit is a great *point d'appui* of the "Shamrock" Club. Everywhere the sweet Irish accent salutes my ear, and now and then some Irish pleasantry, until I fancy I am at home amongst my own people. The girls try to push themselves within the ropes, that they may have a better view; they are gently and smilingly repelled by the policeman on duty, a Cork man, named Falvey, with the genuine brogue of the Southern country. "Come now, girls, keep back, if you plaze," but the girls do not keep back. "Ah! now," he soothingly remonstrates, "do push back. No! Oh! begor, ladies, ye must push back, if ye were twice as handsome." They yield at the behest of that weakness to which woman ever proves responsive, namely, vanity. Another policeman in another quarter tries his persuasive powers with another group of sirens, but he gives up the task in despair, for they vanish at one point but thicken in another. He returns worsted in the amiable conflict, and exclaims to Falvey. "By the law you might as well be wrastling with a ghost?" I thought how different would have been the conduct of the Royal Irish at home—with what a stern face and a still more stern baton they would have pushed the fair daughters of the Emerald Isle outside the ring, nor prove susceptible to the most bewitching smile that would have sought to deprecate their anger.

The posts are fixed at either end, and each bears a flag—the Indian red, the Irish green, of course, and now the melee commences. The athletes appear upon the field, clad in "tights," save one little Indian who insisted on the style known as *sans culotte.* A red belt distinguishes the Indians, a green belt the Irish. The game begins, and the excitement everywhere is intense. Twelve at each side, all armed with the lacrosse. The ball is out and there is great contention for it, each party striving to fling or drive it towards the poles of the adversary, so that it may if possible pass through by main force, or be slipped through by cunning. We admire the marvellous speed of all parties, particularly the Irish. One "Shamrock" catches the ball in his lacrosse and runs with it, like a deer, towards the enemies' poles, but he is chased by an Indian, who strives with his lacrosse to dislodge the ball, or prevent its being flung. The "Shamrock" stoops and the Indian is borne headlong by, and before another Indian can come up, the "Shamrock" flings the ball to within a few inches of the polse, where a half-dozen Indians are posted to repel it. It is once more in the middle of the field, and the contest for its possession is disputed by another half-dozen, the crowd all the while shouting at every clever manœuvre, whether of Shamrock or Indian. I will not attempt to go into details, I can only say that there was evoked by the contest all the pleasurable excitement which ever springs from beholding a contest where physical strength, activity and fleetness are pitted together, and where the mind is further stimulated by the hope of national honour, or the apprehension of national disgrace.

The first game was won by the Indians in six minutes. I should have stated the game was three out of five. There was no shouting for the Indians, and when the band played up it was not a lively air. After an interval of ten minutes the second game began; it lasted thirty-five minutes, a fearful contest under the red hot sun, and was won by the Irish. Then, indeed, there was shouting and throwing up of hats, and the band played its most exultant strains. The third game continued twelve minutes and was won by the Irish, and the same sounds and sights of jubilation prevailed. The fourth game continued forty-five minutes and was won by the Indians in perfect silence. Now comes the last game, the game of championship, and scarcely a breath disturbs the silence. We were not long kept in suspense. After six minutes fortune decided for the "Shamrock." I cannot attempt to describe the wild joy of the spectators. All rushed madly into the field and embraced the victors, who stood puffed and perspiring and with hands all livid from the blows of their enemies' lacrosses. The air was filled with cheers, and I fancy I was the only man in the field who felt an emotion of sympathy for the defeated Indians. It was a tremendous triumph, and Father Hogan was in ecstacies. He passed through the throng, and shook hands with all the "boys," presenting the spectacle, so often witnessed in the old country, of men contending for glory with the blessing and under the admiring eye and stimulating presence of the "Soggarth Aroon." A few evenings after Father Hogan entertained the whole "Shamrock" Club at a supper in his own house. I was present. We spent a very pleasant evening; we had toasts and songs and plentiful draughts of ginger beer, a great deal of talk about old Ireland, and strong expressions of hope for her future prosperity. Such was my experience of the Indian game of Lacrosse.

How strongly is the history of Ireland interwoven with the history of America! It was well for the persecuted race that so rich a country lay open for their reception, when all but Providence had appeared to have abandoned them. And yet for how many was the ordeal of transportation the most trying period of their unhappy lives, and for how many was this land of promise a land of doom and desolation! I have been lately speaking to a most respectable Irish clergyman in one of the great cities of Canada, who emigrated here in the year 1835, when he was only fourteen years old. He and 250 others left Ireland in a small brig—a sailing vessel—and the voyage lasted over three months. During that time the unhappy passengers were all herded together like swine; there was no distinction, day or night, between age or sex in any kind of accommodation; they ate and drank and slept and were sea sick together promiscuously. He remembers with a shudder the starvation, the foul air, the stench of ejected and stagnant bile, the disease and death that prevailed through these three long months on board that melancholy ship; how he lost all consciousness, and cared not to live ; how he forget what was decent, or even human, and landed without a sensation of relief, deeming that no better fate could be in store for him on land than he had experienced at sea. And this was the case of many, very many. In Ireland, in 1847 and thereabouts, there came the memorable famine. The landlords were too glad to get rid by any means of their starving and insolvent tenants. They shipped them off in large numbers to America, paying their passage—oh! yes, paying their passage, as they would pay for pigs or sheep, and little recking how their fellow-creatures should be treated on that long sea voyage. The poor people obeyed the behests of their tyrant, heartless lords, and, in " poverty, hunger and dirt," with famine in their cheeks and disease in their vitals, and despair in their hearts, like " dumb driven cattle," they went to the great ship, and entered, "anywhere, anywhere, out of the world " where nought but the worst and most appalling of deaths stared them in the face.

Thousands sailed thus for Quebec in sailing ships, at low prices. It would not be a paying concern if they were properly fed, and so the starved were treated to congenial starvation. They were stowed away in the "fever ship;" the typhus broke out ; the plague infected the hold and the deck and the rigging. Week passed after week, and the disease, the grim disease, slew its unresisting hecatombs. Every day the sack—ah! no, the victims had not even the dignity of a sack, but such as they were, in their tattered clothes, reeking with fever and crawling with vermin, they were launched into the deep, where they found at least a resting-place from man's implacable and unrelenting cruelty. The fragments of humanity whom God had spared reached their destination. They dragged their faltering limbs up the steep heights of Quebec. Some were billeted to Montreal, and there debarked. Of those two cities they walked the street, more like animated corpses than living men, such, perhaps, as walked the earth when Christ died, and the veil of the temple was rent. Here humanity was moved. The starving, dying thousands found sympathy with the French-Canadians of Montreal. Sheds were erected for them, where at least they might live as long as God would let them. The Mayor—a worthy man, Mr. Mills—was so unremitting in his kindness that he sacrificed his life to his benevolence. The Sisters of Mercy came to their aid, and some good priests perished in their efforts to allay the agonies of the sufferers.

But, to be brief, for it is a harrowing tale, no less than six thousand Irish men and women fell victims at this time in Montreal alone, to famine and fever. As they died they were buried, many without the poor honours of a coffin, outside the sheds at a place called Point St. Charles, just near the great Victoria Bridge, to which I have already alluded. I came down with Father Hogan to see the spot where so many of my fellow-countrymen so miserably perished. There was the desolate spot, enclosed by a fragile paling— there the numerous mounds—and, above all, in the centre, an enormous stone placed on a pedestal—a huge boulder from the bed of the St. Lawrence—commemorating the tragic circumstance, with words somewhat as follow :—

"Here lie the remains of 6,000 immigrants [why did they not say Irish?], who perished of famine in the year 1847. Erected by [I forget the names of the builders of the Victoria Bridge]. May God have mercy on their souls!"

That I may not be wanting in justice to the memory of Mr. D'Arcy McGee, I must say that he was a stern Catholic, and always, and in all kinds of company, stood up bravely for his religion and its practices, when they were assailed by bigotry or contempt. In this matter he never flinched, but was ever a valiant and uncompromising champion. When twitted, for example, with abstaining from the use of meat on Friday, at a dinner party, amongst Protestants, he defended the practice of the Church by arguments worthy of an accomplished divine, and was never guilty of that cowardly weakness by which some of his co-religionists sacrifice their principle to their appetites on this point. Again, he was a man of intense charity and compassion for the poor, and I have heard some well-authenticated anecdotes illustrating this feature of his character. These things I feel bound to mention, as I have at all alluded to him, having no desire save that the full truth should be known about him.

After my sermon on Sunday, the 17th, a gentleman presented himself to me in the vestry-room as Captain Duff, of the ss. "Tweed," of the Red Cross Line, now lying in Montreal. He reminded me that he and I were brought up in the same street in Cork. I remembered him very well. He had been accidentally at Mass, and, to his great surprise, recognised me in the pulpit. He invited me to lunch on board his ship the following day, which I did, where he had some company to meet me. Before I left he gave me an invitation to his house in London, and expressed a desire that I should, on my return from America, make a tour on board the "Tweed" along the coast of the Mediterranean. I hope I shall be able to do so. Many people flocked about me who had been from Cork, and put various enquiries, which I answered as best I could. One poor woman, a servant, from Cork, insisted on my taking from her four dollars for the object of my mission, and only asked in return a little picture or other token, no matter how insignificant, which would tell her it came from her native city. Of course I complied with her request. I was able to send the Bishop before leaving Montreal a draft for £200, the first instalment of the large sum which I hope to collect before my return. It was with considerable regret that we prepared to leave this city, consoled by the hope of returning in the winter. We spent one whole day in driving about and paying farewell visits to all the friends whose acquaintance we had made.

CHAPTER V.

QUEBEC AND THE SAGUENAY.

At seven o'clock on the evening of Thursday, July the 21st, we left for Quebec, by steamer. The vessel was one of those magnificent ones I have already described, and there was an immense crowd of people on board; yet there was no crushing or embarrassment of any kind. The scenery down the St. Lawrence from this point is very beautiful; but, unfortunately, no boat goes to Quebec except in the evening, and night falls too quickly to admire it.

Here I met Father Hecker, of New York, whom I had previously met, as stated in its proper place, at Delmonico's Hotel. Father Hecker is a distinguished American priest; he is a convert to Catholicity, and is most energetic in the discharge of his priestly duties. He is the head of a new society of missionary priests established in New York, called Paulists—indeed he is the projector and founder of the Order. Their chief occupation, after the performance of their church duties, consists in promoting the interests of the Catholic Press, which they regard as one of the most powerful agents for the propagation of true religion. Father Hecker is editor of a very excellent Catholic periodical, entitled the *Catholic World*,* and has made a mark amongst the Americans. He is much of an American himself in appearance, but much more in character, imparting into the sanctuary that activity and "dash" for which the American is distinguished. Seated on deck in an armchair, vested in light coat, an ordinary shirt-collar, a straw hat, and gold spectacles, he discoursed with me up to 11 o'clock. He impressed me as being a man of more than ordinary ability.

Of course we slept on board, and rose next morning at five, to get the earliest possible view of Quebec. The river was broad, majestic and calm; the banks precipitous, wooded and uninhabited. But soon the houses began to grow more numerous, and fields to appear. At a distance, on the left bank, rose a bold cliff, to a height of some 350 feet, on which I could discern a citadel. Beneath were the masts of many ships, and around the spires of churches, and tin roofs glittering in the morning sun. This was

---

* New York possesses also a Catholic Weekly, the *New York Tablet*.

Quebec. At the other side of the river were villages and towns, one named "New Liverpool," the other, I think, "South Quebec." We were soon moored, and the city rose precipitously above us, the citadel crowning all. We drive by a "'Bus" to the St. Louis Hotel, and how the horse dragged the heavy machine, well loaded with passengers, up an inclined plain, little short of perpendicular, was to me mysterious.

Our first business was to call on Father Magauvran, Pastor of St. Patrick's. We found him at home, and though he evidently did not like the object of our mission to Quebec, he received us with sufficient courtesy. He insisted on our coming and staying at his house, and we of course consented; meanwhile we drove out to see the Falls of Montmorenci, some eight miles from the city. They are one of the sights of Quebec. We drove through a very beautiful country, and in due time reached the Falls. They are much higher than those of Niagara, being I believe 250 feet from the river beneath. This river is very shallow, so much so, indeed, that in the year 1759, when England was at war with the French in Canada, the celebrated General Wolfe led his soldiers across it on foot; it flows into the St. Lawrence, and from that river it is quite possible to see the Falls. They descend rather slowly, one might say leisurely, at least in summer, for then the water is shallow. The bulk of descending water is not much, and the whole spectacle might be called pretty rather than majestic. Just above the falls was a few years ago a suspension-bridge, which broke one day as a cart was passing, containing a father, mother and son. They were all precipitated to the bottom, and only the body of one, the father, was recovered ; the rest still lie in cavities covered by the falling water.

We remove to Father Magauvran, and meet his curates, one of whom is a very nice young clergyman named Maguire, son of Judge Maguire ; another a Father Neville ; a third a Mr. Connolly. They are all very agreeable and gentlemanly. After dinner, Father Magauvran takes us out to see the city. He brings us to see Durham Terrace, an elevated plateau at an enormous height over the lower city, and commanding one of the finest views I ever beheld. At an immense depth below is the great St. Lawrence, with its far-off windings at either side—with its multitudinous rafts, and ships, and the towns and villages on its banks, and long ranges of houses stretching in every direction, and, beyond all, tall mountains in the distance. To be admired it must be seen. Durham Terrace is a fashionable lounge, and on certain evenings a military band plays here.

Quebec is a strongly-fortified city, although it could not well withstand the assaults of modern warfare. A great wall, with five massive gates, surrounds it ; but a vast portion of the city too is outside the walls. One of those suburbs is called St. Roch, where a few years ago was an immense fire, which destroyed three hundred houses. We passsed through it, and it reminded me very much of pictures I have seen of the disinterred cities of Herculaneum and Pompeii—ruin and desolation on every side. We inspected the citadel, from which, as it is far higher, there is a better view than from Durham Terrace. Father Magauvran showed us several places of interest—the University, the French Cathedral and Cemeteries, and a spot where some years ago about 200 people were burnt to death while viewing a diorama in a theatre. Fire appears to be the special agent of destruction in Quebec. Periodical conflagrations take place, and hundreds of houses are burnt; even the woods in the neighbourhood often take fire, and for several days clouds of smoke overhang the city, while an occasional bear, driven before the flames, seeks refuge among the haunts of men.

On Sunday I preach, and with permission of Father Magauvran and Vicar-General, a French gentleman, announce the object of my mission. About 3 o'clock in the afternoon, although the weather in the morning had been the most excessively hot I had ever experienced, a most fearful thunderstorm took place. It was far more violent than the one which occurred in Montreal a week before, and which I have described in its proper place. The rain fell so thick that it presented almost the appearance of snow, and it was impossible to see through it more than a few yards. The wind was terrific, and the thunder and lightning appalling. All who witnessed the storm, admitted that they had never seen its equal. In the evening Father Magauvran drove us out a few miles in the country, and everywhere our way was blocked up with fallen trees. From one road we were forced to turn aside altogether, six trees lay prostrate right across our path; we heard the following day that more than one life was lost, of men who were surprised boating on the river. During the drive of which I speak we passed through the " Plains of Abraham," the scene of the great battle fought in 1789, by General Wolfe, on the part of the English, and General Montcalm, on the part of the French, on which occasion both generals lost their lives. We passed close to a pillar indicating the spot where Wolfe fell, a scene which forms the subject of a picture, "The death of Wolfe," familiar to everybody.

The place of our visit was the parochial residence of the parish known as St. Columb Sillery, of which the pastor is the Rev. Mr. Harkin, an Irish clergyman. He was not at home, but we were hospitably received by his curate, a French-Canadian, Mr. Fourmier. The house, in the midst of woodland, commands a charming view of the St. Lawrence, through a vista of trees, while the church in the vicinity looks down also on the river from a great height. This was the spot where, in the early years of the colony, and during the missionary sway of the Jesuits, one Sunday, while the people were at Mass, the Indians rushed down on them, destroying "at one fell swoop" four hundred families, and roasting and eating many unfortunate victims in the sight of the few who escaped, and who beheld the horrifying spectacle furtively from a spot where they lay concealed.

On the following day we waited on Mr. Sharples, an English gentleman, living in Quebec. We had letters of introduction to him from a firm in Cork, with whom they have dealings. Mr. Sharples proved to be "a fine old Englishman, one of the olden time," one of the old Catholic families who were not allured from their faith by the terrors or emoluments of the Reformation. He received us very kindly, and promised to call on us in a few days. This evening we drove out into the country, and stopped at the residence of a Mr. Thomas Delany, an Irishman from Kilkenny, who has risen to opulence in the trade of butchering. He showed us through his garden, which was admirably kept, and where we had the pleasure of meeting his wife and one of his daughters. There was with him also an old man named Dunne, aged 86, but wonderfully strong and hale, who discoursed with great familiarity of the Irish Rebellion of '98, of which he preserved a vivid memory. The whole scene was Irish to my fancy, for we had green fields, distant hills, and the sweet brogue everywhere about.

The geniality of these people was astonishing—they were so delighted to have two genuine Irish Priests with them. They showed us their cattle, and such cattle I never saw. One field contained an immense number of bullocks, of whose beauty I shall say nothing, but of whose size I shall say that one, a great white one, was like an elephant, and though he is only about to be *fattened*, already stands over *one ton weight*. Mr. Delany pointed to him with peculiar pride, and seemed to regard him as a rare possession. He then showed us his pigs, numbering about 100. His farm consists of over a hundred acres of prime land, and is his own property out and out. He has a large family, one or two being married, and he has abundance of means for all the rest. "And yet," said Mr. Delany, "the day we landed in Quebec we had very little." "You astonish me," I said. "And how did you get on so well." "I will tell you," said the outspoken Thomas. "I was determined to get on, so the day after I landed I got employment in a butcher's stall, and when he saw I knew the business, for I was brought up to it at home, he took a fancy to me. But he was a Canadian, and they are mighty close, and the wages he gave me would not support us, so I looked out for something else. I went down to the docks and gave myself out as a shipwright, although I knew no more about shipbuilding than I did about making a steam engine! There I got on pretty well for some time, but they found out I was no use, and they discharged me. Then I turned to the brewing, for I could not be idle, and there I scraped a few dollars together. My heart was always set on the butchering, so I quitted the brewing and bought a few joints of meat in the market, and went about from house to house selling them. I knew the good article from the bad, and people began to have confidence in me. At last I scraped together so much as would buy a whole cow, and one day Mr. Gunn, manager of the Bank of Quebec, was passing by my door. He was a customer of mine. 'Good morrow, Tom,' says Mr. Gunn. 'Good morrow, sir,' says I. 'Why, Tom, who owns the cow?' 'It is I own it, sir,' says I; 'and I am just going to kill it.' 'Well, Tom,' says he, 'I never saw a beast killed, and I will look on at the operation if you have no objection.'" "Not the least, sir," answered Tom.

So the beast was killed, and Mr. Gunn had to "pay his footing," as is the rule among butchers on such an occasion; and more than that, he ordered a quarter of the cow. When Tom brought the quarter to Mr. Gunn's house that gentleman asked him why he would not kill half-a-dozen of cows instead of one. Tom replied that he abstained from doing so for the obvious reason that he had not the money. Mr. Gunn offered to lend him money out of the Bank if he could get any kind of security. Tom succeeded, and when Mr. Gunn lent him £20 Tom opened his eyes on the enormous amount of wealth in his hands. But he went on until Mr. Gunn would be glad to lend him £5,000; but Tom did not want it, for he was now an independent, rich, and happy man. Here, then, was an instance of an Irishman rising to wealth and independence by pure industry and honesty. He took us into his house where we had tea, and where his daughter played and sung at the piano for our amusement, and I could not but feel charmed on witnessing the comfort that reigned in that happy homestead, and contrasting it with the position which the same group would occupy if they had remained in the old country.

One evening Mr. Sharples came with his carriage, and having paid his respects to us proposed to drive us to his house, some three miles from town, where we might have tea, and return at a convenient hour. We willingly accepted his offer. His house is only a very short distance from the church of St. Columb Sillery, of which I have already spoken, but it is on the low ground not far from the river, while the church is in an elevated and very remarkable position. We found Mrs. Sharples and her children to be a very interesting family. She comes from Clonakilty in the County of Cork, her maiden name being Alleyn, and the whole family had sojourned for some months, three years ago, at the Queen's Hotel, Queenstown. The children are all young men with the exception of one daughter, a very pretty young lady. Here a Mr. James De Witt O'Donovan was on a visit, and in him I recognised a gentleman whose face was as familiar to me as that of my dearest friends. I have many a time seen him in Cork. It turns out that he comes from Middleton, and had only just arrived to make a tour of pleasure in America. We spent a most agreeable evening. There was also present the Rev. M. Fourmier, already alluded to, and a young gentleman named Wade, just arrived from England. We sat on the piazza and chatted about Ireland, and particularly about Cork, with which the whole family were well acquainted. One young gentleman was very much amused by the fact that everyone in Cork seemed disposed to accompany him in any tour of pleasure which he wished to make. Young men who, he fancied, should be at their places of business, came with him freely as if they had nothing to do. No one seemed to be in a hurry. The business was left to take care of itself.

We spent a few hours here enjoying the balmy air. The view of the broad river, the ships, and rafts, and nearer to us the beautiful garden, of which, by the way, the presiding genius was an Irishman named Flood. Mrs. Sharples spoke highly of the gardener as a man of taste and orderly habits, and held him up as a living proof that Irishmen of the humble classes are not, as is generally supposed, dirty and unappreciative of the comforts of life. She insisted that we should all go and pay a visit at his house unawares, so that we might judge for ourselves whether this was true. We went and found Mr. and Mrs. and Miss Flood at home, and certainly I have never been in a house, whether of the rich or poor, where there was so much neatness, and, for the means, so much elegance displayed. The front door led into the parlour, which was papered and carpeted, and well stocked with pictures. There was a sofa, and on the centre table were books and ornaments, all gracefully arranged, and in the middle a lamp. In a word, everything was in the best style, and clean to scrupulosity itself. Off the parlour was the kitchen, in which there were two large stoves, one for winter and one for summer, and both as bright as brush and black-.ead could make them. We were obliged to go up stairs to see the bed-rooms, of which the pillows and counterpanes were of spotless purity. Indeed, if the family expected a visit, it would be impossible for them to be better prepared. Mrs. Sharples was proud of them, while the poor people themselves were delighted at the honour of the visit. They flung themselves on their knees, and begged the blessing of the priests, which was freely and cordially given. We returned to the house, and resumed our entertainment, which was rendered very agreeable by the warm-heartedness of Mrs. Sharples, and the unaffected manners of her children. Mr. Sharples sent us home in his carriage, very much pleased by all the attention paid to us. We spent two other evenings there before leaving, and took our final parting with sincere regret.

One morning Father Maguire, one of the clergymen of St. Patrick's, prepared a great treat for us. I must mention that he is the son of Judge Maguire, one of the most respectable citizens of Quebec, and now living at Bay Des Chaleurs, some 400 miles down the St. Lawrence, and that he is an extremely gentlemanly young clergyman. Born here, his parents are Irish, and though he never saw the Emerald Isle, he loves it as though it were his native land. This morning, by the kindness of a certain Captain Russell, he procured a small steamer belonging to the "River Police," in which he wished us to go to New Liverpool, a village at the other side of the river, some three miles up, that he might visit the church of that place, which now that it is complete, is regarded as the prettiest church of its size in Canada. We went, accompanied by two or three ecclesiastical students, who are on a visit in the house. The morning was very fine, and we enjoyed the trip very much.

The church, which presents a very fine view from the river, is of an unpretending exterior, built of limestone, and with the usual tin-covered spire, but the interior justifies all that has been said in its praise. It is quite a gem. The style is Grecian. There is a nave and two aisles, and the whole is decorated and adorned with frescoes of the highest artistic excellence. The ceiling is all painted, representing scenes from the life of Our Lord, and the sanctuary is perfection itself. My limited knowledge of architectural phraseology forbids me to describe in a proper manner my views of this church; but I will sum up all in this, that for its size and style, it is without exception the most delightful church I ever beheld. The pastor, the Rev. Mr. Saxe, led us through it, and was charmed with our praises of it. He is himself a very charming person, with as little as possible of priestly seeming in his manner; good-humoured and large-minded, having with much that is human the one absorbing spiritual passion, a love for the beauty of God's house, nor was his own dwelling out of keeping with the church. On the contrary, order and beauty reigned everywhere. Before we enter we must see his exquisite garden, cultivated entirely by himself. He has a vinery worthy of a ducal mansion, and such a variety of flowers that the atmosphere is laden with perfume. The interior of his house is elegant, in the extreme, wanting in nothing, and when we complimented him upon the beauty of all we saw, he said "Well you see a priest has few pleasures,' and he ought to provide himself with as many as he can legitimately enjoy. That is my idea, and I act up to it."

Having bade him farewell after tasting his wine, we re-entered our steamer, and went still further up the river to a point where a river called the "Chaudiere" joins the St. Lawrence. We have resolved to pay a visit to the "Falls of Chaudiere," celebrated next after those of Niagara and Montmorenci. In order to accomplish this little journey we were forced to look out for some kind of land conveyance, for the Falls were three miles up the river, and the water was too shallow for the steamer to go any further. Accordingly we proceed on foot up a rather steep acclivity, to a place where we see some houses. We enter one and find it the house of a French Canadian peasant; we state our want and they immediately answer that we can be accommodated. While the men prepare the conveyances, for we require two, the woman of the house treats us to some milk. The French spoken by these people is not very intelligible to me, but Father Maguire was quite at home in it. We drive a few miles and then stop. We have to walk across a few fields to see the Falls; here they are beneath us, a very respectable flow of water, indeed, but after the two great Falls we have seen, rather insignificant. Owing to the dryness of the season the river is very shallow, and the Falls are not full, but there is a long portion of river which, though now empty, must in the spring time be full enough, in which case the Falls must be very grand to look at. High as we were above them the spray reached us from the rocks on which the descending water broke. Around the scenery is splendid, woods spreading behind the Falls on both sides, the river running over brown rocks between, while beyond, at an immense distance, spread the fields, forests and mountains of the North. We rejoined our crew on board the steamer in due time, weary and wet with perspiration from all we had to walk, and steamed to Quebec, delighted with our trip.

On Sunday the church was crowded, for the sound had gone forth that a priest from Ireland was to preach. I delivered a sermon on the respect due to the House of God and then made my special appeal. I collected 247 dollars. During Mass I was somewhat surprised to hear the organ playing several Irish airs, such as "The Last Rose of Summer," "The Meeting of the Waters," and "Savourneen Dheelish." In the course of the day the organist was introduced to me, a young French Canadian. He spoke English imperfectly, and I was amused by one of his blunders. When I complimented him upon his performance of the melodies during Mass, he assured me that he was very fond —indeed, passionately fond—of the Irish airs, and that, of them all, his favourite was that lovely lyric "Mary, you are now sitting in style!" (evidently, "You're sitting on the stile, Mary"). Thus we had every reason to be content with the munificence of the Irish in Quebec, for, owing to their frequent fires, their charity has been sadly overtaxed; besides, it is now a poor city owing to the substitution of iron for wood. The latter branch of industry has been almost eliminated from the place, which is a great misfortune, as in consequence of the abundance of timber brought here from the Western country, ships were built in large numbers in Quebec. The people, however, are very kind and good, and our stay here was very pleasant.

Before leaving we were advised to visit the River Saguenay, one of the great sights not only about Quebec, but in all America. This river, rising in a certain lake (St. John) joins the St. Lawrence at a point about 100 miles down the St. Lawrence from Quebec, and steamers run from the latter place three or four times a week, to enable tourists to visit the beautiful scenery for which the Saguenay is distinguished. On Tuesday morning, August 1st, we left the wharf at Quebec in the "Union," to make this little tour. The morning was very unpromising for purposes of sight seeing, for it rained and thundered with unmitigated ferocity. But the very vehemence of the storm was the surest augury of its short duration, and in point of fact it soon cleared up, and the weather became all that could be desired.

Descending the river, we had a very good view of Quebec, situated at the junction of the St. Lawrence and the St. Charles, and surmounted by the citadel, which protects the river on every side. We soon caught sight of the Montmorenci Falls, which present from this point a magnificent spectacle—falling in copious volume from their great elevation, and filling the surrounding air with spray.

Further down is the large and beautiful island of Orleans—very picturesque, wooded, and cultivated, and thickly inhabited; and, still further, Gros Island—an island of melancholy recollections to the Irishman who becomes acquainted with its terrible history. Here, in the fatal year of 1847, the fever ships from Ireland, already alluded to in these pages, were placed in quarantine. Here, as at Point St. Charles in Montreal, were sheds erected for the sufferers. Here they died—first in tens a day, then in hundreds. Here perished with them many good priests and nuns. Here arose, with appalling suddenness, a huge Necropolis—a City of the Irish Dead, where, in addition to the victims of the grim tyrant, were interred (horrible to think of!) many live human beings, as I have heard asseverated by more than one witness of the tragic scene. When the fatal work was accomplished it was ascertained that from 8,000 to 10,000 souls had perished, whose bones lie now beneath the sod in this lonely island as I pass. I inquired from several persons whether any sufferers survived this terrible pest, and I was answered "a few did," but that they were scarcely worth counting. Some four hundred children survived, whose parents perished; and, let the Irish at home ever remember it with gratitude, the present Archbishop of Quebec, Monseigneur Bailleargeon, animated by the spirit of the great St. Vincent de Paul, appealed from the pulpit of his cathedral to the public on behalf of those poor little children. With tears in his eyes he begged of the people to adopt them as their own. The appeal was not made in vain. On the contrary, a holy rivalry sprung up amongst the inhabitants of Quebec, Canadian as well as Irish, for the possession of the children. Not one was neglected, and at the present day many of those survivors are pointed out as persons rescued by charity from a terrible fate, and, I am happy to add, as persons who reflect the highest credit upon the parents of their adoption. Some are wealthy, some sit in Parliament, and what is strange to think of—some who were brought up by the Canadians cannot speak one word of English. The French language, as well as French parents, has been adopted as their own.

At one side of the river, as we drop down, is a large range of mountains, known as the Laurentia range, from the river's name, and in some places descending right to the water's edge. At the other side the banks are more flat and fertile, and a line of villages appears to run the whole way. Here and there the houses accumulate, and we have a town such as Riviere-du-Loup, and Cacouna—fashionable watering-places. One watering-place only lies up the left side, and this is called Murray Bay. At all these places we touch, and give and receive passengers. On board we have a large number, principally Americans, who are all very agreeable, and show a fraternizing spirit. We are specially taken up by one family—a lady and gentleman, and their daughter, from New York, who are very interesting. We spend almost the whole time in their company.

About seven o'clock in the evening we reach the mouth of the Saguenay, on the left bank, and land at a little village called Tadousac, the very earliest settlement, I believe, of the French in Canada. We catch one glimpse of the river, and it seems to realize all we have heard and read about it—precipitous banks, and copious woods at both sides, and a pervading aspect of solitude, with the placid water between the hills. We can stay as long as we please at Tadousac, for the steamer will not go up the Saguenay until midnight; not that we are expected to view the river then, but that we may reach the highest point before morning and view it on our return. Tadousac is situated in a very wild region, reminding me much of Glengariffe in the old country. It is evidently frequented by pleasure-seekers and vacationists, for there are many pretty cottages, and there is a fine strand for bathing, and the water is sufficiently salt, for the air is strongly impregnated with the odour of sea-weed. Here is a fine hotel, which, for the honour of Ireland I may add, is kept by an "O'Brien." At Tadousac is a little church which is said to be the oldest in Canada. It is built of wood. If it be the oldest, it must have been frequently rebuilt, as wood could scarcely survive the wear of three centuries.

We adjourn to the steamer, as it grows dark, and the rest of the evening is spent very pleasantly listening to a performance on the piano by a person of very remarkable musical talents. He is nothing more or less than one of the waiters who assist at table on board the boat, but his education and bearing are evidently far above his present occupation. His performance on the piano was simply marvellous. When he had played for some time, he got an accordean, mounted like a harmonium, which he played with one hand, accompanying himself at the piano with the other. A third variation was created by a fellow-waiter accompanying himself at this performance with a penny whistle. The effect of the whole was very striking. On inquiry I found out that the pianist was the son of a celebrated piano-maker in London, that he came out to America only a few months ago "to seek his fortune," that he could get nothing to do, and was forced, by way of a beginning, to become waiter on board this steamer. He is on the eve of something better he told me afterwards. Another waiter, who happens to be a native of the "beautiful citie" of Cork, hears by some means that I am a Corkman, and his delight is unbounded. His name is Howard, he was born in Evergreen, and the greenest spot in his memory is the "Botanic Gardens." During the voyage he was specially attentive to me, and could never pass without giving me a confidential smile, as if he would say, "You and I understand each other, we are from the same city of Cork, you know." All he possesses he would give to catch another glimpse of his native city, of the vegetables that grow in the market-garden of Evergreen, and the tombstones that grace the final resting-place of the dead, amidst the trees and shrubs of the Botanic Gardens.

In due time we retire to rest, and in the morning, when we dress, we go on deck and find ourselves anchored in a pretty cove, with hills all around, some rocky and barren, others wooded to the water's edge, while two small villages grace the banks—one just at hand and one at a considerable distance; but both so quiet that not a sound strikes the ear. This is " Ha-ha Bay "—a curious name, and one arising from a strange circumstance. When the French first rowed up the Saguenay in a canoe, they turned in here, thinking it a continuation of the river, but soon their little craft came in contact with the ground, and looking backward, they saw themselves shut in on every side. They cried " Ha, ha," in surprise, and, turning back, found that the course of the river lay in a northerly direction.

Our vessel will remain here until 10 o'clock, and then we proceed down the river to view its celebrated scenery. The morning is lovely — bright, calm, and warm. After breakfast we land, and go up on the most elevated of the hills in our neighbourhood to fulfil a twofold object—namely, to take some exercise, for we had been very confined for the last twenty-four hours, and to take views of the country all around. There is a portion of the river much higher up than that to which we ascend, but the boats rarely go so far, for in some parts it is fit only for a canoe, and there are rapids which can be got over only with considerable difficulty. At 10 o'clock we start to do "the Saguenay." We have sixty-five miles to traverse before we get back to Tadousac.

And now for the river. All along there are mountains on both sides; in some places they are quite bare, in others thinly wooded, while for the most part foliage of every hue extends from the summit to the very water. Here and there a cataract leaps down from the top, perhaps from a height of fifteen hundred feet, peeping out through the woods, and then hiding itself again—the only thing of life, and that only life in a figurative sense, distinguishable in this awful solitude. Barrenness and desolation are around us on every side; not even a bird passes in the air or makes the wood resound with song; not even a solitary goat browses on the herbage, for here no herbage grows. Animal life seeks in vain for sustenance in this inexorable soil. Silence, oppressive silence, reigns on every side. The voice of the tumbling cataract is the only sound that salutes the ear. We reach Trinity Rock, an enormous pile of naked granite standing right over the river at an elevation of nine hundred feet. The steamer steers immediately under it, and steam is shut off, that we may view the scene. The huge bluff rocks look down from above, and seem to threaten us with destruction. A revolver is fired off to awaken the echoes, which are very fine, but cannot compare with those of the "Eagle's Nest," at Killarney, to which, indeed, Trinity Rock is not unlike. Here we experience a curious optical illusion. While standing under the rock we fancy we are very near it, and the captain, as is usual, had provided at Ha-ha Bay a bucket of stones, that persons relying on their powers of projection might try to strike the rock at the nearest point. Several attempted, but all failed. The distance appeared so little that one would fancy a child might hit the rock, but the stones flung by a dozen volunteers invariably fell into the tide; they appeared to go straight towards the rock, and then, at the last moment, they made a curve backward, as if the rock repelled them. One gentleman went very vigorously to work. He told us that he was always remarkable for throwing a stone well. He went so far as to take off his coat, and yet, after a vigorous effort, failed in the attempt.

The point of interest is Eternity Bay, where there is another elevation, somewhat about fifteen hundred feet high, all beautifully wooded and very precipitous. The whole river is magnificent, and at some points presents the appearance of a lake, entirely shut in by wooded hills, the most abandoned solitude it is possible to conceive. The depth of the water at some points has never been ascertained; it is considered unfathomable, and its colour is as near as possible approaching to black. It was in this neighbourhood, but higher up, that the fire took place by which so many houses were burnt and the inhabitants were thrown upon the charity of the public. The woods somehow were wrapped in one wild conflagration, which spread over a distance of three hundred miles, destroying all the human habitations in its way.

We reached Tadousac at half-past two o'clock, and continued our voyage on to Quebec, admiring on the one hand the mountains, on the other the villages that graced the banks of the majestic St. Lawrence. We reached Quebec at 2 a.m., but did not disembark until morning. The day we spent in visiting our friends, in procuring a bill of exchange for the money we had received, and making other preparations for our voyage to Halifax, Nova Scotia.

CHAPTER VI.

THE LAND OF THE BLUE NOSES.

Quæ regio in terris nostri non plena laboris!

August 5.—At 4 p.m. we went on board the "Georgia," a very fine ocean steamer (Captain Connell), bound to Picton, Nova Scotia, the farthest point to which she goes; the journey from Picton to Halifax to be accomplished by rail. The evening was fine and warm. Our passengers were not numerous, and amongst them were six nuns, bound to Charlottetown, Prince Edward's Island, and two Christian Brothers, bound to the same place, the former to join a convent, the latter to found schools. The nuns were under the protection of a French Canadian priest from Montreal, from which place they had come by this same ship the previous day. When passing Gros Isle, to which I have already alluded, the captain told me some startling things of the unhappy sufferers, to whose misfortunes he was an eye-witness. At that time he had been a pilot on the St. Lawrence.

Next morning we reach a place called Father Point, where some of our passengers land. From this place the bank of the river on the right-hand side becomes very hilly and wooded. Mountains beyond mountains appear, some about three thousand feet high, and so close are they in many places that the captain assured us the snow and ice of winter is never melted in the valleys. The bank on the other side can scarcely be seen. The river at the farthest point is thirty miles wide; it then spreads and become the Gulf of St. Lawrence. The weather is bright and cool, and we have a moon at night, and while we sit in groups, and tell stories on deck, a beautiful *Aurora Borealis* appears, and charms us with its ever varying form, and the dancing movement of its rays.

On the second morning, about seven o'clock, we pass between the mainland and a long, curiously-shaped rock. This rock is several hundred feet long, very high, and cut quite sharp, so that its summit cannot be reached by any creature, save a bird. And accordingly, as if conscious of their security, crowds of birds swarm upon it, conspicuous amongst which is the penguin. In this rock Nature has carved a large round hole, through and through. The name of this isolated mountain of stone is "Percy," called from this carved hole, the rock being in the French language "percé"—*i.e.*, pierced. Such is also the name of a small village just here on the main land, at which we touch. Farther out is a considerable island called "Bonaventure Island," mostly cultivated, and with many houses scattered over its surface.

We now fall right out into the deep, and for some time lose sight of land altogether. On the night of the second day after leaving Quebec we stay at Shediac, a small seaport in New Brunswick. Here we remain over night. Next morning, while the vessel is being unloaded of a miscellaneous cargo, chiefly flour, we saunter about the shore; some of our party, principally young folks, go and fish, and are very successful in their attempts, as we found at breakfast and dinner; others go to bathe; some walk to see the town—a small thing some two miles distant. The weather all through the voyage was lovely. Remote as the place is from the inhabited world,

I find an Irishman from Dungarvan, who shakes my hand with all the warmth of brotherly affection.

About 12 o'clock we weigh anchor, and steer for Prince Edward's Island. By this time the passengers have all become more friendly with each other. There is a Mr. Barker, from Picton, an elderly gentleman, and his daughter, Miss Barker, a clever and interesting young lady. There is a Dr. Haight, from the same place, a Mr. McLord, from Montreal, a young man of family, for he tells us of his ancestry, and particularizes one who was an officer under Wolfe, on the plains of Abraham. Here is Mr. Brown, of Montreal, and two young lads, his sons, a quiet, very gentlemanly and social man, who gives me a good deal of information about Canada, and confirms all I have said about the Canadians. There are many others, but one is remarkable above the rest. A handsome young man, with very black hair, dark complexion, black eyes, a moustache, and a very French air, he wears a Turkish fez and looks picturesque with his suit of tweed, and a meerschaum. This is M. Turgeon, an advocate of Montreal. He speaks English just enough to increase the interest you feel in him for the beauty of his person. He and I understand each other at once; he has travelled over Europe, and knows life and the world. Thus we get to Prince Edward's Island, which at length discloses itself to view from the bosom of the ocean, a long island, over 130 miles in length, and about 35, at the widest, in breadth. It reminds me much of Ireland; isolated from continental lands, green as emerald, and fertile as Nature can be, with pleasant harbours, and—but here the comparison ceases—with a happy and contented population, self-governed, and only wanting to be let alone by the world, which it is to be feared will not let it alone, but which, despite its inexhaustible treasures of land, is still crying out, "annexation! annexation!"*

We do not reach the harbour's mouth that opens to Charlottetown until dark, but we have a full moon and a clear sky. We see, as we approach, the dim outlines of ships and wharves and houses, and church spires, and this is the metropolis, the mother city of Prince Edward's Island. We are moored about 8 o'clock, and Turgeon and I go ashore together, after having bade farewell to the nuns and the two Christian Brothers. We stroll through the dimly-lighted streets—the main street; gas has not yet found its way in here. We wish to find a decent hotel; it is called the "City Hotel" (for the Prince Edward Islanders call their town of 7,000† inhabitants a city). We reach it, and enter. Our chief desire is to hear the news of the great European conflict now waging between the Prussians and French. Up to this time no serious engagement has taken place, nor has the dignity of either Power been compromised. We find ourselves in a place that might be called the reading-room of the hotel, and we take up the paper of the day, Prince Edward's Island *Examiner*. Here we find news from Europe, *three days old*, exactly the same that we had heard before we left Quebec. This was disheartening; but it happened just as we were deploring the telegraphic shortcomings of P. E. Island, that

---

* Prince Edward's Island was incorporated (as a distinct State) in the Dominion of Canada in 1873.

† Now over 11,000.

a written telegram arrived, giving an account of a terrible battle between the Prussians and French, in which the latter were defeated with wholesale disaster.

On our way towards the ship we reach the cathedral, a fair church enough, with a very great tower and a very short spire. Next door was the bishop's palace, outside was a carriage and horse, and the two Christian Brothers were urging the nuns to enter, and proceed to the convent. The nuns, no doubt believing that the carriage was too small, were resisting and expressing a determination to walk, as the night was so fine. There was a good deal of argument between the brothers and sisters on the subject; but at last the horse brought matters to a speedy conclusion. He seemed to have grown weary of listening, and so in brief he simply " took head." Away he dashed at full speed, the nuns aghast and the two brothers stupefied. We followed the runaway, who went right round the next corner, pursued by a few young men, who had been standing by, and found that he had toppled over, having done very little injury to himself, and only broken the box of the carriage.

We proceeded towards the ship, which we reached in time, as all things are reached. We slept on board, for the ship stayed here as at Shadiac over night, and next morning in like manner a great part of the cargo was discharged. In the morning again Turgeon and I sally forth together to do Charlottetown. But there is nothing to do. It is a very plain city, with the streets broad, and cutting each other at right angles. A voice from a window salutes us. It is that of Miss Barker, who has taken up lodgings here. A judge from Montreal is also staying here, for it is a watering-place, and rather frequented by people from the continent of America. The Judge breakfasts with us on board.

We got some notions of Prince Edward's island. It is a very fertile island, and produces a great quantity of grain. The clay is of the old red sandstone description, and it is said that there is scarcely a stone in the whole island. The population is 80,000 ;* the Catholic religion appears to be predominant. Bishop McIntyre is the present prelate, the whole island being one see, with 22 priests to 43 churches.

The people are independent and proud, regarding themselves as quite able to manage their own affairs, and scorning to belong to the Dominion or the States, not reflecting that but for the protection of *some* greater power they should become the prey of the first that wished to invade them. There is no poverty on this island, and the people are lazy and indifferent to advantages of labour. Thus the captain offered some loungers one shilling an hour to assist him in unloading, and although they admitted the payment to be just and fair, they declined, much to his annoyance and indignation. During the winter the island is icebound, and for several months the inhabitants devote themselves to the pursuit of literature, with a zeal proportionate to the vast store of knowledge to be acquired. If those people, despite their insular views, die happy, why disturb them? The population are chiefly of Scotch and North of Ireland descent. The land is undulating, and there is scarcely a decent hill anywhere. There is a submarine telegraph to Nova Scotia, which is some connection with the world.

At 11 o'clock, August the 9th, we proceed to Picton, a distance about 60 miles across the Northumberland Sound.

---

* Now about 110,000.

The air is very warm, and the voyage consequently very pleasant. We reach Pictou at 3 o'clock, about an hour too late to catch the train to Halifax. We must be content to stay here all day and night, and leave for Halifax next morning. Pictou is a pretty town, situated on the side of a gently-sloping hill, not very high. The harbour is narrow, and opens into a large basin, which looks like a lake, not quite so picturesque, nor so large as that of Queenstown, yet resembling it somewhat. We go on shore, and seek the chief hotel, where we first of all look for the news. Unfortunately for Mr. Turgeon, the intelligence from the seat of war thoroughly confirms all we had heard at Charlottetown, and adds the account of fresh disasters. His incredulity is too sorely tested, and he takes refuge in resignation.

We walk through the town and are surprised at its dulness. It is as quiet as any Irish town I ever saw. We return to the ship. Some go to bathe, including Turgeon, McCord, and the young Browns. They return to tea, after which we all go boating in the lovely water, smooth as glass. The beautiful moonlight forms fiery serpents dancing on the water in our neighbourhood, and illumines it into one silvery sheet farther on. We sing, and are, of course, pleased with the effect of our own voices. We are very happy. Turgeon sings French songs, and we applaud as well as we can. We return to the vessel and spend an hour or more on deck enjoying the loveliness of the scene and the balm of the air. I know not how it is, but strangers as we all are to each other, we feel as if we loved each other, and condensed into an hour the pleasantness of a communion which, for most of us, must be soon broken for ever. We retire early, for we must be up early in the morning to start for Halifax.

We leave Pictou at 6 a.m. Three rivers flow into this harbour, and are navigable to about 60 miles up the country. Here also are coal mines of great value. We journey onward through a very wooded country all the way (112 miles in eight hours) to Halifax, very little diversified with signs of cultivation. The land is poor, oats being the chief crop. Wheat is not much grown in Nova Scotia, as it becomes the victim of a small insect called the "weevil," which destroys it in the first stages of its ripeness. Consequently there is a large importation of flour.

The population of Nova Scotia is only about 350,000,* about one-tenth of the population of London. Shipbuilding is carried on to a great extent here, and some of the wealthiest shipowners in the world are said to be Nova Scotians. Certainly there is wood enough on the peninsula to build all the ships of the world, and much more.

The Indians are protected here, and we see several of them and their very rude wigwams — horribly ugly creatures, especially the women. Several beautiful lakes lie between the woods, one fifteen miles long. The scenery round those is magnificent, and one cannot help thinking how one of them would adorn a nobleman's demesne, and what pleasant times one could spend sailing over them in a yacht, or fishing, as fancy would suggest. Truro is the name of the most important town, about halfways on the route.

In due time we reach Bedford, a pretty place at the head of Halifax Basin. The first glimpse of this basin which we have here is fifteen miles from the city,

---

* Now about 450,000.

which is here visible—a very lovely view of hill, wood, water, and islands. I begin to think Killarney is in danger of losing its post of pre-eminence in my admiration. It so happens that there is a large pic-nic party at Bedford, and the sight of many ladies strolling through the fields and along the rocky shore makes the scene very picturesque. The conductor points out a pretty pavilion-like building raised by the Duke of Kent, the Queen's father, when he was Governor here. It commands a view of marvellous beauty.

At length we reach Halifax, and put up at the "Halifax Hotel," Hollis Street, with which we were very much pleased. Halifax is a pretty city, long and narrow, situated along the shore of the sea with a commodious harbour. The ascent from the shore is very gradual and of small account. The summit behind the city is crowned by a fortification called the "Citadel," which commands a splendid view of the city, the bay, and the country beyond. At the other side of the water also on the shore is a very thriving town called Dartmouth. Halifax is built in "blocks," with the streets running parallel, and intersected by others running parallel. There is a good sprinkling of trees through the city; it is remarkably clean, and quiet almost to dulness. Instead of a quay there are several wharves in the midst of the water. Just in front of the town rises a large island, which is mounted with cannon, and forms a great protection for the harbour. The population is, I believe, about 35,000, about half being Catholics and the rest of different religious persuasions. The Mayor, Mr. Stephen Tobin, though born here is the son of a Cork mother. Mr. Kenny, Governor *pro tem*, *vice* General Doyle, a man of immense wealth, is an Irishman. Several of the leading merchants are Irish. The Archbishop (Connelly) is a Cork man. Few come here from Ireland of late years, and those who are here are chiefly from Waterford and Kerry. The British money is used here commonly, and it is pleasant to me once more to handle sovereigns and half-crowns.

In the evening while airing myself on the steps of the hotel, a gentleman accosts me and tells me he heard me preach in Quebec, but what is more astonishing, he adds that he often heard me preach in Cork. I am amazed, and think of the line:—"*Quæ regio in terris nostri non plena laboris?*" The clergy receive us kindly. We call on the Mayor, a fine young gentleman, who takes us to his office, contributes to the object of our mission, and invites us to his house. Mr. Kenny, the Deputy Governor, is equally kind. The citizens in general treat us with great courtesy, and we soon feel quite at home. I preach in the Cathedral on Sunday, and we dine with the Mayor the same evening.

Monday (August 15) is a holiday, and there is a procession through the principal streets of the Temperance Association, men and boys with scarfs, &c. The procession begins at the Cathedral, and ends there. The Glebe House, where the clergy reside, is close by. The men stop and cheer, and then, to my surprise, the band plays "God save the Queen," and all uncover. Irishmen can be loyal in Nova Scotia, but not at home.

The loss of the "City of Boston" threw a great gloom over Halifax.* About thirty notable persons were

---

*The *City of Boston* left Halifax for Liverpool on Jan. 28, 1870; and was never heard of again.

drowned in that vessel. Mr. Kenny, the deputy governor, lost a son, a fine young man. Mr. Patrick Power, member for the city, lost a son, his partner and his nephew. One day, travelling in a street car, I saw a nurse in charge of two lovely children, of whom one was in arms. I admired the children, and told her so. "Sir, their father was lost in the 'City of Boston,'" she said. Indeed, wherever we turn we find some person who has to deplore the loss of a relative or friend in the ill-fated ship.

The Mayor is very kind. There was a regatta on Monday, and in the evening there were public amusements in the Gardens. To these gardens the Mayor took us. It was very pretty. The show was what the papers call a "decided success." There was a band of the 78th Highlanders, and several gymnastic feats were performed by soldiers. The whole garden was illuminated by Chinese lanterns, Kerosene lamps, &c., and the attendance was very large. That night twelvemonths I was gazing on the illuminations of Paris, in honour of the Fête Napoleon. Had any one told me then, that on the next 15th of August I should be viewing illuminations in Halifax, how surprised I would have been, and what speculations I would have indulged in, as to how such an event was to be accomplished.

The Hon. Mr. Kenny is a man of great wealth, as well as high position. He is a Kerryman and made his own fortune. He invited us to spend an evening at the house of his daughter-in-law, Mrs. Kenny, which we did. The house was magnificent, just over an arm of the sea, and the opposite shore all wooded. The company was very large and embraced clergy, laity and ladies. We had a grand supper at 7 o'clock, and then various amusements, cards, singing, billiards; everything was elegant, yet easy and homely. I met some Cork people here and some few who had been in Cork. It was very agreeable to converse with them about the "beautiful citie." Mr. Kenny has invited us to his own house for Friday. In this part of the American continent people generally dine early. The hour for dinner at the hotel is 1 o'clock, while supper comes off at 6. At Mrs. Kenny's we had not supper, but what is called "high tea," that is to say tea with meats, pastry and fruit—somewhat like our *déjeuner à la fourchette* at home.

As we are on the local names of things, I may here mention that the name for a Nova Scotian is "Blue Nose," because in winter the extreme cold imparts a peculiarly cerulean tinge to the olfactories of the natives. It is quite common on asking a man where he was born, to hear him reply, "I am a Blue Nose," meaning that he was born in Nova Scotia. We find the people here very generous. They contribute largely and with pleasure to the object of our mission.

As in most parts of America, the Irish occupy all positions, from the highest to the lowest. If you find a man in Halifax who has raised himself by his talents and industry to a post of wealth and influence, the chances are almost entirely in favour of his being an Irishman. If, on the other hand, you find one occupying a wretched house, in squalor and wretchedness, he too is a Hibernian; one thing is certain, namely, if an Irishman does not succeed in America it is not the fault of his nationality, the failure can be traced to his own personal shortcomings in some fatal point. Nothing is so remarkable in Halifax as the extreme quietness of the city. There is no noise, no thronging of carts or carriages, no crowding of people, no hurry or bustle of any kind; I never before saw so much absence of business apparent in a city. There are no manufactories here, although the natural resources of the country are very great. In the neighbourhood of Halifax are mines of gold, tin, lead, silver, iron, and coal; there is an abundance of water-power and yet no manufactures. The people complain that the wealthy inhabitants are "close" and unenterprising, and almost three out of every four are anxious for annexation to the States.

We dined at Mr. Kenny's own house on Tuesday, the 25th, a beautiful cottage just over the basin already spoken of, and buried in foliage, through vistas of which one can catch charming views of the water. The weather is all that can be desired. Indeed the climate of Halifax, or rather of all Nova Scotia, is remarkably mild and quite free from the extremes which render other parts of the American continent so disagreeable. The heat in summer is seldom unbearable, and the cold in winter never excessive. Thunderstorms are very rare and the mosquitoes, those plagues of the South, never torture the epidermis of a "Blue Nose."

At Mr. Kenny's we spent a very pleasant evening. Several of the clergy were present, and some ladies. Mr. K. sent us home six miles in his own carriage. Mr. Davy, son of the late R. M. of Bantry, was also very attentive to us. He had us to "high tea," which was got up very sumptuously indeed. In a word, we received all manner of kindness in Halifax, and prepared with great regret to leave it. I sent home from here £200 (the second to the Bishop) by the "City of Baltimore." The more we went amongst the people of Halifax the more reason we had to admire the depth and sincerity of that two-fold attachment which seems to be the birthright of Irishmen—namely, the love of their religion and the love of their native land. Whenever we entered a house we were received with a smile of welcome, and a shake hands which placed us at once at our ease. We were then ushered into the drawing-room, and all the members of the family were summoned to meet us; in many places they kissed our hands, and fell on their knees for our blessing. The subscriptions we received were sometimes apparently so far beyond the position of the donor, that we declined accepting them until we were assured that they could afford them. "Oh! dear, you cannot afford to give so much." "Indeed I can, sir; and since God was so good as to give me more than enough, the least I can do is to give Him a little when He asks me for it." We were often touched by remarks of this kind. The Catholics here are excellent in their devotion to the faith and the general practice of religion. The clergy assured me that the highest in rank were the most exemplary in this respect, which is not always the case.

We were very hospitably treated by the clergy of Halifax. The Vicar-General, the Rev. Dr. Hannon, invited us to dinner. Father Daly, another member of that body, gave us a grand entertainment, at which several of the local gentry were present. Father Allen (a native of Kinsale) had us to a grand pic-nic at a place called Dutch Village, some three miles from town, a spot exquisitely picturesque. Here also we met a number of lay gentlemen.

On the last day we spent in Halifax we were invited by the same Father Allen to a "children's pic-nic." This children's pic-nic is quite an American institution. During the summer months, the children of the various schools all proceed on a certain day appointed for the purpose, either by railroad or steamer, to some place where they spend the day in all kinds of sports, under the guardianship of some priest or other teacher, then dine *in globo*; and again, like the Israelites of old, after feasting, rise to play. *Ex uno disce omnes.* From Father Allen's pic-nic you may learn of what kind are all the rest. A carriage was sent for us to our hotel, at 2 o'clock, p.m. The pic-nic was to be held on the grounds of the Archbishop's country-house, some three miles from the town. Thither we proceeded, and reached the place in almost half-an-hour. A magnificent mansion indeed, very large, and built in a style of great architectural beauty, although of wood, as are most of the houses in this part of America; wood is warm and cheap, and durable, and though it may imply that the owner is not able to rise to the dignity of limestone or granite, for all practical purposes it is as good as either. Why should we sacrifice so much of our happiness to idle sentiment?

The house is at present rented (during the summer months, in the absence of the Archbishop) by a Mr. and Mrs. Dwyer, a young couple only recently married, whom we met at Mr. Davis' "high tea" a few evenings before. Mrs. Dwyer was a Miss McTavish from St. John's, N.B., a very charming young lady, and her sister-in-law, Miss Dwyer, whom we also met there, is on a visit with her. We call, and they receive us very kindly.

We then go through the grounds, which we find to be splendid. Woods and forests abound in Nova Scotia, and here are fields, surrounded by trees, shut in from all the world. A few hundred children, boys and girls, are disporting themselves in various ways. There are several "swing-swongs," where the little ones enjoy the pleasure of oscillation. There are two or three spots covered plentifully with boards, where boys and girls move on the light fantastic to the music of a violinist hired for the occasion; the big boys amuse themselves with foot-ball. Some parents and friends of the children are about, and we see enacted the spectacle described by Goldsmith, of "the young contending as the old survey." Father Allen is the presiding genius—a good-natured and very gentlemanly young man. Long tables are arranged for the dinner, and there is a respectable staff of servants, for the thing seems to be got up regardless of expense. The children are almost all Irish, either by descent or birth, and while they have lost some, they retain many characteristics of their race. They are very tastefully dressed; very self-possessed and intelligent. When spoken to, they reply with confidence, and always address themselves to the point. They prefer Irish airs for their dances to all others; and in their games of contention they display all the vivacity, enthusiasm, and pugnaciousness of the Celt. This latter peculiarity was manifested strikingly in the game of foot-ball. Twenty-four boys played twelve aside, and they called themselves the French and Prussians. The battle raged with as much fury as the contest just now being waged between the original nations they represented. The sympathy of the bystanders was strongly carried in favour of the French, but the Prussians fought nevertheless with unflinching pluck. At length of course the French triumphed, and it was hard for the beaten Prussians not to join in the general shouts of congratulation.

We had a splendid dinner, and when the viands were

consumed, toasts, speeches and songs followed, in all of which amusement we were obliged, not unwillingly to share. We then adjourned to the house where we met Mrs. and Miss Dwyer, whom we induced to come out on the steps and witness several running matches between the boys on the lawn. These were admirably contested, under the admiring gaze of the young girls who ranged themselves in front of the house. Just as the games were contested, a gentleman, accompanied by two ladies, rode on horseback into our midst. These were a Mr. Stubbins, and two cousins of Miss Dwyer—namely, the Misses Tobin. We spent the evening with the Mayor's family, and returned about midnight to our hotel.

Before leaving Halifax, I had an opportunity of seeing one of her Majesty's men of war, the "Royal Alfred," through which I was shown by Mr. Oliver, an Irish gentleman, one of the Admiral's staff, whose acquaintance I had made here. He introduced me to a lieutenant on board, a Mr. Gladstone, nephew to the Premier. I also visited the Citadel and expected to meet there a Dr. Clarke, another Irish gentleman whom I had met at Mr. Davy's. He was not *chez lui* at the time, but by the courtesy of an officer I was shown over the whole place. The view of Halifax and the neighbourhood from this point is truly grand. In the evening, just before we left, a telegram arrived from Archbishop Connolly, saying that he had left New York and might be expected in Halifax next day. This was unpleasant, seeing that we were so near making his acquaintance and yet so far. We were delighted with everything in Halifax; with the charming scenery on every side; with the people, and above all, with the success of our mission. We received here the sum of 875 dollars—namely, £175.

CHAPTER VII.

ST. JOHN. GOOD-BYE TO CANADA.

Thursday, August 5th.—We leave Halifax by train at 6 a.m. The first ten miles are along the basin whose beauties I have already described; the next nineteen miles lead to Windsor, an important town at the head of the creek, and those nineteen miles present a scene of barrenness as wild as it is possible to imagine, always excepting the desert of Sahara. The ground is one mass of jagged rock, rising and falling in confusion most confounding, with interjacent herbage, scarcely sufficient to satisfy the cravings of a goat. Trees and forests there are no doubt, stretching far, far away, but for every one that looks green, ten seem charred or withered, as if by some blasting pestilence. In some places whole acres of wood have been cut down and the blighted stumps remain, and will remain, for the land is unsusceptible of tillage. At the termination of this vast wilderness starts up Windsor, a brisk, lively, bright little town, with good streets and a business-like air; and we see in the creek the masts of ships, and new ones building.

Away we fly from this little nest of human life, and Nature now, with that caprice for which she is so remarkable, robes herself in the gaudiest fashion of the period. The sun is shining so brightly, and there is a vast, oh! so vast a plain, stretching away and away, farther than the eye can see, with cattle that appears as small as ants in the distance, while beyond stand the mountains with their boundless forests, like a countless army protecting this region of beauty. And do you know what is the name of this charming region? Acadia. And what is this valley—this one smiling meadow called? It is no other than Grand Prê, immortalized as the scene of Longfellow's " Evangeline." The village of Grand Prê is near; the train pulls up there, and I long to get out and visit the spot from which the perfidious soldiers of Albion banished the guiltless children of this peaceful and happy land.

But we must on. The scenery from Windsor to Annapolis —129 miles—is famous for its beauty all over the world; mountain and vale and endless woods; the forest primeval; a broad river, teeming fields, and lazy cattle, some browsing on the herbage, some bathing in the water that seems loath to tear itself away from so much loveliness. We reach Annapolis, at half-past one, a very small village like Windsor. At the head of a creek we embark. We steam away. The captain is an Irishman of course, one O'Leary from Dunmanway. Co. Cork. At the end of an hour we reach Digby, a very small watering place within the harbour. Having given and taken passengers, we proceed. We pass through the harbour's mouth, which is very like a mouth indeed, and find ourselves in the Bay of Fundy, a portion of the Atlantic Ocean.

At Digby we took in a gentleman who was evidently a votary of Bacchus, and who had been very recently pouring libations at the shrine of that merry god. The unfortunate man soon becomes the laughing-stock of everybody. He will talk to every one, and in a very loud way. His perpendicular is constantly seeking the acute angle, and as we sit on deck he topples into our laps one after another. We have all to look out for our corns, at least such as have them. He makes a dead set on me. He devotes himself to me, and imparts all kind of knowledge about the coast, for he has been in the Bay of Fundy, forty, aye, a hundred times. He is continually mistaking the cardinal points, and frequently takes the bow of the boat for the stern, and his information is conveyed in such a jumble of speech, that no one can discern one word from another. He asks every one down to the bar, and as he can get no one to obey he goes himself, and returns after every visit with increased lubricity of tongue, and fresh unsteadiness of understanding; poor man, he becomes an object of universal commiseration, and preached by his conduct an admirable sermon on the vice of intemperance.

It is the hour of twilight as we steam up before St. John's. The city is built right on the sea, and looks very pretty, with its lamps, and dim church spires. It is built on an elevation, too low to be called a hill, and too large to be called a mound. The St. John river runs up from this point. On the right hand is the city, on the left the town called Carleton. We land and proceed to the Waverly House, the first hotel in the city, kept by Mr. Guthrie, an Irish Catholic. The Mayor of Halifax, who had been here last week, told us that we would find it hard to get rooms, and so he telegraphed to-day to say we were coming, and begging of Mr. Guthrie to make us comfortable. When our carriage arrived at the hotel, Mr. Guthrie looked through the window, and said in simple language, but with an expressive air, "All right."

August 26th.—At 6 o'clock in the morning I was waked out of my sleep by a noise; it was only a knocking at my door. "Come in," I cried. It was a young man like a waiter, with a very long nose. All Paul Prys have long noses. "Well, sir," said he, "Are you Father Buckley from Cork?" "Yes." "Why, then, sir, if you please," said he, and he spoke, oh! with such a sweet Cork brogue, "Are you the Father Buckley that was in Drinagh long ago?" "I am," I said. "Oh, sir, I thought so. The minute I saw your name in the book last night I said it was you. I knew you well, sir, and was often speaking to you there. My name is Donoghue. My father kept a forge in Drimmindy." "Ah, yes," I said, "I remember well." "Oh, Lord, sir," said he, "I am wild with joy at seeing you, and how in the world are you, your reverence?" Lest Mr. Donoghue might manifest his wild joy, in any peculiarly savage, however affectionate manner, I informed him that I would send for him in the course of the day, and have a long chat with him about the old country. He was satisfied, and I resumed my sleep.

We waited on the Bishop (Sweeny), who lives in a magnificent palace close to the Cathedral. This palace is built of stone, and its interior is quite in keeping with the exterior, tasteful, and elegant, and rich. The Bishop himself is a man of middle stature, gentlemanly, and good-humoured. He permitted us to collect, and invited us to dine with him on Sunday. We called on Mrs. Anglin, sister of Mrs. Dwyer, of Halifax, already alluded to, and wife to Mr. Anglin, editor of the St. John's *Freeman*. She said Mr. Anglin would call on us. So he did. He is a native of Clonakilty, Co. Cork, a thorough Catholic, and Irish patriot. He promised to notice our mission in the *Freeman* of to-morrow (and did so).

We visit Mr. MacSweeny, one of the wealthiest Catholic

Irishmen in St. John, N. B., a Corkman. We find him and his wife our best and staunchest friends during our stay in St. John. They came out from Cork in the year 1826, and by hard industry and good luck prospered, and now scarcely know how rich they are. They have no children, but they adopted various orphan children of relatives, whom they esteemed, and brought them up in the best manner that the resources of the province would allow. Mr. MacSweeny is a blunt man, very warm-hearted and munificent, extremely undemonstrative, silent; but when he does speak, talkative to some purpose, full of common sense, and large experience, an unflinching Catholic, and steadfast friend to all who need his assistance. Mrs. MacSweeny is an excellent woman, generous and hospitable, and straightforward. Both are highly, and from what I can see, justly esteemed by the inhabitants of St. John.

We called, as I have said, on Mr. and Mrs. MacSweeny. They entered warmly into our projects, and promised to assist us by every means in their power. Mr. MacS., who appears to be a man of large influence in St. John, immediately issued a summons for some of his neighbours to attend, and the summons was promptly obeyed. Arrangements were made for conducting us through the city. From all I saw I augured that our mission here was likely to be attended with success.

We call on Dr. Travers, the Bishop's brother-in-law, a member of the Travers family in the County of Cork, and a convert to the Catholic faith. We had a letter of introduction to him, and he receives us with the barest courtesy compatible with the conduct of a gentleman, for which, of course, we are very grateful. After dinner I am visited by Mr. T. Coghlan, a young gentleman, very well-mannered, intelligent and agreeable. He places himself entirely at my service, and I accept the offer. Thus the ground is becoming gradually broken all around, and I begin to feel quite at home. The hotel is excellent; the host genial. Indeed, the house resembles, not only to me, but to everyone, a home more than a hotel. I am not twenty-four hours in St. John, and I feel as if I had lived in it a year.

From inquiries and observation I am able to make some reliable remarks concerning St. John, N.B. It is a pretty city, with very good broad streets, and some excellent shops, or, as they are called in America, "stores." Two streets are particularly fine, Prince William Street and King Street, in the latter of which is our hotel. There is considerable bustle and animation in the streets. In this respect the city is very different from Halifax, of whose indolent air I have already written. In the evening there is a good deal of promenading, and the inhabitants are very lively and chatty. From some points there are good views of the sea, and the sights of ships in the river, and the thronging of the wharves is pleasant to a stranger. Ferry-boats, such as first excited my surprise at New York, ply here constantly between the city and Carleton, already alluded to. There is also a fine suspension-bridge leading across, under which are very respectable "falls," at low water. High water fills the chasm, and the falls disappear. Fogs are very frequent in St. John, but, as they come from the sea, however unpleasant, they are not unhealthy. The climate is mild all the year round as a rule, but exceptions are frequent. In the suburbs there are some excellent mansions, but not many, for St. John contains only a population of 35,000*, and is of a comparatively recent growth. There are no manufactories worth talking of, and scarcely any public buildings. One or two small "squares" with their grass and trees relieve the eye; cars are confined to one point as the streets are hilly, but good carriages may be had for moderate fares. This seems to be all that can be said of the city.

The people are very agreeable in their manners, social, easy, good-humoured and polite. It is very much to be regretted that religious bigotry prevails here to some extent, a far greater extent indeed than the people seem willing to admit. The population is about equally divided between Catholics and all other denominations. The former have only one church—the cathedral—an ostentatious building erected at an expense far beyond the result in proportion. There are several churches of other religious bodies, whose towers and spires lend a picturesqueness to the scenery, and no doubt fulfil loftier and worthier ends. The hatred of Catholicity was very great in St. John long ago, that is to say in the last generation; but the growth of that Church has disarmed contempt and opposition. An old man one day said to me, "Sir, when I came out here from Ireland, some forty years ago, it was a dangerous thing in St. John to you if you were a Catholic; but now we have it all our own way." Few Catholics, however, hold wealth or prominence in St. John; perhaps four or five is the highest number. Hence they find it hard to bear up against the spirit of ascendancy which belongs to the other party. The Press does not strive to allay the pernicious feeling, and during my stay the

---

* This includes Portland. The population at present is about 42,000.

Protestant *Telegraph* and the Catholic *Freeman* had a smart passage of arms on the religious aspect of the Franco-Prussian War.

Trade is not active in St. John. Some time ago shipbuilding was a large source of wealth and prosperity, but it has fallen away. In America the sunlight of commerce seems disposed to shine only on the States; the Dominion languishes in the "cold shade of opposition." Here again, amongst a large section, the cry is "annexation," which some few, however, persist in regarding as the certain forerunners of failure and disaster.

That spirit of disunion which has become the proverbial source of Ireland's misery, is here apparent among her children. The Catholics do not agree amongst themselves; they have cliques and parties, and petty hatred. I am told that there are three classes of Catholics in St. John, distinguished by a conventional estimate of their relative respectability. I must say, however, for myself, that I found the people of all classes to be generous and courteous in the highest degree. The Catholics are justly praised for their attachment to the faith; and in no place did I find this quality so strongly developed. With it, as usual everywhere amongst Irishmen, grew and flourished an ardent love of their native land. And here also, as in other parts of the British Provinces, did I find that the love of Ireland is as strong, if not stronger, in those of Irish descent, as in the Hibernian born. I suppose this is owing, in a great measure, to the vivid imagination of our people, who from their infancy upwards picture to themselves in colours even more heightened than reality, the loveliness of Erin and the virtue of her children.

In going about from house to house, from garret to garret, I was able to see very clearly the condition of the Irish emigrants, and I regret to say that in few instances was their condition improved. Many had as well have remained at home, for they live here as in their former dwellings, in poverty, and in no wise different because they have changed their position on the globe. In St. John I met an immense number of people from Cork City and Cork County, the great majority of whom had come out here some eighteen or twenty years ago, few later, but they, save in few instances, had risen to no higher position than that of an humble tradesmen or shopkeeper, while they alone are the hewers of wood and drawers of water. One thing is very clear, as I have already remarked, and it is that the generation who emigrate do not as a rule rise in the social scale, but their children born here, imbibing that love of freedom which, as it were, floats in the atmosphere of America, and meeting their fellow men on the same platform, grow independent and self-asserting, and become an honour to the land of their ancestors.

Every day the impression grows deeper and deeper on my mind that the Irish, with all their faults, are the noblest race in all the world; they have qualities of head and heart superior to the rest of mankind, and but for the centuries of iniquitous persecution to which they were victimised, would long since have displayed those qualities, so as to extort the admiration of their fellow-men. Weeds grow in every garden. The Irish mind and heart have been left untilled, uncultivated for ages; the atmosphere around them was poisoned by hatred, contempt, persecution, and neglect; but another day has come, they have been transplanted to a more genial climate, and to a more productive soil, the sunshine of freedom prevents their decay, the waters of peace develop their vitality, they grow and flourish from year to year, from generation to generation, destined by their triumphs of industry and skill to confute the prejudices of the old world, by founding and perpetuating the greatness of the new.

We proceed on our collection, Mr. MacSweeny opening the list with a cheque for 100 dollars. On the subject of our collection I may say that we realized in St. John altogether the sum of 1,100 dollars and were enabled to send home to the Bishop the third £200. Nor did we experience any difficulty in making up this large sum of money; the people gave with great generosity. Not one person said an unkind word, and we met very little meanness. The donations in general were small, but everyone gave something.

I met a great number of Irish people as I passed from house to house, and the vast majority of those I met were from the County or City of Cork. Some knew me, having come within the last few years; but immigration to St. John has ceased; people prefer going to the States. Several spoke the Irish language and were delighted to hear me converse in it. I need not repeat all the complimentary things they said about my appearance, &c., nor all the loving expressions they used to show their predilection for a priest fresh from the old country. One woman said, "Wisha, hasn't he the rale look of the ould sod." Another, "Oh, then, father, I would like to be following you all day." When we got into a street the news of our coming went abroad. All had their subscriptions ready for us, and if by chance we passed by any house a messenger was sent after us to remind us of our mistake. Our progress was slow, as we had for the most part to sit down, and tell the people some news of the dear country they had left behind. No one was poor, that is to say, absolutely poor; even in the humblest houses the good women had their twenty-five or forty cents ready for us, and gave them with a good heart. In many cases they gave and then inquired the object. It was sufficient for them that they gave to an Irish priest. Indeed no words could exaggerate the intense love of religion and fatherland that animates the breasts of the Irish abroad as well as at home.

We attended a large pic-nic given for the St. Vincent de Paul Society, at a very beautiful place seven miles from town, on the banks of the river "Kennebekasis," a tributary of St. John river. The house and grounds belong to the Bishop, whose mother occupies them at present. A pic-nic such as they have in America is altogether different from ours. It is a means of raising money for some specified object, chiefly charitable. It is advertised that a picnic is to come off on such or such a day, at such or such a place, and that the people can go to it either by rail or steamer. The committee hire the rail or steamer for that day for a certain sum, and receive by the sale of tickets a sum that leaves a large surplus to their account. Then there are various sports on the grounds, such as foot-racing, leaping, archery, dancing, quoits, and several other amusements. Tickets are got for admission to the grounds. Refreshments also are to be had, and the total receipts go for the object specified. Great crowds gather on these occasions, and the number varies with the popularity of the object. All are well dressed, and apparently happy. No excess or disorder of any kind takes place; no intoxicating liquor is sold on the grounds, and although on such occasions the majority of those who assemble are Irish, yet you miss the broad, loud-voiced hilarity of such gatherings at home, and however you may be a lover of peace, you are inclined to sigh for one flourish of a shillelagh, and one cheer for the successful wielder of the national weapon. We drove out in a carriage and pair with Mr. Guthrie, his daughter, and Miss McDonough. Some hundreds were assembled. The day was all that could be desired, the Bishop also was present; we walked through all the grounds, several persons asked for an introduction, and we were nothing loath to satisfy them.

A party of us was arranged to go up the St. John river to Fredericton, on Saturday, September 10th, and we all looked forward to it with great pleasure. On the principle of the "more the merrier," we endeavoured to recruit as many as possible for the day's enjoyment.

Who is not acquainted with the American's love of advertisement? Of this their newspapers give striking evidence, for three quarters of every journal are crowded with advertisements of every description, while only one quarter is devoted to local, foreign, or general news, and lest the ordinary mode of advertising may prove ineffective, considerable ingenuity is shown in attracting the reader's attention to special notices. Thus in the editorial columns, where you expect to read something peculiarly novel and startling in the way of intelligence, you find yourself decoyed by a startling heading into a description of some potent quack medicine or other "Yankee notion." But I need not give examples of what every one knows. For my part I was excessively annoyed one day when reading, amongst other things, a very startling story in a newspaper, to find that towards the conclusion, where I anxiously expected the *denouement*, I was treated to a description of the wondrous qualities of " Helmbold's Bucha " or " Parson's Pills." One of the most artful dodges in the way of advertising that I have yet encountered was one I witnessed in St. John. A splendid open carriage is driven through the streets by four spanking horses. The equipage and harness are superb. At some public square or market-place, where people most do congregate, the horses pull up, and the gaudy vehicle is transformed into a kind of platform, on which four or five musicians, sumptuously attired, take their places. A concert, vocal and instrumental, is improvised, and the programme is really excellent. In the intervals of the playing and singing, Coryphœus expounds the merits of a new and powerful medicine, just invented, possessing in itself all the qualities of all the medicines ever known before. No disease can stand before the redoutable nostrum, and the cure is wrought not slowly, and only in part, but suddenly, effectually, and for ever. This wonder of the world, this miracle of Pharmacopœia, is entitled " Flagg's Instant Relief," and is sold for the ridiculously small sum of *one dollar per bottle*. Will it be believed that thousands are gulled by the blarney of these itinerant musical medicine vendors, and the great unseen Flagg realizes a gigantic fortune by the credulity of an innocent public? No less than twelve equipages of this kind do the work of advertising and selling his " Instant Relief;" and it is said fifty dollars a day is about the amount received by each troupe, an enormous receipt in return for a trifling outlay.

Saturday comes and at twelve noon we leave by steamer for Fredericton, by the St. John river, a distance of eighty-five miles. This river is considered one of the beauties of America, and we are naturally anxious to see it. But, unfortunately for our hopes, it is foggy and wet all day. The river charmed us much more than we were prepared to expect. Perhaps because its beauties were veiled, our imagination clothed it in loveliness it had not, or perhaps because we were all on a friendly footing, we were disposed to admiration. Howbeit, we were excessively pleased and happy, and consoled ourselves with the hope of seeing the river to greater advantage next Monday on our return. We arrived at Fredericton at half-past six o'clock, and stopped at the "Queen's Hotel," a very fine new one, on the principal street. Messrs. Guthrie and Coghlan are known to every one, and we feel quite at ease, though in a strange place. We visit the Parish Priest, Father McDevitt; he lives in a fine house, and is very popular. Fredericton ranks next after St. John in respectability in New Brunswick.

We return to our hotel, and spend a very pleasant evening, chatting, singing, story-telling, and in what pleases the Americans beyond anything, in conundrums, good, bad, and indifferent. The morning up to dinner we spent at church. Out of a population of 6,000 scarcely 2,000 are Catholics, and almost all those are Irish. The congregation was very respectable; there was not a single badly-dressed person in the church. The church itself is decent, quite finished, with a spire, and evidently in the hands of a good and holy priest. We dine at one o'clock, and immediately after prepare to drive out.

The weather since yesterday has taken a violent and

sudden change from hot to cold. It is quite dry and bracing, but the thermometer can scarcely get beyond 50° in the shade. In Fredericton it frequently goes up to 100°, and higher, during some days in summer. The place is remarkably hot during that season. Fredericton is prettily situated on the St. John river; its streets run at right angles, as in most American towns and cities; and the principal street is that which runs nearest to and parallel with the river. It is a one-sided street, that is to say, the houses are all at one side, if we except the part occupied by the barracks, and a wall running outside. There are about four churches of any note in town, and their tall spires are very ornamental. The Cathedral, at one end of the town, is very beautiful, within and without. From the summit of one church spire rises a hand, with the forefinger pointing heavenwards. I did not like it, for it seemed too practical a representation of that to which the spire itself has been poetically compared, viz., a finger pointing to heaven.

We admired the Exhibition building, the "Hermitage," a beautiful wooded place, purchased by the Bishop for a Catholic burying-ground, but, above all, the College, magnificently situated on a rising ground, and commanding a splendid view of the river and the surrounding scenery. We passed by the Governor's house, and would have called but that he is somewhat of a Puritan, and would not understand visiting on a Sunday.

The British troops have been quite withdrawn from Fredericton. While they were here the place was lively and gay, and a great deal of money was spent—something about £60,000 per year. What a falling off in the prosperity of the city the loss must create—I say "city," for Fredericton is the capital of New Brunswick, and the Parliament of the Province sit here, in a house of wretched style and dimensions. By the way, it is singular that in many parts of America the local Parliaments should sit in places of less than fifth-rate importance. Witness Ottawa in Canada, Albany in New York, and Fredericton in New Brunswick.

About thirty miles from this place is a colony of Cork people, known as the Cork "Settlement." However they came here I know not, but they are almost all Cork folks— once there was no exception—about 60 families, all very comfortable and happy. Speaking of Fredericton, I find that Lord Edward Fitzgerald, according to his "Life" by Tom Moore, was some time stationed here, and that he travelled from Quebec on snow-shoes, a distance of some three hundred miles. The allusion to Lord Edward reminds me of the fact that during our drive to-day we passed by the house of a certain Colonel Minchin, who was actually on guard at the execution of Robert Emmet. The man is still alive, and must be an enormous age. At that time he was lance-corporal in the Irish Volunteers.

We return to the hotel, after which we cross in a ferry-boat to the other side of the river to inspect an Indian village situated just on the bank. When we arrive, a short walk brings us to the outskirts of the village, where we find about a half-dozen Indian girls walking. Civilization has done so much for them that, instead of the blankets which we associate with the idea of a squaw, they were dressed in very pretty garments, and showed no symptoms of savage breeding, except the taste for gaudy colours, for indeed their gowns were of every conceivable colour of the rainbow, and had a very pretty effect to the eye of a spectator. They seemed very bashful, for the moment we addressed them they scattered and fled. I think, however, that their bashfulness arose rather from their ignorance of our language, for they speak only their own tongue, with the exception of a few who have to transact business with their white brethren. A slight shower of rain afforded us a good pretext for taking refuge in one of their houses, and here again we observed the traces of civilization, for the hut was no longer a wigwam (with which, however, the country abounds) but a decent wooden house—small, to be sure, but well built and sufficiently clean. There was a stove, on the top of which was what *we* call a "bastuble oven," and in the oven, no doubt, a cake was being baked. I observed on the walls two pictures, very highly coloured, one representing the Madonna and Child, the other St. Michael killing the Dragon. Here were the indications of Catholic training and on inquiry I found that everywhere amongst the Indians who have been at all affected by civilization, the Catholic is the prevailing religion.

A young man stood leaning against the pipe of the stove. He wore a jerry hat, a black velvet coat, much the worse for the wear, of which doubtless he had been made a present of by some one. He spoke English fairly, and without reluctance. Two young women were present, each with a child; one child her keeper had just taken from an old shawl lying on the ground. A little hammock swung close by the child's cradle; a small puppy, a duck, and a kitten formed a happy family reposing on the only thing like a bed that lay in the corner. The children were very different from each other, one rather white, the other extremely sallow, but both with the inevitable black eyes and black hair. We conversed with the man. He was a Catholic, so were all the tribe—the "Maniseet." He could read, and had a small book in his own language, the "Gospel of St. John," which he presented to me, and which I now have; he said he had another. It was translated, he said, by a missionary (Protestant) who came out from England, and learned the language by living amongst the people of this tribe. He never essayed to convert them to the religious views of his sect, content to learn their tongue and strive to help civilization by letting them know the truths of inspiration.

This young man told us that the Indians subsist during winter by hunting. The moose and the caribou are the favourite objects of their sports. They feed on the flesh and make clothing of the skins or sell it. Of the moose's hair they make exquisite ornaments, for it is dry and hard, and bears the dye well. I have seen some cigar cases made by the Indian women with flowers on the sides of moose hair, and nothing could surpass them for beauty; other ornaments the women also make and baskets, and the men fish in their canoes. They need little, and that little they can easily make out. Begging comes quite natural to them; it appears to be a profession almost universally exercised.

We go to the next house, and here a more curious spectacle meets our eyes. The house consists of only one room, in the middle of which is a stove. Around this stove on the ground are squatted about a dozen women, young and old. A few men are sitting on chairs, as if to indicate the superiority of their sex. In one corner a man and woman are playing a game, and a very curious game it is. Sitting on the floor, a cloth is spread before them, and they have a wooden bowl rather shallow, in which there are about six or eight things like buttons, one side of them is plain white, the other side is dotted with black spots. The man shakes the bowl and tosses the buttons, as a cook may turn a pancake. He then hands it to the woman who performs the same operation. The play seems to consist in an effort to bring all the buttons with the plain or dotted side uppermost without exception. A silly game apparently. They did not desist while we stood at the door except for a moment. A general chatter went round in the Indian tongue, and we were perfectly at sea until one of the women pointing to me said "Bishop." She was then informed who I was, and she seemed pleased by her having hit the mark so nearly. The young women were not bad looking, but they were far from handsome according to our notions. Their hair was jet black, and some of them wore it in long flowing locks down the back. I remarked though very glossy it was very coarse. Their eyes also were black as coal, and these were the characteristics of all without exception; the men's eyes and hair were black, but their hair was cut short on their polls. Men and women alike had high cheek bones, and very yellow or dark complexions. Their look was highly intelligent, and it is a pity that greater efforts are not made to civilize them. Prince Arthur some few years ago when he was out here, took one of them home with him, and had him educated at Cambridge. The young savage became a young gentleman, and one of very engaging manners. He is a doctor, I saw his name, but I forget it. It was one of extraordinary length. He practices at Toronto, but he is cut by his tribe for having condescended to mix so freely with his paler brethren.

Before we leave some young Indian lads volunteer to show us their skill on the bow and arrow. We fix a cent on the ground, and they compete with each other in the effort to shoot it from its position. They seldom miss. We then fix it at a greater distance on the top of a short stick, and their success is the same. One young lad particularly distinguishes himself, and bore off a great many prizes, for we gave ten cents for every successful shot. Here we saw a beautiful canoe just finished, which the owner placed on his head for our amusement, and ran a considerable distance.

We returned to Fredericton very much pleased with our visit to the Indian village. The evening we spent with the MacDonalds, a most respectable family, who treated us with the greatest kindness, and did all in their power to induce us to prolong our stay. Next morning, Monday, Sept. 12th, we rose early, because the boat was to leave at 9 o'clock. The morning was bitterly cold, just like winter, and the wind was skinning, but it was fine and bracing, and on the whole agreeable. I see at one of the wharves a steamer named "Olive." It reminded me of a dear friend far away, of whom that is a pet name. We are escorted to the boat by "troops of friends." Fredericton looks pretty as it sits on the gentle river, and I forgive the spire for its hand as it points to the region of sunshine and eternal peace.

And now the river, for there is nothing to-day to mar its beauty. It is a lovely river, broad, sinuous, with flat, grassy banks, great meadows, and beyond ranges of wooded hill all the way. The scenery is tame, and all around the land is more or less cultivated; but we see no grand mansions such as adorn the river banks of our rivers in Europe. Art has done little. Nature is left to herself; but she is always beautiful. At a point called Oromocto, we witness a strange spectacle, one that I never witnessed before. About a quarter of a mile in front of us we see large black bodies projecting out of the water, to the number of about ten or twelve. When we come near we find them moving across the river, and as we approach quite close we discover that they are horses swimming from the mainland to an island in the river. They had to swim at least a quarter of a mile, and some were foals following their dams. The man at the wheel told me it was usual, and directed my attention to a man on the bank who had driven them across. It appears cattle cross in the same manner. When the horses had got across they spoiled the good effect of the cleansing they had got by rolling in the sand.

There are some projections on the river called by strange names, for example, "The Devil's Back," "The Minister's Face," and "No Man's Friend." Some places in New Brunswick have very queer names, all of Indian origin. I may instance a few. "Quispamsis," "Nauwigiewauk," "Ossekeag," "Apohaqui," "Plumweseep," "Penobsquis," "Magaguadavic," and "Memrancook." The most picturesque part of the St. John River is that which extends to ten miles above the city. The scenery is bold, and trees grow in abundance from the bare rock to a great height over the water. There are a hundred spots of which you would say, "Oh! if it were given to me to live until the day of my death in that sweet spot, with a competence, and companions of my choice, how happy would I be." It is a pity to spoil the charms of so pretty a thought, but alas! to darken your pathway would come the clouds, and blasts and snows of winter, and the companions of your choice would die when you would most choose to love them. It is better strive to be happy wherever we may be than to sigh for happiness we cannot attain. Real contentment is a blessing; imaginary contentment a torture. We had great fun coming down the river, and the Trulls were very much amused by some puzzles we gave them, puzzles familiar to us from our childhood, but apparently quite new to them, such as the fox, goose, and sheaf of corn—the eight, six, and five gallon casks—the men and their wives crossing the river, the snail, and 14 feet pole, &c., &c.

But here we are again at St. John, about $3\frac{1}{2}$ o'clock. The city has grown quite familiar to me, and the people nod to me as I pass. I return to it with a kind of affection, for we have received more kindness here than anywhere in our lives before. On our arrival at the hotel, several gentlemen called to see us and pay their respects. Some had called during our absence. There were letters containing donations, and letters inviting us to supper parties. In fact we were missed out of town, as if we were leading citizens. Colonel Drury had called and left a note. The faithful Major McShane was on the watch for our return. We were almost "ovated." We could scarcely get time to dress for an evening party, to which we had been invited by a Mr. Henry Maher whose relatives live near Cork. We got there, however, in time, and his supper was, indeed, magnificent. On my return to the hotel, I had to begin again with the Guthries, the MacDonoughs, and the faithful T. Coghlan. Mr. Guthrie one afternoon took me out driving, and pointed out the remarkable places about St. John. The most beautiful residence in the suburbs was that of a Mr. Reid, one of two brothers, Irish Protestants from the North, who "began at nothing," and are now owners of the "Blackball Line of Packet Ships." The house in question is as fine a mansion as I ever saw, situated on the very topmost summit around St. John, and commanding a splendid view of the city and the sea. The house of the brother is near but not half so grand. Here is also the house of a Mr. Robinson, another self-made man. America is full of such men. We mounted to the "Observatory," which commands a beautiful view, and was once a French camp or fort, until they were driven from it by the English. The celebrated William Cobbett was stationed at this fort, as a private soldier, and found his wife in the neighbourhood. Walking one evening with a friend he saw a young woman washing, and then and there resolved that she should be his wife. The matrimonial negotiations were not long doing, as there was not much to win or lose at either side, and the washerwoman was united for life to the philosopher.

Some few evenings after Mr. Reid, the owner of the grand house, gave a "promenade concert," for a Ragged School, and Mr. Guthrie and Miss Guthrie and I attended. The word Ragged School, to our Irish ears, are suggestive of proselytism. Not so here. The institution is purely charitable, though it has an unhappy name. It was quite a sensational event in St. John. Everyone went to it. The roads around the demesne were thronged with carriages and foot-passengers. We entered. The house and grounds were splendidly illuminated with Chinese lanterns. All the avenues were gracefully lit up, and the whole scene looked like fairyland. The night was calm, nay, breathless, and the moon and stars shone out, and beneath the placid sea lay in silver light, as if sleeping after the toils of a tempest. A band played in front of the house, and there was no other amusement worth mentioning. But the people here are easily amused. It must be said also that they are very well conducted, and orderly. I very much fear if such a place were thrown open to our young folks in Cork, the "boys" would not behave themselves with exemplary propriety, but all went merry as a marriage bell. On our way home, we passed over a suspension bridge, beneath which are curious falls. When the tide is going out they fall outwards; when the tide is flowing, they fall inwards, and when the tide is full they do not fall at all, but are flooded over.

Thus feted and feasted, dining, and supping with new friends every day, honoured and respected, our appeal successful beyond our hopes, taking our pleasure in the interval of labour, the companions of gentlemen, the beloved of the poor Irish, who watched and pursued us, happy in our hotel as in a home, we deemed it high time to depart from St. John, and not wear out a welcome so cordially offered and so admirably sustained. We therefore fixed on Wednesday, September 14, for our voyage to Portland. Mr. McSweeny insists on having us the last day. He has a country house, and we must have a good drive, and dine with him. Accordingly at 10 o'clock we arrived at his house. There are three open carriages, with a pair of horses each, ready for us, and some friends whom he had invited to meet us. T. Coghlan, of course, is of the party. The day is lovely, and so we all drive away. Our route lay eastward from the city, and the chief features of the landscape were cultivated fields, undulating land, very much forest, half reclaimed woodland, with the stumps of trees still adhering to the ground, the soil in some places barren, in others fresh and green, an occasional homestead, snug and comfortable, and now and then a splendid mansion, the country seat of some wealthy merchant. Mr. McSweeny's house is situated at a distance of about seven miles from the city, and he has about 150 acres of land, a fine house, sheltered from the north by a gentle hill, and with a river flowing in the valley below. Land is had very cheap in New Brunswick. It can be purchased for a half-dollar an acre; but, before the purchaser becomes proprietor it must be cleansed. He is then owner in fee. What a grand opportunity for young men who have any means at home to come out here, work hard for a few years, and then become lords of the soil, independent for ever.

We drove farther westward for about nine miles, the scenery presenting the same features the whole way, and the road as good as one would wish to travel over. Population is very sparse in these parts. The same may be said of the whole province, whose population does not exceed a quarter of a million. The great object of interest to which Mr. McSweeny wishes to invite my attention is Loch Lomond, a lake more than twenty miles long, by an average breadth of four miles. But, before we reach Loch Lomond, it is resolved that we diverge from the main road, and visit the scene of the Munroe murder.

The circumstances of this murder are so singular that I cannot forbear describing them. In the month of October, 1868, a young gentleman named Munroe, about thirty-two years, exercised the profession of architect in the city of St. John. He was of respectable birth and connexion, but his moral character was far from irreproachable. Though a husband and a father, it was generally believed that his wife did not monopolise his affection. Nor was public suspicion incorrect, although the precise object of his attachment was unknown; and he conceived the desire and formed the determination to rid himself by violent means of the unhappy partner of his guilt. The absence of his wife in Boston presented him with a good opportunity of effecting his purpose. One day he hired a carriage and drove the young lady with her child along this very road which we have just traversed. They arrived at a tavern situated just by the borders of Loch Lomond, and called Bunkei's, from the name of the proprietor. Here they dismounted, and Munroe informed the coachman that he and the lady were about to pay a visit to a friend—a Mr. Collins, who lived some short distance off the high road— and that they would soon return, except (what was highly probable) that the Collinses would insist on the young lady staying with them for some days. They took their way through a narrow road with thick woods on either sides, and were soon lost to view. After half-an-hour's absence they returned, took some refreshment at Bunkei's, and returned to the city. It is greatly surmised that the unfortunate man intended to commit the murder on that day, but postponed it for some reason; while some are of opinion that he only came to inspect the ground. He told the coachman that

K

the Collinses were not at home, but that they would be in a few days.

On the following Saturday the same coachman was hired, and the party proceeded as before to Bunkei's. The murderer and his two victims diverged again into the wooded road, and after twenty minutes he returned alone. He took a glass of brandy at the tavern, chatted loudly on the topics of the day, lit a cigar and drove home. Nine months elapsed, and no breath was uttered of the missing young lady, much less of the horrible crime by which her life was sacrificed.

After the lapse of some long period, however, some niggers who lived in a settlement not far from the scene of the murder, while cutting timber in the wood, suddenly discovered buried beneath branches of brushwood the bodies of a woman and child very far advanced in decomposition. They gave the alarm, and great excitement was created by the intelligence in St. John. An inquest was held, but the police could suspect no one for the crime. At length a man named Kane, a person of bad reputation, who could give no account of his missing wife, was arrested; and the evidence went very hard against him. Munroe still exercised his profession in St. John, and was at this time actually engaged in repairing the gaol wherein poor Kane was confined. A gentleman told me he heard Munroe say that the ruffian who perpetrated so gross a crime deserved to be hanged, drawn, and quartered. Yet he was the coolest man in town during all this fearful investigation. He trusted to his respectability and the influence of his friends, and nothing seemed likely to compromise him. At length the coachman who had driven Munroe and his victims felt himself bound to reveal all he thought of the transaction; and this gave a new and startling aspect to the whole affair. Once that the authorities got the proper scent they hunted up the matter so well that a case of circumstantial evidence, perhaps the strongest on record, was made out against Munroe. He was tried, found guilty, confesssd his crime, and was executed February 5, 1870. He shot the young woman through the brain ; I have not heard how he despatched the child. A pamphlet of the whole affair is published, and a friend has promised to send me a copy by post to Boston.

We turned our horses up the road from Bunkei's corner, and after going about a hundred yards a pole stuck in the ground at the left hand side, with a white cloth tied round the top, indicated the point at which the murderer and his victims entered the wood. We dismounted and followed a swamp path made by the frequent visitors who come to view the spot, until we found ourselves in an open place surrounded by wood. In the centre was a large white stone, on which it is supposed they sat some minutes previous to the murder. The ground all round was damp. Another pole with a piece of cloth on the top was stuck in the earth close to the stone. Here the crime was committed, and here the bodies were laid. A tree in the neighbourhood was pointed out, and we observed several cuttings from which the murderer had with his pen knife procured branches to cover the bodies. No lovelier spot could be conceived, nor one so hidden from human gaze; but the eye of the All Seeing watched the murderer and exacted blood for blood.

We came away with feelings of sadness and reach Bunkei's,

where we do not stay. We push on to Loch Lomond, and it must in truth be said that it is a magnificent lake. The hills all round are wooded; the highest is called Ben Lomond. Having never seen the originals of these places of Scotch nomenclature, I cannot draw comparisons; but I only hope the Scottish scenery is equal to that of its namesake of New Brunswick. I need not describe the dinner at Mr. M'Sweeny's country house on our return. Suffice to say it was Irish—Irish in its style, Irish in its profusion, Irish in the warmth of feeling that existed in the breasts of hosts and guests. Mrs. M'Sweeny was present, and all her young *protegees* were with her; some other ladies also lent a charm to the feast. Champagne flowed profusely, and other wines graced the board. Our host was in high glee, and broke from his taciturnity by repeated exclamations of delight. I proposed his health, which was drunk with enthusiasm. He tried to respond, but his feelings overpowered him and he burst into tears. When he had sat down and recovered he called it the happiest day of his life, and indulged in various commendations of his reverend guests, which my modesty forbids me to record. After tea we drove back to town, and took a last farewell of Mr. and Mrs. M'Sweeny, the best husband and wife I ever met, and amongst the very best of human kind.

I should have mentioned that amongst the parties to which we were invited one of the most elegant was that of the Coghlans. Here I had an opportunity of making the acquaintance of Mr. Coghlan and his daughter, a very agreeable young lady. Mr. Anglin, editor of the *Freeman*, gave us a splendid party, quite a sumptuous affair, and the leading citizens were present. One guest is Major

M'Shane, an Irishman, who stays at the "Waverley." He is a lawyer in town, and an officer in the Volunteers. He is unmarried, is a Catholic, and is a scholar, a virtuous and patriotic gentleman. He takes to us, and becomes a warm, attached, and devoted friend.

The last hours of our stay in St. John were spent at the hotel where all our friends met *in globo*. Several gentlemen had called and left P.P.C. (*pour prendre congé*) cards during the day, and some had left their subscriptions. One poor woman, who had not seen us hitherto, called to ask our blessing before parting; she was from Cork. In fact the last few hours were essentially sensational, and as hilarity waxed fast and furious the hours grew on and it was one o'clock before we were permitted to retire. We had to rise next morning at the early hour of 6 to do our packing— by no means an easy task—and when that was near finished my friend Coghlan was at his post, namely, at my bedroom door, soliciting permission to aid in the final function of "speeding the parting guest." We breakfasted and proceeded in a carriage to the wharf. There our friends were assembled. Some three hundred passengers crowded the steamboat; there was the usual bustle, the hurrying to and fro. At every step to the boat we encountered some new friend come to bid farewell, and when the bell sounded for strangers to go ashore, there was the last shake hands, and the blessing, and the hope to meet again, however diffidently entertained. We cannot bear this idea of *never* meeting again. A something in our very nature advises us of another world where we meet to part no more. "I shall see you again," I say. "Oh, yes," is the reply; "I shall go to Ireland some time before I die, and I know where to find you. Good-bye. God bless you!" "Good-bye," I say, "good-bye." The moorings are loosed, the steam ceases to make that horrid noise that precedes the parting of the vessel; our distances from the shore increases. Now no token of friendship remains possible but the parting glance, the flutter of the handkerchief, and the silent prayer. A fog, so frequent in St. John, shortens the period of mutual recognition. A moment and the very church spires of St. John are buried in mist. The morning is soft, breathless and balmy, and the sea is gentle as a slumbering babe.

We steam slowly away, and the very silence of our passage through the water calls up by contrast the excitement of the past three weeks. I feel a disposition to gloom, but strive to shake it off. We go once more to a land of strangers, and we know not what our success may be. We look around amongst the passengers, and we who were so feted and feasted during the previous weeks, nay months, see no familiar face. All are strange; none known us, and we know none. Our spirits would droop if we let them, but we argue that we have heretofore had those feelings of despondency, and that we fared better than we anticipated. Who knows what good luck may be in store for us yet.

Here is "Partridge Island," just in the harbour. It was to St. John what Grose Isle was to Quebec—the quarantine of the Irish during the year of plague, and their burial place. Some thousands of our countrymen lie buried in this small island.

The scenery from St. John to Portland—for Portland (Maine) is the place of our next visit—is not of remarkable interest. The vessel coasts the whole way as far as Eastport, by the New Brunswick shore, keeping very close

The weather is so fine that she can keep close. There is nothing to note about the coast. It is low, woody, and the soil is bad. We reach Lubeck, a pretty village, where we do not touch, and steer out through a narrow harbour, passing between some islands and the mainland.

About noon we reach Eastport, the first town on the American continent belonging to the States in this direction. The State is that of Maine. Immediately opposite, at a considerable distance at our left, is the island of Campo Bello, which the Fenians once "occupied." All the islands here belong to the British. How lovely is the weather, and how pretty the boats look—some large and some merely of pleasure—with their white sails on the smooth, sparkling, placid water; and how charming is the town of Eastport, sitting just on the water's edge, and ascending therefrom gradually with its few church spires, lending that peculiarly pretty effect to a town, especially a town on the water to which I am so sensitive. I do not know if others are. Here we stay about an hour, discharging part of our cargo, and receiving more. Then we start again, and I can see nothing further to note as we lose sight of land at both sides for some time, or approach it only at a great distance. The steamer is a magnificent one, the saloon runs the whole length, and is exquisitely furnished; but the crowd is too great. There is hardly room to move about. I am depressed and lonely after leaving my St. John friends. We retire at 9 o'clock, so I snatch a few hours of slumber.

CHAPTER VIII.

THE "ATHENS OF AMERICA," AND SOME OF THE ATHENIANS.

Sept. 15*th*.—At four o'clock we are awakened by the noise of a gong and the cry of "Portland." We dress as hastily and get on shore. The city lies along the shore a great length. We see it only dimly in the twilight, but it looks very important with its numerous wharves, tokens of commerce. There is some delay, for the luggage has to be examined, as we come from the British provinces. Our luggage was not examined. They took our word for it. We hire a "hack," and proceed to our hotel, the "St. Julian," a distance of about a quarter of a mile, for which the cabman charges us two dollars, the first striking indication that we had got into the States.

We dress and strive to look bright after our voyage and the shortcomings of Morpheus' visitations, and come down to breakfast. The weather is very warm, and flies are abundant. We are amused by the circumstance of a waitress standing at our table during the meal, with a large fan brushing off the flies, and cooling us at the same time. I could not help remarking it was "rather cool."

What are we to do in Portland? To collect? I am opposed to it; but I press my opposition gently. We have a letter of introduction to a Father O'Callaghan, one of the priests of the place. The Irish population of Portland is not much, and larger fields are open before us elsewhere. There is Boston only five hours journey from us and full of Irish. My wish is to go there.

But I let things work themselves out. We stand at the hotel door, and resolve to visit the Bishop. Father O'Callaghan lives at the palace and so we will inquire for him first of all. He may make our access to the Bishop easy. We reach the episcopal palace, and well worthy of the name is that magnificent building. We were told it contained forty bedrooms. The Cathedral is just at hand. They are both built of red brick, but the interior of each is simply superb. "Is Father O'Callaghan at home?" "No," replies the servant, "nor will he be at home for days." "Is the Bishop at home?" "Yes, but he cannot be seen just now; if you call at two I guess you can see him then right off." Despondent and gloomy we retire to our hotel. We can scarcely admire the splendour of the streets, for they are splendid. The first cloud has crossed our horizon and we are impatient with it.

We call at two and see the Bishop. He is a very gentlemanly middle aged man, with regular round features, a very good expression, bald head and white hair on his poll. His dress is that of a layman, shirt and collar, white socks, and shoes with silk strings, and nothing indicates his profession save the large ring on the fourth finger of the right hand. This is Doctor Bacon, first Bishop of Portland. We announce our mission. He smiles and shakes his head. "I cannot allow it—in fact, I forbid it," he says with decided firmness. He then went into a long statement of the wants of the American Church and the burden which lay upon the people everywhere. The Bishops of America, he said, had resolved peremptorily to refuse all patronage to beggars. The market was drugged with them. What claim had we on the people? "They are Irish, you say;

then why not keep them at home ; we have the burden of them ; they are poor, and we want all their resources to provide for their spiritual wants." We remained respectfully silent, and then bowed ourselves out. But we thought it hard that Bishop Bacon should have undertaken to answer for all the bishops of America.

We resolved to leave for Boston immediately. We see nothing to encourage our staying here. We could scarcely see an Irish name over any shop. The Catholic population is only 6,000 and they are poor. We spent the evening strolling through the streets. The greater part of this city was burnt three years ago, but it has been rebuilt on a sumptuous and magnificent scale. The Post Office, which is nearly completed, is a structure of immense beauty ; a square edifice, Grecian in style and built of white polished marble. Throughout Portland there is the unmistakable Yankee bustle; the genius of the dollar animates the place, and the Briareus of Commerce moves his hundred hands.

September 16*th*.—At 3 o'clock this afternoon we leave for Boston by "the Cars ;" the lower road ; distance 111 miles ; time five hours. The country is not good-looking, although here and there we see some vast meadows and wooded uplands. The soil, for the most part, is sandy and scarcely an inch deep. Amongst the underwood in some places we are struck by the blood-red tint of the leaves of some trees ; the effect is striking and pretty. On the route are some pretty towns, such as Biddeford, Kittry and Ipswich. It grew dark about 6 so we could see no more. We reach the " Parker House," a magnificent hotel, of which I may say more as we go on. There is great bustle in the spacious hall, occasioned by the constant thronging in and out of guests. Having made our toilette we entered the drawing-room, a superb affair, and sit down. The waiters stare at us and smile, and soon a round half-dozen fresh ones come in and parade before our table. On enquiring we found out that I am known to some of them and they come to make assurance doubly sure. After tea the head porter, a man named Barrett, addressed me by name. He is from the parish of Blackrock and was at home two years ago, when he often heard me preach. He inquires tenderly for Father James, whom he enthuastically describes as "a great man." Another man, a waiter named White, knew me well in Bandon, where he was a waiter at French's Hotel, and often served me a dinner there. A third was from the South Main Street and left Cork only a few years ago. They were all delighted to meet us. This was a bit of sunshine amongst the clouds, but it was only a passing ray. We stroll out and are astonished at the irregularity of the streets, and their narrowness, two qualities so uncharacteristic of American cities. We make arrangements for the morrow and retire early.

September 17*th*, 1870.—How will Bishop Williams receive us? *nous verrons*. After breakfast a fine carriage and pair is waiting at the hotel door to convey us to the palace. We find this was "arranged" by Barrett, the head porter, who understood our want and provided for it at his own expense We drive to the Bishop's; we reach the house—a very modest unpretentious house; we enter; within it is the same This argues well. At least we shall not meet a Bishop such as he of Portland. We send up our cards and the Bishop comes down, in his soutane. He receives us civilly and asks us up stairs. I briefly state the object of our mission; he listens and then says, "Gentlemen, I can give you no encouragement; were I to do so, I should injure our own charities, which are abundant and pressing enough; we are, as you see, building a great Cathedral, it exhausts all our resources. In a few weeks I shall be making the annual appeal for it; I could not therefore, in decency, make or allow to be made an appeal for you, but I do not forbid you to collect as much as you can; we owe all to the Irish people, and especially to the people of Cork. I owe them a debt of gratitude—do your best. Publish in the *Pilot* that you have my permission. What the people give to you will not stand in their way when we make our usual appeals to their charity. I shall give you a letter certifying that you have my authority to exercise priestly functions while in Boston." The cloud begins to disappear.

We next proceed to the office of Mr. Patrick Donahoe, of the *Boston Pilot*. I explained our mission, and reported the Bishop's conversation with us. Mr. Donahoe immediately wrote a paragraph for the paper, which was just being printed, and promised a larger notice in the next number. He told us it would be well to have a paragraph also in the *Herald*. So we went off and followed his advice. We were determined to lose no time. Wonderful is the progress of Catholicity in this country. In the year 1810 there was not a single Catholic, much less a Catholic priest or church, in all New England—a country embracing six States—viz., Maine, Vermont, New Hampshire, Massachussets, Connecticut, and Rhode Island. Now there are five dioceses in these States. In Boston alone there are 100,000 Catholics and twelve churches, and the professors of Catholicity are by a sweeping majority either Irish or the descendants of Irish, the Catholics of other nationalities being infinitely few. Ireland has achieved miracles for the faith in America.

We travel again in the street cars. The Americans talk much of their respect for women, and in hotels and steamboats there is an ostentatious display of regard for the sex. There are ladies' drawing-rooms and ladies' staircases, and ladies are always accommodated with the first floor. In large cities special policemen are told off to conduct ladies across crowded streets, lest they come in contact with horses or waggons. All very well; but the Yankees prefer their own comfort to the display of politeness. This setting aside of special chambers and special policemen for the convenience of the sex is very pretty, and does not hurt anyone. But take the street car, for example. A number of gentlemen fill the car; a lady enters, and in very few instances will a Yankee rise to offer her a seat. An Irishman will show this politeness, but the lady does not thank him, and the Yankee rather despises him. An anecdote I read on this point is rather amusing. A Yankee is represented as saying, "The fair sex are entitled to all the attentions man can bestow upon them. Thus, when a lady enters a street car, I am shocked to observe the coolness with which men retain their seats, and permit her to stand all the time. For my part, when a lady comes into a crowded street car in my presence, I look around me to see will anyone rise; I see, alas! that no one has the decency to do so. Shame overcomes me. I bury my face in my newspaper, and blush for my sex."

In Boston I met many Irishmen well to do, and when I

asked, to what do you attribute your success in life, such as it is? their answer is, *I worked hard, and I was a teetotaler.* The drunkard is idle; he does not respect himself. No one employs a drunkard, because no employer can depend on him. One man, a shoemaker, said to me, in his own way, " I made the first pair of shoes ever I wore. I then began to make them for others, and from that day to this, thank God, I never saw the bottom of my purse." This head-porter, Barrett, said:—" I am nineteen years out here; I would live in Ireland if I could, but there is nothing for me to do there. I never possessed a cent in America that I did not work for. Here is work for all, if they only wish to do it. I never taste intoxicating drinks. I send money to my father and friends, and have more than enough for myself."

Another obstacle to the Irishman's success is, the Yankees hate him. They regard him as one made to work. Of course they see around them every day Irishmen who have risen, but that does not remove their ingrained prejudice against the race. Where headwork is necessary they will not employ an Irishman, if they can help it; but where they want labour they will engage Paddy as they would a dray-horse. If an Irishman achieve any daring deed, they will not admire his valour or pluck. They call him that wild Irishman, that madman, or fool; whereas if an Englishman or one of themselves accomplished the same, they would make the world ring with his praises.

Thus, within the last few days a Mr. John Charles Buckley has arrived in Boston, after having performed one of the most astounding feats recorded in the history of navigation. He left Queenstown in a small craft not much bigger than a whaleboat, called the " City of Ragusa," accompanied by a man and a dog, and steered for America. The voyage extended to ninety days, at the end of which time he reached this city, safe and sound, with his human friend, but deprived by death of his canine companion. He is exhibiting his boat here, and realizes a good deal by it. And yet the papers make no flourish about this wonderful achievement, and the man is not regarded as anything more than a madcap—he is only "a wild Irishman;" whereas if he had been a John Bull, or a Jonathan, what a cry would be raised to extol his indomitable perseverance and his unflinching courage. Some go so far as to deny that he ever performed the voyage. They say he was picked up with his boat and brought along somewhat in the style of Darby Doyle in his famous voyage to Quebec. But, never mind. As I have said elsewhere, our countrymen are capable of distinguishing themselves in every department, whether for good or evil. Few will approve of Captain Buckley's foolhardiness; but where will you find so foolhardy a Jonathan or a Bull? As soon as the gallant Captain landed he was interviewed by the Press. A long account of his voyage was inserted in the *Boston Herald*.

It is very hard to form a correct notion as to the advice which ought to be tendered to the Irish people wishing to immigrate here. I make it a point to ask everyone I meet what is his opinion on the subject, and their invariable answer is—"Let no Irishman come to this country who can make a livelihood at home." There is more happiness in the old country, more sociality, more friendship, more chance of saving one's soul. Come to America, and you must work hard, and work without ceasing. In summer the heat is so killing that you would wish it would kill you outright, and not mock you with only the phantom of death. In winter the cold is so bitter that you long for the summer, with all its calorific terrors. I called to see a young woman, the sister of my servant, Ellen Colbert. This young woman left Ireland about three years ago. I remember her then. She was a fine young, healthy, rosy-faced peasant girl, with a face like a very ripe peach, such as we see in America. "Ah," said I to her, "I fear you will lose that fine complexion of yours when you shall have crossed the Atlantic." My words were verified; I saw her this day. She was pale, and the perspiration sparkled like dew-drops all over her face. "Ah, sir," said she, "many a time since have I thought of your words, that my complexion would fade in America."

"Would you advise your sister Ellen to come to this country?"

"No, sir—a thousand times no. If she can live at home on half a loaf, it is better than to live here upon two loaves. At home there is some pleasure—here, it is nothing but work, work, work." I thought of the words of Tennyson: "Better fifty years of Europe than a cycle of Cathay!"

And yet, in conversation with a very respectable and wealthy man, who left Cork in the year 1843, when he was nineteen years old, and made a fortune here, I was taught to reconsider my notions on this subject of emigration— "Sir," said he, "If it were possible for me to put all the Irish people into one vessel, I would bring them all over, and plant them in America. This is the country to live in—a free country, where labour is prized and rewarded, and where every man is the equal of his fellow." It is hard to form a conclusion; but I write my impressions just as they are made, fairly and dispassionately, nothing extenuating, nought setting down in malice. They will probably become more worthy of estimation as I go on.

Sept. 18.—We officiate in St. James' Church, Albany-street. I go first to Charlestown, and stand under the monument on Bunker's Hill. A large pyramid of granite 221 feet high and thirty feet square at the base, marks the scene of the great battle, in which so much of the interests of America have been involved.

I then go to Cambridge, to see the parish priest, Father Scully, a Corkman, whom I met at home last February. I find him in his church, a very beautiful one, and presiding at catechism, where there are about 1,000 children present of both sexes. He takes us into his house, is extremely kind and hospitable, invites us to stay with him while we remain here. We decline this invitation, because Cambridge is "out of town." He opens our subscription list with a handsome donation, and promises every assistance in his power. The prospect begins to brighten.

Sept. 19, *Monday.*—We begin operations to-day by hiring a carriage, and telling the driver to take us to the principal Catholic citizens. To be brief, we receive 180 dollars the first day. On my return to the hotel, I find a card for me, "John Charles Buckley, Knight of the Order of St. Sylvester, Captain of the City of Ragusa." Accordingly at ten, accompanied by a friend, the truly gallant captain appears. He expresses great pleasure at making my acquaintance, and I very heartily reciprocate the compliment. When he is seated I sketch him in my mind's eye. He is a man of ordinary stature, with brown hair, and a very long bright brown beard, apparently very muscular and healthy, and

L

notwithstanding his recent exploit, with nothing to indicate the seaman. His features are not remarkable, but they express good nature and good temper. There is nothing in them from which you could imagine that you saw a man who had voluntarily undertaken and accomplished one of the most heroic deeds ever performed since Noah launched his big ship. Captain Buckley conversed freely on his wonderful voyage, but with an amount of modesty hard to conceive. He stayed two hours, and left the most favourable impressions on my mind. I have seldom met, in my sphere of life, and least of all in a sailor, so Christian a bearing, so thorough an attachment to the old faith, so much confidence in Providence (of its kind, for the Captain, no doubt, tempted Providence most culpably), so much genuine patriotism. He undertook the voyage because he was "doing nothing," and could not bear idleness.

It reminded me of the story of the shoemaker who was found to take charge of the Eddystone Lighthouse: when asked his reason for so doing, he replied that he did'nt like "confinement," alluding to his workshop at home.

The captain made up his mind "to do something," and he resolved that should be something novel, startling, and likely to reflect credit upon Irishmen. He would do something that no man ever did before. The Atlantic had been crossed in 1866 by a boat called the "Red, White and Blue." She was 26 feet long—he would cross in a craft of only 20 feet. Fool-hardy the adventure no doubt was, and all his friends advised him not to try it, but he would do it, and he felt he would succeed—it might be tempting Providence, but he felt assured he would get across under the protection of the very Providence he tempted. The reasoning was not very solid but the Captain did not much care for logic. He had a father, mother and sister; he told them nothing about it. He loved peril—he had been volunteer for the Pope, and fought at Ancona, because he liked the excitement of the thing. "Was he not afraid?" "No, he never feared anything but God."

He left Cork harbour on the 16th of June and arrived in Boston, Sept. 9th. He recounted the whole story, all he suffered, all his mate, an Austrian sailor, suffered, and the death of his dog, the worst calamity that befel him on the voyage.

But nothing, I repeat, struck me more than the quiet unassuming manner of the man and his utter want of vanity. He gave no credit to himself. He only thanked God for his success. He knew how wrong a thing it was to venture; but he never lost hope, never despaired. Even when on the coast of Newfoundland a gale raged that caused many wrecks, he still cherished the strong hope that he would come safe. He never would attempt the same again: he would learn wisdom from the past and strive to be good as well as heroic henceforth. He called the boat the "City of Ragusa," for two reasons—first in compliment to his mate, a Dalmatian from that city, and secondly because "Ragusa" is the smallest walled city in the world, and his boat was a structure of the smallest wooden walls that ever encountered a bombardment by the waves. Captain Buckley strove to prove his relationship to me, but even his voyage was an easier task than this.

Sept. 20th.—We could find no pilot to conduct us from house to house, so we had to go by ourselves. We heard Federal Street was full of Cork people. We went there and out of the whole street found scarcely ten people that were not from some part of Cork City or County; several I recognised. They were anxiously expecting a visit, for they had heard I was in America. Anything like the generosity of these people I never experienced. It was simply romantic. No ancedote of their kindness can be told, for they were all equally kind. One house we passed by because we saw the name "Archamleau," and did not care to call upon any but Irish. When, however, we had passed the door a woman ran out and followed us. She called us in and in a very Irish accent rebuked us for passing. This was Madame Archamleau, a County Cork woman married to a Frenchman. We fared well here, for the wife subscribed and insisted on Monsieur subscribing for himself.

The mosquitoes have fearfully disfigured my hands and face. I had no notion that they paid their visits so late in the year. They have made me a special victim. The first morning I woke in Portland I observed my hands were full of sores like "hives," and that my forehead had got a great increase of bumps. I thought it was "summer heat," but soon found that it was the work of mosquitoes during the night. The sensation of itchiness is perfectly intolerable. Those creatures cannot be seen at night, but when I wake I hear them buzzing about my head, and every morning reveals new mischief *at* their hands *on* mine. I must have patience with them as with other crosses.

September 25th. At the invitation of Father Scully of Cambridge, to whom I have already alluded, I preach in St. Mary's at High Mass. A large and attentive congregation—all Irish. I announce that I am to "go around" during the week. I do go around, and raise a very respectable sum. The hot weather appears to me to be one of the most unpleasant things to be encountered in this country. Now at the end of September, it is simply intolerable. I sit with Father Scully in his garden : the air is dense, and there is not a breath of wind. I can do nothing but sit and perspire and look at my hands all sore with mosquito bites. At length the sky becomes dark as night, and a fearful thunder-storm takes place, like those I have already described in Montreal and Quebec. It rains in oceans, but after an hour all is dry and warm as before.

The following day in going about from house to house I go into several rooms where there are stoves. How any human beings can bear the heat of those stoves in such weather is to me inconceivable. I cannot go beyond the door—the rooms are hot as a Turkish bath—and how do those poor infants live in cradles within a foot of such furnaces, all wrapped up in warm clothing? This Cambridge is a pretty place; the houses, to be sure, are all of wood, but they are elegant in style and warm and durable almost as stone. The damp has little effect on them for the seasons are nearly always dry. There are little gardens in front, and the streets are regular, and lined on both sides with trees—I mean the suburban streets. Indeed, Cambridge is almost buried in foliage. Yet in some of those houses live very poor people, all Irish. There is none of that squalor and filth we see in the old country, but there is poverty hiding itself in clean rags. On the other hand there are Irishmen very rich and well-to-do, and a great number very "comfortable." I enter one house, that of an Irishman from Clare, named Griffin. A very pretty garden fronts his house, and all around the house itself are wall-trees, such as ivy and other creepers, conspicuous amongst which is the vine all thick with ripe grapes. Mr. and Mrs. Griffin give me a hearty welcome, and their drawing-room is as pretty as anyone could desire. They fetch a large basket containing fruit, the most delicious pears of their own growth and a huge cluster of grapes; they also produce a bottle of their own wine, made by themselves, and I am glad to taste it so that I may be able to say that I drank the *genuine* juice of the grape once in my life. This couple were very happy, and blessed Providence in a truly Christian spirit for the comforts with which they had been enriched. Need I say that I wished them a continuance of such happiness?

Father Scully is beloved by the people, and justly. He is an excellent priest, and has provided amply for the religious and educational wants of his flock. His house is very pretty —white with green blinds outside the windows, and with a very charming colonnade, Grecian style, forming a piazza all around, and separated by a lovely garden in which fruit trees abound. Yet he is happy only on principle. His heart is in Ireland.

The American priests have no society, they are thrown completely on themselves, and no consideration reconciles them to their ostracism but the high obligation of their sacred duties.

The poet, Longfellow, lives at Cambridge. I am most anxious to see and converse with him, if only for a short time. I was in the house of Mr. Luby. Said I, "Would you kindly tell me where does the poet Longfellow live?

"Longfellow, Father? Oh, bless you, he is dead this many a day!"

"God help us," thought I, "no man is a prophet in his

own country." I endeavoured to persuade Mr. Luby that he was mistaken, but he could scarcely be convinced. He appealed to his daughter, who told him that he must be thinking of Mrs. Longfellow having been burnt to death long ago; he began to shake in his opinion.

" Or perhaps," said the daughter, " you are thinking how his son was married last year."

"Ah! that's just it!" cried the clear-minded Luby, "that's just it. I knew there was something in it."

My constant intercourse with the Irish gives me abundant opportunities of studying their character, and the change wrought in their manners by settlement in this country. One thing I remark, and that is that they are extremely polite and courteous. When I knock at a door, it is opened by the " Lady" of the house, for in all ranks of life men and women are gentlemen and ladies in America, from the coal-heaver up to the President. She says, with a very smiling countenance, " Good morning, sir; won't you walk in?" and she immediately opens the drawing-room door, if there be a drawing-room; if not, the door of any other apartment, places a chair, opens the blinds, and apologizes for any shortcomings that may appear about the place. She then opens the conversation on some topic, and discourses with perfect ease, in many cases with the dignity of a duchess. When she ascertains the object of my visit, she is not the least embarrassed, but addresses herself to it with a very business-like air, and evidently speaks the truth in everything.

There are very few Irish people who do not pick up the American accent, and the American form of speech. The expressions most frequently used are, " I guess," and "right off," or "right away." Some Irish folks who come hither in their maturer years, never alter their accent or language in the least, always excepting the use of "I guess," and "right away." But young girls in a very short time become perfect Yankees in speech and accent. I met one whom I had known at home in a country district, the daughter of a farm-labourer, eight years ago; she was now married, was smartly dressed, and thoroughly Yankeefied—in fact, she spoke so grandly, that I grew quite ashamed of my Cork accent in comparison with hers. What she had done with her own Cork accent I could never imagine.

It is very much to be deplored that in America the Irish are extremely "clannish." The Northerns look down on the Southerns, and both dislike the Connaught-folk. The "far-downs," *i. e.*, the Northerns, are despised by the "Corkeys," while the latter are odious to the former in a similar degree.

All, when spoken to on the subject, admit how baneful these distinctions are, but all act alike in accordance with them. What curse is on our people, that dissension must be the brand of their race at home and abroad?

Sunday, October 2.—This evening I deliver my lecture on the Bible to a dense audience. The Church was literally crammed. Mr. Boyle O'Reilly was present, a young gentleman of rather chequered career. He had been at one period of his life a soldier. During the Fenian agitation he was arrested on suspicion of corrupting the allegiance of his fellow-soldiers. He was tried by court-martial in Dublin and sentenced to transportation for life. He was imprisoned in Millbank, escaped, and was apprehended. He was then removed to a prison in Chatham, whence he also effected his escape. To lessen his chance of eluding his gaolers he was removed to Australia, but there he was more successful than ever, for he escaped to some purpose, having by a variety of adventures found his way to the protection of the "Star-spangled Banner."* He will give my lecture a favourable notice in the *Pilot*.

The president of the United States visited Boston a few days ago, for the purpose of placing his son at Cambridge University. He put up at St. James's Hotel. As he came in a private capacity, his arrival created no sensation. There was no demonstration of any kind, except a few flags hung out in some places. There were no salvoes of artillery, and no addresses from mayors or corporations. The President was allowed to smoke his Havanna in peace, and he was not worried by bores, or interviewed by "gentlemen of the Press." That was a blessing. Well for him he was not a monarch, such as we have in Europe, or even a monarch's shadow, he would be grudged the very slumbers demanded by inexorable nature. That evening the President went to the "Globe" Theatre, and a large crowd of roughs filled the streets to catch a sight of "Ulysses," but few enjoyed the pleasure. On reaching his box a faint clap proclaimed a welcome, but beyond this gentle demonstration, Democracy was too proud to venture.

This was a lovely day; the great heat of the weather has entirely disappeared, but the sun is still warm and the air

---

* Sir W. Vernon Harcourt lately, in the House of Commons, alluded to this gentleman as "the man O'Reilly." There may be, perhaps, some readers who need to be told that the ex-convict is now one of the most successful men of letters in the States; and, what is better, the author of poems distinguished by a peculiar delicacy and nobility of thought. He is at present editor of the *Boston Pilot*.

balmy. I had arranged to visit Harvard University in company with Mr. Aloysius J. Kane, of the law school, a Roman Catholic young gentleman, whose acquaintance I had made at St. John, N.B. He was to meet me at Father Scully's. True to his appointment he came, and we both walked a short distance to the University. Cambridge is a large place, and embraces various divisions, such as Old Cambridge, East Cambridge and Cambridge-port. I have stated elsewhere that the whole place is buried in foliage. The University is peculiarly so. It consists of a large number of long red-brick buildings, perhaps five storeys high, all detached, and about three edifices built of granite, one polished, viz., the University Hall—the other two rough; of the latter one is called Gore Hall, from the name of him whom I suppose to have given it an endowment—Christopher Gore, whose marble bust stands within. It is built in the style of a Gothic church, and is nothing more or less than the library, containing 120,000 vols. Between these buildings are large grass plots intersected by walks running in various directions. The students have no peculiar costume. The American idea is opposed to all kinds of insignia, because they distinguish one man from another, and that would not be democratic. The president's house is within the grounds. We called, and sent in our cards. After a short time Mr. President Elliott appeared, quite a young man. I had seen him a few hours before in one of the streets, and had passed him without knowing who or what he was. I told him so, and he said he had seen me too, and was equally at a loss to know who I was. He was very polite, and volunteered all kinds of assistance in having me shown through the place, but I did not wish to put him to any trouble. I said I called merely that I might do myself the honour of making the acquaintance of the president of so great a university. After some desultory and unimportant conversation, I retired with Mr. Kane. We visited the various schools. The number of students attending the university last year was 1,200.

We next proceeded to visit the great American poet, Henry W. Longfellow, who lives in the immediate neighbourhood of the university. This was an honour I was long ambitious to enjoy; for in common, I believe, with all readers, I admire his poems excessively, and I have conceived from their perusal a love and esteem of the soul from which such pure outpourings of thought have flowed, and assumed forms of rarest dignity aud beauty, at the magic touch of language. We walked along under the trees, and saw in an open square a large monument just erected to commemorate the death on the late battlefields of America of the soldiers of Cambridge. On the summit of the monument stands an ideal soldier, leaning on his gun, and on the slabs beneath are the names of the fallen. Of these more than one-half are Irish. We walk still further, and reach another open space, where is an immense tree enclosed by railings, outside of which stands a large stone, with words inscribed as follows:—"Beneath this tree Washington first took command of the American army, 1772."

We find ourselves in Bratle-street, which is not a street according to our notion—that is, a succession of houses fronting the public way. It is rather a road, off which are detached suburban villas. In one of those villas Washington lived. We see it from the roadside. It is a large, old-fashioned house, evidently much the senior of its wooden neighbours, with grass-plots and flower-beds in front, and a conservatory at one side. This is the house now occupied by Longfellow. We knock at the hall-door, and a servant appears. We send in our cards, and are instantly permitted to enter. There are two gentlemen in the large room, of whom one stands writing at a desk, and the other approaches us. In the features of the latter I recognise those of the poet, with which the infallible photograph has made me familiar. He is tall, but not remarkably so, and his head is the great object of the spectator's regard. A large, well-shaped head, with very regular features, an expressive forehead, eyes, I think, blue, a very bushy white beard and moustache, and long white locks, flowing loosely behind. His expression is mild and calm, and his demeanour singularly modest.

"Sir," I said, "being a stranger in Boston I could not think of leaving without doing myself the honour and pleasure of paying my respects to you, the great American poet, and of thanking you for all the pleasure I have derived from the perusal of your works."

"Sir," he answered, "you are very kind. I have been forewarned of your visit by a gentleman from Cork, who came to see me a few days ago."

In conversing with Mr. Longfellow, he asked me had I seen the University, and I said I had. I told how I had seen the President in the morning without knowing who he was."

"Yes," said he, "Nature seldom helps us to discover a man's rank or genius."

I replied that it was so, and that in his own poem *The*

Belfry of Bruges, there were some thoughts expressive of the same idea. I had forgotten the words, but the idea was that the common wanderer through the streets at night hears the chimes, and can discover nothing in the sound, while the poet on hearing them revels in a thousand strange and delightful fancies.

"Have you been to Bruges?" he asked.

"Yes, sir," I replied, "I was there last year and I well remember in my bed at night keeping myself awake that, like you, I might hear the chimes at the midnight hour, and conjure up the thoughts with which they inspired you."

I am by nature very averse to flattery. I hate to give or to receive it: but I could not resist the temptation to convey my feelings of affection and admiration for him who sat before me, the great mind that had moulded such thoughts, and clothed them in such exquisite language. He dwelt on the chimes of Bruges with great pleasure and described the plan on which they are played. He asked me had I heard the bells of Antwerp, and I replied in the affirmative, adding that the chimes which pleased me most were those of St. Gertrude's Church at Louvain. These he said he had not heard. I told him how I had lately passed through the now immortal valley of Grand Pré, the scene of the early part of *Evangeline*, which thereupon, I said, I read again for the fifth time. He told me that though he had written of Grand Pré he had never seen it. He asked my opinion of it, and I described it in terms similar to those already contained in this book. I asked his opinion of the lakes of Killarney, which, as I saw by the papers, he had visited last year, and to my astonishment, he told me he had never seen them! He had seen an account of his travels in Ireland in the newspapers which amused him excessively—but although he was once in Queenstown harbour, he had never put his foot on Irish ground. After he had addressed a few words to Mr. Kane, I said, "I have one sister in Ireland, a passionate admirer of your poems. How delighted she will be to learn that I have had the honour of an interview with you, and how she will envy me that honour! This very morning I received from her a letter in reply to mine which I sent some weeks ago, describing my passage through Grand Pré, and she says that once more she took *Evangeline* that she might picture herself on the spot where I had so recently been."

"Your sister," said the poet, "must be very much attached to her brother. When you write, tell her from me how grateful I am for her appreciation of my writings."

Mr. Longfellow then asked me where I was staying. I said the Parker House, and after a few more words, not wishing to trespass further on his time, I rose to depart. He accompanied us to the door and shook our hands at parting. We were very much pleased with the simplicity and urbanity of his manners, and I fully realized by an analogical process the joyous sensations of Boswell after his introduction to Johnson in Mr. Davis's back-room.

Oct. 11th.—The American people with all their shrewdness seem to be very gullible. There seems to be developed amongst them a strong taste for candy, bull's eyes, and other sweet things, but these tastes are only symbolical of their love for the sugarsticks of praise. I had an opportunity this evening of witnessing their passion for flattery. Mr. Thomas Hughes, M.P., the author of *Tom Brown's School Days*, was invited to lecture at the Music Hall, and being an Englishman and a politician, and above all an author, he was greeted with an immense, an overflowing audience. The subject of his lecture was "John to Jonathan," or in other words, "What England had to say to America." He had been in the country for two months and had received most profuse and cordial hospitality everywhere, but when he mentioned the name of his country a shadow came over the kind faces. Now he should set them right in their estimation of the attitude of England. She had been accused of siding and sympathising with the Southerns during the late revolutionary wars. Of course she was, Mr. Hughes, and it is strange if you doubt the allegation—it would be strange if America could forget it. But, poor, easily hoaxed, Yankees! Mr. Hughes undertakes to prove to you that during the whole struggle England and the English people were your friends and sympathisers, and you shout and cry hurrah! He tells you, with regard to that Alabama question, England is ready to settle it, she only desires to have the matter referred to arbitration and she will abide by the result. In fact that Jonathan has only to present his little bill and it will instantly be paid.* And then Mr. Hughes becomes lachrymose. He contemplated the possibility of England veering to bankruptcy and seeking among the Nations for a rescuer.

"And," said he, "if the strong old Islander, who after all is *your own father !!!*" (Where is the paternity of Germany, and of Ireland?) "should happen some day to want" (Here Mr. Hughes' voice faltered with emotion and the audience burst forth in sympathetic applause) "a name on the back of one of those bills, I for one should not wonder if

---

* Plainly Mr. Hughes' reading of the situation was the right one here. And it may be said, too, that while the English governing classes and their organs were Southern, the English Democracy, even including the Lancashire cotton-spinners, sympathised strongly with the North.

the name of Jonathan is found scrawled across there in very decided characters." "Hurrah! hurrah!" shouts Yankeedom, "hurrah! hurrah!" Mr. Hughes was successful, he offered Jonathan a sugar-plum and Jonathan swallowed it with the gusto of a child. The most distinguished citizens were present and some remarkable strangers. The poet Longfellow was conspicuous in his chosen obscurity by his copious white hair, and loud cries for Sumner after the lecture indicated the presence of that popular statesman.

Such, also, was the character of the American's mind in relation to Charles Dickens in his *American Notes*. He said some hard things of Jonathan, and Jonathan was very angry—but years rolled by and the great novelist came and made the *amende*. He was sorry for what he had said, he was mistaken and all that; and the Yankees forgave him. They went further, they took to worshipping him, and when he died the event caused a far greater sensation in America than in England. The pulpits rang with his praises—the morality of his life and writings was held up to admiration, and in America, the ridiculed of Boz—the repentent lecturer found at last his apotheosis.

Pulpits! alas for the pulpits. Read one of Monday morning's New York papers, where all the sermons of all the churches preached the previous day are summarized, and what a medley! I take up by chance last Monday's, the "leader" on the sermons sufficiently explains their variety of characters, and I shall merely quote it word for word :— " There was a marked increase in the number of attendance at church yesterday. Every place of worship was crowded. Resplendent fashion, having temporarily retired from Paris, shone in all her original grandeur, until it became a difficult matter to say whether the dresses or the sermons were the best, both, in some of the churches, being the last sensation. The Rev. Mr. Hepworth, at the church of the Messiah, delivered his third lecture on 'The Moral Aspect of Europe,' in which he gave Napoleon some very hard raps; on the other hand, Father Ronay, a French missionary, in a most eloquent sermon at the church of St. Louis, in Williamsburg, praised the emperor highly, and predicted his early restoration to the throne. His picture of the sufferings of France was quite touching, and affected his congregation to tears.

"Dr. Dix, at Trinity, declared that the crowning sin of Rome was in proclaiming an enthroned God, and said many hard things of the Catholic Church. There are, however, two sides to every question; and, consequently, those who do not agree with the anti-popery doctrines of Dr. Dix can read our reports of sermons of the Catholic churches— where the recent misfortunes of the Holy Father were made the subject of much eloquent argument, and where infallibility, and all other dogmas of Catholicism, were explained and extolled. We would, however, suggest that there might be good policy in reading but one side of the question, lest a perusal of both may end in the believing of neither.

"Sermons of a more general nature, and in some respects more instructive, were delivered at the other churches. Brother Beecher was particularly pathetic on the subject of the woman with seven husbands, and the future life. And well he might! We should think that the contemplation of such a domestic arrangement, even in the future life, would incline one to pathos and even anxiety. At Lyric Hall Mr. Frothingham took piety for his theme, and administered a severe rebuke to cant. He seemed to have a tolerably clear idea of what piety is, and he thought that it was not displayed by mankind exactly as he believed to be right and proper.

"At the New England Congregational Church Rev. Mr. Richardson discoursed on the renovating power of Christianity; while at the Elm-place Congregational Church, in Brooklyn, the kingdom of heaven was the theme. In the same city, at the Grand-street Methodist Church Rev. Mr. Hendricks gave the young ladies some sound advice on subjects matrimonial, and a few hints on the same to husbands expectant. 'Though he may have a boundless fortune,' he said to the fair maidens, 'Will you marry a man who will bring upon you not only poverty but disgrace?' How a man with a boundless fortune can bring poverty upon his wife we cannot imagine."

Oct. 12 — This is the anniversary of the discovery of America by Christopher Columbus, and the Italian residents of Boston have celebrated the event with due *éclat* At 9 o'clock, a.m., a procession of Italians, numbering a hundred, with a band and a banner—the latter representing the landing of Columbus at San Salvador—proceeded through the principal streets, and stopped at the City Hall, where they paid their respects to the mayor, and made him a suitable address. His honor replied appropriately. Will I be accused of hypercriticism if I comment unfavourably upon one passage of his honor's speech, or rather upon a quotation from an American poet, which he adopted.

"If I could have my say," said his honor, "I would give your illustrious countryman his true deserts, and call our beloved country by its real name—Columbia. I think we could all exclaim in harmonious feelings, in the language of Barlow, the Yankee poet :—

> "Columbia, Columbia, to glory arise,
> The queen of the world and the child of the skies."

I only ask, what is the meaning of saying that Columbia is the " child of the skies ?" Were she called " child of the ocean," there would be sufficient *vraisemblance* in the idea to divest the hearers from too rigid an examination of the words; but " child of the skies" is too absurd, too inconceivable, or, if conceivable, too prosaic to awaken a poetic sensation. The idea of America, a large continent, falling from the boundless skies, and settling in an ocean small in comparison to the firmament, is an anticlimax annihilative of all poetry.

There was a good deal of cannonading in Boston Common commemorative of the great event, and festivities and convivialities crowned the joyous celebration.

Oct. 13*th.*—We had a letter of introduction to the celebrated comedian, Mr. Barney Williams. This gentleman lives in New York, and while we were there we made inquiries and found that he was staying at Bath—a fashionable watering-place, on Long Island—consequently we did not call, resolving to do so at some future time when it would be more convenient. This week Mr. B. Williams and his lady are performing at the Boston Theatre and staying at the St. James Hotel. We called and Mr. Williams returned the visit. He appointed this day to call on us, and drive us in his carriage around the suburbs. He kept his word. At 11 o'clock he called in a magnificent landau (he is famous for his carriages) and a pair of splendid horses—the day was beautiful and we had a very charming ride. He is an interesting man, small in stature, with a handsome face, a bright intelligent eye and a rather fashionable style of dress. He is Irish Catholic and a native of Cork, where he was born, June 4th, 1826. His father, he told us was a man named Barney Flaherty, a full colour sergeant in the British Army. His name of Williams is assumed. His wife is a convert, an American lady, and a very staunch papist. He and she have made thirteen converts since they were married. He is a great lover of Ireland—they have grown very wealthy by their talents and much good may it do them.

Mr. Williams discoursed a good deal about the Irish in America, and his points, put very briefly, were these :—The Irish are matchless for brain-work, and handiwork. He instanced the making of the Erié Canal, one of the grandest pieces of engineering ever seen in the world as a proof of his statement on the subject of Irish talent. It was designed by an Irishman, and made by Irishmen. It is 500 miles long, and is cut through mountains and rocks, in many places at great length and difficulty. The Irish are kept in big cities by cunning politicians who wish to have their votes in election times. The unfortunate creatures receive no encouragement to go West where land may be had for nothing; but are crammed like "Sardines in a box," in tenement houses, in New York and elsewhere. They are honest in every sphere of life, except when they become politicians. The Yankees prefer an Irish servant to all others—Irish servant girls are saucy and hard to put up—but it is better to bear sauciness than to be robbed. And Yankees insist on them going to confession at certain times. They justly regard confession as a great check of crime, and the safe-guard of conscience. Mr. Williams has been in almost every hotel in America, and he could not remember a single instance where the night watchman was not an Irishman and a Catholic. To no other would they entrust the awful responsibility of life and property, which could be so sadly jeopardised at the dead hour of night by collusion between the watchman and a burglar. He fully concurred in all that had been said of the Irishman's attachment to the old faith, and witnessed all that have been done in America for its sake of late years; and he justly observed that the preservation of that faith, under so many trials, was one grand proof of its being divine.

On Sunday, Oct. 17th, a great celebration took place here, the laying of the corner-stone of a New Home for Destitute children. It was altogether a Catholic affair. The funds for the erection of the building are the voluntary offerings of the Catholic people, and the thirty thousand persons who were present belonged to the old faith. It was a great event in this city, once the strong-hold of Puritanism. The day was beautiful, and so warm that many butterflies were abroad. All the Catholic societies and confraternities, and school-children of both sexes, marched in procession arrayed in the various costumes indicative of their orders, through the chief streets of the city, with banners but without bands. On the ground two platforms were erected, on one of which the societies, &c., took their places. A band performed here, and some concerted pieces of sacred music were well sung by the children. On the other platform, the Bishop and clergy took their places, and the ceremonial usual on such occasions was proceeded with. A sermon was preached by Bishop O'Reilly, the newly consecrated bishop of the new See of Springfield, Mass. The great point of the whole ceremony was the means it afforded the Catholics, that is the Irish, of showing their power, and they showed it to some purpose. Great order prevailed and the whole spectacle contrasted in every respect to my mind very favourably with similar displays in the " old country."

Mr. Patrick Donahoe of the *Boston Pilot*, is the chief promoter and largest subscriber to the New Home, and he took, as far as a layman could, a very prominent part in the ceremony. When it was over a large number of carriages were ready to convey the clergy and some laymen to Mr. Donahoe's house, where supper was prepared; we were amongst the invited guests, and a carriage was placed at our disposal. The Bishop (Williams) was as usual extremely courteous and introduced us to the other Bishop (O'Reilly). Before supper we all assembled in the drawingroom, supper came off and was something novel to me; two black servants helped us. No one sat down, not even the Bishops. All stood and were helped from the table. There was nothing like a general blending of sentiment or conversation, the meal was consumed in a business-like fashion and did not occupy a very long time, not half an hour; after which all adjourned to another room where cigars were provided, of which almost all partook.

Bishop Williams is an excellent man; his dress on this occasion was simply that of an ordinary gentleman, there was about him no vestige of the priest, much less the bishop, and as he is a very handsome man, and personal beauty is a rare thing in gentlemen of our profession, the thought of his being a clergyman could enter no one's mind.

Oct. 23rd, Sunday.—I deliver my lecture on the History of Irish Music this evening in the Boston Theatre. Mr. Barney Williams says this is one of the finest theatres in the world. My lecture was a great success, an audience of about 2,500 were present, and considering I was a "new hand" it was very patronizing. I was introduced to the Honourable P. A. Collins, a young gentleman of very great promise in Boston; he is among the chiefs of what is called the "Young Democracy," a very clever person only 26 years of age, yet already a senator, a native of Fermoy, County of Cork, but living here since his infancy; he is only a law student, and yet there are few men more respected in the city.

Immediately after the lecture Judge Russell, a gentleman of great respectability in Boston, now collector of customs, waited on me in the green room, and in very choice language congratulated me on my success. He said he was anxious to testify in some manner his admiration, and the only thing he could do was to ask me to proceed with him the following afternoon on board the revenue cutter, when he would show me the harbour, and take me on board the "School Ship." This latter is, as it were, a floating reformatory for boys who have violated the law; they are placed on board this ship, educated in the Naval art, and learn to become sailors in the marine of the United States.

I accepted the Judge's invitation, and the following day (Oct. 24th), as was duly recorded in the papers the day after, I proceeded on board the revenue cutter with the Judge, his wife and family. The afternoon was lovely, the scenery pretty, and all passed off very pleasantly. We went on board the school-ship and the boys were put through their various exercises for my entertainment. They "boxed the compass," sang Naval Songs, performed Gymnastic's, showed their skill in Geography; and, in a word, went through a synopsis of a sailor's theoretical duty. The Judge suggested to me that I might deliver a short address. I complied. I assured them how grateful I was to Judge Russell for the honour he had done me, in bringing me amongst them, that I was delighted with the exhibition which I just witnessed of their proficiency in the Naval Art, and that I had no doubt they would hereafter make brave sailors under the banner of the United States, the greatest country in the whole world. I reminded them of their duty to their country, but reminded them also of the still higher duty which they owed to God. They were mostly all Irish, and I trusted they never would disgrace the country of their ancestors, but would be to the end, brave sailors and devoted Christians. The Judge and suite, including me, then went on board the cutter for the purpose of leaving. Meanwhile the boatswain's whistle sounded, the boys formed on deck, and in an instant manned the yards—the effect was very pretty.

"I suppose," I remarked to Judge Russell, "that is a part of their daily drill."

"Not at all," replied the Judge, "this is intended for you—they wish to give you a parting cheer."

And, accordingly, as we moved off the boys set up a hearty cheer, which, as the papers say, was again and again repeated. I was very much pleased with the compliment thus paid me.

Curious coincidence. The evening I was at M. Tarbell's that gentlemen showed me the family album containing photographs of the celebrities of the day, especially American celebrities. Amongst the latter the generals of the late war were conspicuous. "You miss the photograph of

General Lee," said Mr. Tarbell; "I am sorry I have not got it. He is a man I admire very much, and his personal appearance is as magnificent as his manners are gentle and amiable. You will, doubtless, see him as you go down South. Call upon him, and you may be sure of a cordial reception." The papers next morning all over America contained telegrams of the "death of General Lee" on the previous day. The event occurred almost at the moment Mr. Tarbell was addressing me.

Another remarkable coincidence of the same kind occurred the day before my lecture. After tracing the history of the Irish Bards from the earliest ages down to the present, it was my intention to pay a tribute of admiration to the distinguished Irish composer Balfe in some such words as the following :—" At the present day Balfe sustains the honour of Ireland in the field of music, &c." But on taking up the paper that morning I read the death of Michael William Balfe, the Irish composer, at his residence in England the day before. In my lecture I had to substitute the past for the present tense. Here are two remarkable instances of the uncertainty of human life.

As a rule, I find amongst those whom I meet very little education of a high order. Perhaps I do not meet the educated classes; but there is an impression on my mind that even the clever men of America are not very well read, and that amongst them English literature is at a large discount, and a knowledge of languages as rare as a knowledge of hieroglyphics. In America the great ambition is to be rich, and for the acquisition of riches much book education is not necessary. Boys are "put to business" when very young, and it is no rare thing to see them employed at occupations which seem to demand not only brains but large experience. They grow fast here. Our boys at home spend years at Latin and Greek, and other years in forgetting those languages, while the lads of America are hard at work piling up dollars. In England and Ireland, and indeed most countries of the Old World, the great ambition of young men is to shine in the intellectual arena. Hence, they seek in crowds the Bar, the Pulpit, the Senate, or, failing those high aims, they are content with some profession where intellect is required, such as Medicine. They study the languages and music, and are most eager to acquire a reputation for literary culture. Not so here. He is the most esteemed in this country who makes the most money, and the only intellectual power admired here is that by which some new scheme is invented for the easier acquisition of wealth.

But every day I spend in this country the more do I admire the democratic character of the people, the apparent equality of intercourse that exists between them, and the more absurd appears to me the aristocratic spirit at home, the lines of demarcation between the different ranks of society, and the cringing respect with which those of the lower rungs of the social ladder regard those above them. Somehow here in personal appearance there does not seem to be much difference between man and man. You have a colonel who gained distinction in the wars now keeping a beer-shop, and serving the customers from behind the counter in his shirt-sleeves; majors and captains occupy positions of the same social respectability.

And by the way, that word respectability seems to be unknown here. It implies gradation, and there is no gradation amongst a free and equal people. Their Military men have no martial air to distinguish them, where as in England and Ireland, *the air Militaire* is unmistakable. At some public gathering one evening in the Music Hall here, a friend of mine was pointing out the remarkable men to me. While he was doing so, I saw a man (I could not say a "gentleman") enter with some ladies. His whole bearing, and dress, and features, especially an intense stupidity of expression, all forced me to the conclusion that he was a peasant and no more. No, sir, that is Colonel of the Montgomery Guards— one of the most brilliant officers of the late war. "God bless us!" I cried, "to what a depth has colonelcy descended!"

Another day, while I was at dinner in the Parker House, the waiter whispered in my ear:

"A General has just come in, and is sitting at a table below!"

I turned round in the direction indicated, and saw only a waiter standing. I said facetiously, "Is it that man with the white apron?"

"No," replied my waiter, "he does not wear a white apron, although he often appears in the White House!"

I was pleased with the waiter's humour, and then viewed the General at my leisure, a mighty plain, ungeneral-like man. "And," said I to the waiter, "has the general ever distinguished himself by any feat worthy of historical record!"

"Oh yes," he replied, "the general made very good use of his feet on one occasion!"

"How."

"Why he skedaddled at Bull Run."

You seldom see a man in America of what we call *distingue*

appearance, then you very seldom meet with a man poorly dressed, or if you do, he is a labourer and labour is respected. Nothing is so common as to see men of great wealth shaking hands and familiarly conversing with what we call menials, such as servants in hotels. The waiters while they stand at your table converse freely with you, and never condescend to say "Sir." But there is nothing offensive in all this; they have *helped you, and they are paid for it—you help* yourself and *you* pay for it; the balance, you see, lies against you. A man may make "tall piles" and yet retain his humble position. There are waiters in this hotel who own *real estate*, and yet they go on making fresh "piles." The master of the house must take care to handle them gently, they would take none of his dictation, they would not stand being "bossed." A servant, especially a female servant, will not allow herself to be called by that degrading name. If you ask her what business she is at, her answer is that she "lives out," and if you ask her does she mean that she is a servant, she replies, "No," she is a "help."

One day I was going in a horse-car when a very pretty and elegant young lady entered and sat not far from me. The journey continued a good while, and people got in and out as we went along. At length when very few remained the conductor, a young man, like one who would drive a hack at home, entered, shook hands with the young lady and sat down by her. She was delighted to see him, and they soon became very chatty and confidential. For aught I knew this conductor might have been a young man of great wealth, and even social position. There was nothing degrading in being conductor to a horse-car, and he may have retained the office from choice, or to prevent himself getting rusty.

All I knew was that in Ireland, or England, the immense barrier between an omnibus conductor and a fashionable young lady would not have been so coolly and unblushingly broken down.

Every one in America is a "gentleman," or "lady." The man who cleans your boots, and the "cabby" who drives you are "gentlemen," your very chamber-maid is designated "the lady." You may shake hands with them all, they expect it, and it is no social degradation. They live by honest labour, so do you it is hoped. You may have more money; but there are people too who have more money than you; poverty is no crime, though it is extremely inconvenient.

* * * * * * * * *

Soon after my lecture I became so ill with rheumatism and other maladies that I was confined to my room for a week. At the end of that time the *Pilot* did me the honor of noticing the fact. A good deal of inconvenience was caused to myself, and some to other parties, by the announcement. When I was quite well, people who had only just seen the *Pilot* flocked to know how I was. With my friend, Captain Buckley, of the "City of Ragusa," the story took the course once pursued by the three black crows—when the rumour reached him it told him *I was dead!* He telegraphed; I received the missive in bed one morning at 1½ o'clock, but was so vexed for being roused out of sleep, with the silly query whether I was dead or alive, that I deferred my answer till morning; but when morning came, I found that the captain had not sent any more definite address than "Providence." I thought this too vague, and did not reply at all. That night the captain turned up, "all dressed from top to toe"—got up especially by some Providential modiste, that he might present a decent appearance at my funeral. My silence was construed by him into an admission that I was done for. On his arrival he learned that I was spending the evening with Mr. Patrick Donahoe. I dare say he was disappointed ; but on my return from Mr. Donahoe's I met him, and although there was a considerable manifestation of *spirits* on the occasion, he saw very little of the *grave* about me.

He accompanied me the following day to Lowell, a large manufacturing town, about twenty miles from Boston. Here I got a very poor reception from one of the pastors of the place ; he was almost offensive ; he would afford me no assistance towards prosecuting my mission in Lowell—none whatever. I then asked him for information. I said I was anxious to deliver a lecture in Lowell, and enquired if there was a Hall in the town where I might deliver it. He answered that there was.

"Is it a large one ?" I asked.

"You will find it large enough for you," was the reply. I never before encountered so ungracious a person as this old specimen. He is unique, but I forgive him. The other pastor, a Rev. Mr. Crudder, was not at home. I sought the Hall ; it was engaged every evening up to the 11th of December. I came home to Boston, disappointed and chagrined.

The great singer, Christina Nillson, has arrived in Boston, and has been serenaded outside her hotel, the "Revere House," by the Bostonian "Scandinavians." Her pay is pretty handsome—1,000 dollars per night. I do not know shall I go to hear her ; I am indifferent.

During my convalescence I sometimes strolled through

the Boston Common, a very excellent park in the centre of the city, but small. Here is a very fine old tree, railed in. An inscription on the railing informs us that it was in full bloom in 1722, began to show signs of decay in 1792, and was subsequently shattered by a storm. It is swathed in canvas, to keep out the rain from its incisions. It looks like an old man with a diseased leg.

Boston is a very fine city, very large, with a number of suburban towns, which are so connected with it as to form a great whole. It is quite a flat, with the exception of one considerable elevation, on which is the "State House," a very fine building, overlooking the common aforesaid. The State House, from its great height and lofty situation, commands a magnificent view of the whole city; and its cupola is seldom seen without some half-dozen persons, generally tourists, admiring the view from so favourable a point. The city is remarkably clean, and there is an air of elegance and substantial comfort about it. The streets are very irregular, and in some places inconveniently narrow. They were evidently built at a time when no seer could prophesy the subsequent magnitude of the city. One may very easily lose his way in Boston, so sinuous are the streets. Public buildings are few, and not of remarkable beauty, if we except the State House, the City Hall, and a few others. The hotels, especially the Parker House, are fine buildings. The churches, with one or two exceptions, are nothing to speak of. There are in some streets magnificent "blocks" of commercial houses, tokens of great industry and wealth. I doubt if any city can present so fine a pile of public building of its kind as the "State-street Block" of Boston, an immense range of solid granite buildings, of uniform dimensions, welded together, and forming one massive square.

The suburbs of Boston are very much admired, and justly, although the people, I think, exaggerate their beauty. Some streets have been widened by pushing back one whole side. This appears strange to us, but it is quite common here. A plan of machinery is arranged, by which a house, no matter of what dimensions, is moved from its place to any distance the operator pleases. The Boylston Market, weighing 30,000 tons, was moved back twenty feet a short time before I came to Boston, and the business of the market was never for a moment disturbed.

Boston is called the "Hub of the Universe," or, briefly and familiarly, "The Hub." It would appear that "hub" is the name of that portion of a wheel from which the spokes radiate; and the Bostonians are of opinion that from their city, the "hub," as they call it, the spokes of intellect and general moral influence radiate to the whole world. No very modest assumption, to be sure; but who does not forgive that vanity by which men love the place of their birth? At home we, Corkonians, call our city "the Athens of Ireland." I find that the people of Boston call theirs the "Athens of America;" and when I was about to deliver my late lecture, the Hon. P. A. Collins, the gentleman who introduced me, made a point of this circumstance. He begged to introduce to the "Athens of America," a gentleman who hailed from the "Athens of Ireland."

The people of America are wonderfully lecture loving. There is scarcely a night of the year (except in summer weather) when some lecture is not delivered in Boston. I saw by one of the papers that a Miss Anna Dickinson "is engaged to lecture every night for an indefinite period." How I envy the lady her ocean of knowledge, with such multitudinous outlets! They enjoy a lecture here as people elsewhere enjoy the theatre. It is an elegant taste, and, I am sure, productive of good.

The people of Boston are quiet and respectable. There is no rowdyism here. You never see anything sensational in the streets; and such crimes as burglary and other outrages are extremely rare. The ladies dress very quietly, and are generally good-looking; and altogether there is about Boston an air of propriety, and decency, and quiet, hard to be conceived when one considers the general depravity of human nature in big cities.

Fechter, the celebrated actor, is playing here for some months back. I went to see him in "Hamlet." I have not much experience of the stage, but I was greatly impressed by his acting. I think, however, the secret of my pleasure was not the power of his acting, but the master-genius of the great mind that composed the immortal drama. The "Ghost" was admirable. During his long narrative of the manner in which his murder was accomplished I was positively transfixed. Fechter was "Hamlet," and did it beautifully. A few days after the performance, I was standing in the hall of the Parker House, when I remarked a group of three persons speaking together.

"That is General Banks," I asked of a gentleman standing by.

"Yes," he replied, "and that gentleman opposite him is Fechter, the actor." I should never have recognised him.

Have you ever suffered from boredom—I mean on a large scale? I don't ask you whether you have endured the torture for an hour or two, or once in a week, or so—but has anyone ever laid himself out to be your special and irrepressible bore? Not that he meant to bore you—on the contrary, he might have been the best-natured man in the world. But has he ever, with the best intention, watched, pursued, caught, and sat upon you, day after day, night after night, as if you were his property, and he would not part with you? No; well, I have been the victim of this horrible torture ever since I came to Boston. I have alluded, though not by name, to a certain young man, whom I will call Tomkyns. He is my bore. I was not two days in Boston when he introduced himself into my room as one who knew me well in Cork—knew me very well, and for a long time, and was surprised that I did not recollect him. He is a young man, about thirty years of age, with moustache and whiskers, a broad forehead, a very flat accent, and an endless jabber of unmeaning talk. He stands very erect, is bold and confident, although unconscious that he is obtrusive, with a great deal of good nature and affection, but the affection of a spaniel. Of course I was very civil to him the first night, and invited him again. He came again, and again. He took a great interest in all my doings; always wished to know my programme of action; brought a good deal of chit-chat of matters in town; an occasional cockpapet, a cheap novel—anything to amuse.

The evening was his time for coming—he was then free from business. A smart knock announced his arrival. He entered, tall, bold, smiling, and laid down his hat, as one who was privileged to stay, without ceremony. He usually smoked a cigar on his arrival, and kept smoking it to the end.

This went on night after night, and my friend's confidence in himself, and his easy conduct towards me, went on increasing. I began to see that he came because he thought it gave me pleasure. I was lonely, he thought, and I wanted company. He had stories of his interviews with Longfellow and with other celebrities. He was influential with the Boston Press, and got a few notices of me in the papers. His conception of humour was peculiar, because he told anecdotes without point, and laughed most where the point was conspicuous by its absence. Every evening he was particular to ascertain what I was to do next day, next Sunday, next week. He was always bringing some person to introduce to me, and sometimes he would leave a note stating that he would come at such an hour, to introduce Mr. Such-a-one. He and his friends frequently stayed until midnight, when I was obliged to present striking symptoms of weariness. Tales came back to me of Mr. Tomkyns' discourses concerning me. He told his friends how "thick" he and I were, and how I could do nothing without him—how I had him in my room every evening, "private and confidential," and soforth. It sometimes happened that a friend would look in on me in the evening, and, of course, find Tomkyns. I found that I had let him go too far. He came more and more frequently, and earlier than usual. Thus my evenings were being frittered away, and I received nothing in return. I could not read or write, or be alone, or enjoy another's company. He had taken possession of me; I was not my own master—not master of my room, my time or my actions. I saw myself reduced to the condition of a slave, an automaton—all because I had not the moral courage to shake off the incubus. If I came in of an evening he was waiting for me; if I happened to be in the dining-room, dining or taking tea, he was at my side; and, after the meal, I would adjourn to my room, led irresistibly by my bore, to be bored for the fortieth time, as before.

It so happened that I spent some consecutive evenings out with friends, and the feeling that I was freed, even for a short time, from my evil genius, gave new zest to my enjoyment. But every evening on my arrival home I heard that Mr. Tomkyns had called, and said he "would call again to-morrow evening." But when several to-morrow evenings came and he was disappointed, I fancied I was free. Alas! for my ignorance of what a bore can do. One morning, at eight o'clock, there was a knock at my door. I was in bed, got out and opened it. There was Tomkyns! Why, what had become of me—where had I been all the evenings— was I to be out again this evening, and where? He had a great deal to say, after the silence of several days, and he said it while I listened, wishing that some unseen power would take him from my sight to some region where I should never see him more. These morning visits were repeated, until at length he came morning and evening the same day, and I felt like one possessed by the demon, and gone beyond the power of exorcism. I would stand it no longer. It had now lasted for two months. I should stay in Boston one month more, and I would not allow myself to be victimised any longer.

November 13*th*.—I determined to take my stand, once for all, against my implacable tyrant. My spirit was sore, and I should burst if this slavery continued. I went out to Watertown, a village some ten miles from Boston, preached, and made a collection of 284 dollars. I dined with the pastor, and returned to town. I expected to reach the hotel about six, and asked myself what should I do in the possible contingency of meeting my bore. I could not answer the question; but one thing I resolved, and that was, that he should not spend that evening in my room.

I entered the hotel, and the first man I met was Tomkyns, radiant in beard and whiskers, and white waistcoat. He looked as if he meant to say "what kept you so long, here am I waiting for you for the last half hour?" I heard the first clank of the chain; but I did not succumb. I determined to initiate no conversation, I would let him begin—let him propose questions, and I would answer.

"But," I said, "I was going to have tea." "All right," he said, "I will sit with you while you take it," and he sat by me picking his teeth with a wooden tooth-pick, and proposing questions out of his wooden head.

Tea at length was over, and he accompanied me to the hall, where groups of loungers stood chatting. He evidently expected to be asked upstairs, but his surprise and disappointment were great when I asked him to help me on with my outside coat.

"Not going upstairs?" he said.

"No," I replied.

"Then let us have a walk on the common?"

"No," I said.

"What do you mean to do then?" he asked.

"I mean to stand here," was my answer. He could not understand; but he obeyed. I stood and was silent. He could not divine what had happened. Things went thus for *full three quarters of an hour*, when I concluded that he would stop there all night, if he were allowed; and the cure would be even worse than the disease. At the end of that time I took his hand abruptly. "Good night old fellow," I cried, "good night, I have some writing to do, good night!" and I rushed from him upstairs, I locked my door, I was free from my bore, at least for this night, and piously hoped it might be for ever.

Monday came and went and I did not see my bore, but I left town at 4½ p.m. to dine and sleep at the house of a friend at Jamaica Plain; Tuesday I returned. That evening I went to see Hamlet. On Wednesday morning there was a knock at my bed-room door; I was dressing. "Come in," I cried, and Tomkyns came in, fresh and smiling as a daisy. He had been in the two previous evenings and could get no tidings of me. I find I am dealing with a piece of human granite. He brought me books to amuse me, and made the usual queries about my past and future engagements. Now I don't know what to do. Thursday I went to Providence and returned late. It is now Friday evening, 6 o'clock, and I tremble every moment lest I should hear his foot-fall at my door.

On the 8th of November the elections take place all over the United States, the elections to all municipal and senatorial offices. In Boston it passed off very quietly, so quietly indeed that the very day could not be distinguished from any that went before it. On the evening preceding the election I had an opportunity of hearing Mr. Wendell Phillips speak in public. He is considered one of the best if not the very best public speaker in the States. He is very popular also, and was running for the office of Governor of Massachusetts. His war-cry is "Labor and Reform" and "Prohibition," viz., of intoxicating drinks. A large meeting took place in the Tremont Temple. There was no charge for admission, and one would naturally think that on the eve of a political election some excitement would be natural. There was none. The people sat quietly and orderly. When Mr. Phillips appeared there were three good cheers, but then all was quiet.

He is a graceful, quiet, elegant speaker, by no means passionate, but rather seeking to convince by argument than by rhetoric. His diction is admirable, he is one of those speakers of whom it is said they "speak like a book." In the election, however, the following day he was defeated.

Strange about this Liquor Law, no man is allowed to have a license for the sale of liquors in this State, and yet the law is allowed to be violated by hundreds every day. Sometimes the police pounce on some obnoxious liquor-seller, and seize his goods and have him fined; but they allow hundreds who are doing the same to pass unmolested. Thus in this country every day you meet contradictions—fact and theory coming constantly into collision; and notwithstanding the perpetual proclamation of Americans that they are a free people, you are forced to conclude that there are people just as free in countries where less noise is made about it.

In an early part of this Journal I commented rather severely on an American hotel, Broadway, New York, and I have no reason to think that I wrote unjustly of that house. But if I was understood to convey that my censure on that occasion embraced all American hotels, I would be sadly misinterpreted. The only hotels I have yet had experience of in the United States are the "St. Julian's," of Portland, Me., and the "Parker House," Boston. In the former I stayed only twenty-four hours and have nothing to say against it;

in the latter I am now "located" for more than two months, and wish to say a great deal in its praise.

In America hotels are quite an institution of their kind, they take the first rank as institutions in all the world. It is a natural result of the Democratic spirit that in this country, private hospitalities should be less extensive than in countries Monarchial or Aristocratic when all are equal, there is less willingness to receive favours or to be under obligations. The people have a universal taste for independence. Hence the majority of the respectable classes live in hotels, which have thus become institutions and are constructed and managed with all that style and order for which in America, institutions are distinguished.

"The Parker House" in Boston is the best hotel I was ever in. It is a magnificent building, erected by a Mr. Parker, a self-made man, who still presides over it, in partnership with a Mr. Mills. It is situated in School-street, and faces directly the City Hall, perhaps the handsomest structure in all Boston. It is itself an extremely handsome building, being Grecian in style, and faced with polished marble. The number of persons employed is 180, the guests rooms are 250 and are always occupied, but the great business is done by casual visitors who breakfast, dine, and sup. It is the most popular hotel in town, and is always thronged; over 2,000 people visit it daily, and partake of its hospitality. The bill of fare is stupendous and bewildering; but the machinery of the house, complicated as one might suppose it to be, works with the most marvellous regularity.

Let us consider what is an American hotel—*ab uno disce omnes*. You enter, and write your name in the book on the counter; you are told the number of your room, and get your key, while your luggage is taken upstairs by a porter. Having made your toilet, you come down stairs, perhaps you wish for a bath—there are two on every corridor ; you wish to be shaved or to have your hair dressed—there is a hair-dressing and shaving establishment below ; your boots are soiled— here are several shoe-blacks ready for an order. You ascend smiling and comfortable, and you just remember that you have a telegram to send to New York, to London, to Bombay, it matters not whither—here is the telegraph clerk seated at his desk, and the eternal "click, click," announcing his occupation. The news ? why here are papers from all parts of "creation." Your supply of visiting cards is out—a young man is here to do them on the spot. You want to write a letter—here are desk, paper, ink, and stamps, all at hand. Have any letters arrived for you ?—one of the clerks will tell you. You want a novel, or some other light book to amuse your dull hours—see the book-stall in a corner, and the young man up to his eyes in business. Do you smoke ?—here is another little corner, where you can have Havanas, or cheroots at pleasure. Do you wish to go to the theatre ?—this young man at the counter will supply you with a ticket, and point out in a diagram what seat in the theatre is yours for that evening. Take off your outside coat and leave it in the cloak-room—the man will give you a check for it. Enter the dining-room, with at least one hundred tables, made double and treble by the reflection of mirrors ; here is the bill of fare ; find if you cannot satisfy your appetite out of it, you must be an epicure indeed. Over 200 items, including soups, fish, flesh, fowl, and game, pastry, fruit, and wines, ought to satisfy you I think. Do you wish to dine with the ladies?—if so, go to the ladies' dining-room, it makes no difference. In fine, do you wish for a railway ticket to any place, from Boston all round the world and back again?—you can get it at the magic counter of this wonder-working Parker House.

I have gone through the whole house, and observed its machinery. Twenty feet under ground are the furnace and steam-engine, which by the annual consumption of 800 tons of coal, supply the motive power for the complicated operations going on above. I passed into the store-room, packed full of nice things—spices, preserves, olives, oils, nuts, and smelling with a delicious compound of richest odours. Here is the larder! how neatly everything is arranged! how crowded every nook with the raw materials for health, strength and pleasure! See those matchless rows of mutton-chops, and red and white beefsteaks, all ready to broil! they are beautiful enough in their repose to tempt the art of a photographer. What provoking quantities of game, brought from every part of the country, to set the mouths of epicures watering! Here are salmon from the pine-clad banks of streams in Maine, from the icy floods of Canada, and the gold-haven rivers of California. Every air of heaven, every clime on earth, every isle of the ocean has been laid under tribute to cater to the appetites of those who patronize the Parker House, and what quantity of materials, think you, is daily consumed in this establishment? Fourteen barrels of vegetables, one ton of meat and poultry, five-hundred weight of fish, four barrels of oysters, three hundred and twenty quarts of milk, three barrels of flour, one hundred and fifty pounds of butter, one hundred dozen of eggs, and other things in proportion. One can fancy what work goes on in the kitchen after this enumeration. The ranges of tables and dishes, the gigantic soup kettles, big enough to boil down whole oxen in, the glowing rows of fires, with spits and gridirons, and every convenience for frying and roasting and broiling—the long array of white-aproned cooks at their respective posts, twenty in number, all make up a show that fill the spectator with admiration and surprise.

And then the laundry in an adjacent room is another wonder. As we look on the busy scene, and trace the running machinery for cleaning soiled garments, and see the exact order in which every parcel has its own mark and book-entry, and notice the purity and freshness of the place, and follow the busy motions of the girls who wash or iron, or fold, the whole room becomes a beautiful picture of a human beehive.

The wine-cellar with its multitudinous bottles of various wines all packed and stored away in an atmosphere of delicious coolness, makes one feel thirsty, and anti-temperate; and this feeling is heightened by contemplating a huge ice-chest filled with bottles ready for immediate consumption. These are only a few glimpses of the working part of the hotel. There are private dining rooms, where parties are held almost every day, and sometimes when I am retiring to rest, I hear the clapping of some thirty or forty hilarious boon-companions over the speech of some Post-prandial orator. I deplore the envious fate that dooms me to a solitary room, and the unromantic folds of a blanket. But I bear my lot with patience, and feel proud of being a guest where things are done in so grand a style, as in the "Parker House" of Boston.

Boston is called from a place of the same name in Lincolnshire in England, where there is a famous cathedral existing since the old cathedral times—dedicated to God under the invocation of St. Butolph, a Saxon saint. The original name of the original Boston was Butolph's Town, which being too cumbersome for common conversation, was shortened down into Bostown or Boston. The historians here, descendants of the old hard grained Puritans, allowed a great many years to elapse before they discovered this fact—the terrible fact that their new city in New England, the city of all the "(sch)isms" (ca-tholi-cism alone excepted), was called after a Catholic saint; in their ignorance they went so far as to allow one of the streets to be called "Butolph Street," but rather late, no doubt, owing to the researches of some officious antiquarian, they discovered the unwelcome truth, that Butolph was a canonized papal saint, and they changed the name of the street into "Irving Street," which it is to the present day. I knew a gentleman who lived for years in Butolph Street. It was newly called, I dare say, after Washington Irving, who has not been canonized, and is not likely to be. It is only surprising that they did not call the whole city Irvingstown, in their wonderful preference of a pleasing writer, to a head of the Christian religion.

November 24th, 1870.—This is "Thanksgiving Day," and is celebrated all over the United States. It is somewhat like our Christmas Day—at least, as far as festive enjoyment goes. Friends come from distant places to see their friends, and there is great feasting everywhere. Labour is suspended, people go to church; and the theatres are largely patronized. The day was fine, and I walked through the city; it was like Sunday, but I could see that labour was not altogether suspended. I saw people building houses, &c. The day is set aside to thank God for all the blessings conferred during the year, especially for an abundant harvest. I had some invitations to dinner—one especially from a *German Jew;* but I declined them all. I don't care to dine with *people* I don't know well.

November 25*th.*—This morning I went by rail to Worcester, a city (I believe there is no such thing as a "town" in all America), of about 45,000 inhabitants, of whom about 18,000 are Catholics. Worcester is, I think, forty-five miles from Boston. The morning was very fine; it had frozen over night, but it was by no means cold, although at this time last year, as I am informed, there was several feet of snow upon the ground.

The American railway carriages are very comfortable. Such a thing as a rug would be a superfluity, and an overcoat may be dispensed with. The carriages are all heated, and as a large number of people are always travelling, the atmosphere is never cool.

I reached Worcester at $10\frac{1}{2}$ a.m., and found it very like all American small "cities" I have yet seen. The characteristics of American cities appear to me to be these: A number of streets, almost always straight and regular, the houses composed either of red brick or wood. Several streets are insignificant, and the roadways bad; but there are always a few main streets which are very fine, composed of large solid houses, fine shops, with plenty of carriages in waiting outside, and a good many foot passengers, and a fair amount of bustle. In these main streets there is a track, and horse-cars run. The names over the doors are frequently composed of gilt letters, and sometimes a shopkeeper who believes in advertising has a handsome flag suspended at a great height, by a rope reaching quite across the street, with his name and number inscribed on it. This looks picturesque. The bustle of these cities is greatly increased by the constant, I might say the incessant, noise of railway trains running by—running often through the centre of an important street, with a bell ringing at a tremendous rate. A large wooden archway over the track warns you against danger by the words painted on it—" Look out for the engine while the bell rings." How a few dozen people are not killed every day in each of those cities is a marvel to me, for the bell is always ringing, and the engine, or as they pronounce it, the " injine," is always coming.

Churches there are plenty, and now and then a green place with a monument to Daniel Webster, to Washington, or Araham Lincoln, or perhaps some nobody. You sometimes pass a splendid-looking building with a magnificent Grecian portico, and steps leading up; but with your walking cane you find the steps are made of wood, and your suspicion being once awakened, you tap the columns, and a hollow sound announces that they too are only a spurious imitation.

Such are, I fancy, the leading features of those " cities." See one, and you see all. Worcester is contemptuously called a "one-horse city." Why? Because it is not large or wealthy enough to support street cars with two horses, like most other cities, but must be content with one-horse cars. Indeed I have been told that the one-horse cars here scarcely pay, and that they had been actually discontinued for some time.

I came to Worcester to make arrangements for a lecture

which I am to deliver here on December 6th. I visited the college, situated about two miles from the town on a great eminence—a fine house on a fine site. It was a long walk. I went to see a young man I knew there, and who was a good guide to me in Worcester. I called on the Bishop (O'Reilly) and the clergy, and several of the laity. I had great success, and anticipate an overflowing house. I visited, among others, a Father John Power. He was at dinner, and invited me to partake of his hospitality. I was nothing loth. His curate and my young friend, Walsh, made up a *partie carrée*. The chief dish, it being Friday, was fish "chowder," a kind of hotch-potch—viz., fish, biscuits, potatoes, vegetables, sauce, &c.

We spoke of the variety of dishes prevailing in various countries. I said I found it hard to like some American dainties, which the natives seemed to prize very much I could scarcely put up with tomato, I hated sweet "potatoes," but "squash" was to me an abomination! I described my having tasted "squash" once (it is a huge yellow pumpkin), and thought it tasted like soap, but that the saponaceous article seemed to me to have rather the advantage of it in flavour. It is usually served up mashed, like turnips. Father Power was amused by my strong denunciation of a precious vegetable, but foretold that I would yet eat it with pleasure. I sturdily answered, "never."

The "chowder" was removed, and a pie took its place. I was helped, and found it very nice pie, so much so that I finished my share.

"You seem to like that pie," said Father Power.

"Yes, sir," said I, "it is exquisite!"

"Well," said he, "my prophesy is fulfilled much sooner

than I anticipated. You have just eaten the one-fourth part of a squash pie. The laugh was against me, and I admitted the justice of it.

I lectured in Worcester with considerable success. The Bishop (O'Reilly) of Springfield, lately consecrated, was very favourable to me, and the clergy lent a cordial assistance, I had an audience of about 1,000 in the Mechanics' Hall, and realized 163 dollars.

All the while I had been suffering from an attack of rheumatism in my shoulder; but soon after my return from Providence, there appeared symptoms of a more serious visitation of the disease. I felt it in my right knee on Wednesday, December the 4th. On that day I sent home to the Bishop a bill of exchange for the second £1,000, and that night I retired to rest with unmistakable symptoms of rheumatism in my right knee. Suffice to say, I was confined to bed for a whole fortnight, and endured a great deal of pain. My whole system was out of order, and medical care was of the greatest importance. But what physician could I call in a strange city, especially in a city where, as all through America, quacks are so abundant.

Nothing could surpass the care and kindness of the servants of the hotel, of whom about a dozen evinced for me the greatest sympathy. They were all Irish, and many from Cork County. They neglected no means for aiding in my restoration to health. The men-servants could show nothing but sympathy, and they showed it as far as language could go.

Dr. Salter called every day while I was sick, and showed great skill as well as industry in banishing my pains and restoring me to health. Mrs. Salter wrote me a note of sympathy, and sent me books and pictures to amuse, and wine to stregthen me. She then came herself every day, and spent an hour with me. She impressed me as one of the most learned, elegant and accomplished ladies I had ever met. Although the daughter of a Protestant clergyman, she is a convert to Catholicity, and so became every member of her family, including the Doctor. I never met a more intense Catholic than Mrs. Salter. She seems to have not only retained, but to have kept constantly intensifying in her soul the first fervour of neophytism.

I bore my illness and solitude with remarkable patience for some days; but soon, when it got noised abroad, my resignation was less severely tested, for several friends dropped in, and all brought some present which they thought would be of service to me. One brought wine, another fruit, a third, Mrs. Murphy, acted like a Sister of Charity. She came every day, and brought some soup or other delicacy, such as a jelly, which she administered with her own hands, until I found myself as well cared for as if I were ill in my own house at home. Withal, I sighed for the gentle care of my sister and dear friend, Miss Cox, and for the balmy air of my native land. In Boston it blew, one day a hurricane, another day the wind was cold and biting—then it froze for several days together, and last of all it snowed.

As I grew better, I fancied that my condition was not so very disagreeable, and that repose and seclusion from a cold atmosphere were not entirely unpleasant; yet I had to spend the Christmas in my room, while all the world were enjoying the festivities of that merry season. No matter, I had many reflections to console me, and I could not resist the tempta-

o

tion of weaving those reflections into verse. I subjoin a copy of the lines I wrote on this occasion :—

CONSOLATIONS OF AN EXILED INVALID ON CHRISTMAS DAY.

How many a way man is doomed upon earth
   To spend " Merry Christmas," as men love to call it !
For some 'tis a season of frolic and mirth,
   For others, there's plenty of sorrow to gall it.
Here family circles unbroken unite,
   There vacant chairs vainly await the departed ;
Here children's loud laughter enlivens the night,
   There pines the lone father, death-doomed, broken-hearted ;
For me, I have tried, when this Christmas comes round,
   To smile in saloons or to revel in attics—
The last was the jolliest yet, though it found
   Me sick in a Boston hotel with rheumatics.

There, stretched at full length, as I lay on my back,
   I gazed on the ceiling all white that shone o'er me,
A canvas so fair did my fancy but lack
   To paint all its visions of Christmas before me.
One pleasure, at least, was the absence of sound—
   Shut out was the world, with its cares and its troubles,
Calm, holy and sweet was the silence around,
   Unheard were the breakers of life, and its bubbles.
The frosty wind sighed by my cold window-pane,
   But I was wrapped snug from those biting pneumatics,
I tell you, my friends, I'd spend Christmas again
   Thus sick in a Boston hotel with rheumatics.

No doubt, it is lonely thus lying in bed ;
   With patience, however, to bear it I'm able :
Far better my lot than of those whom the dead
   Come haunting at Christmas, and grin round the table.
Far better be captive in bed, when the pain
   Is not unendurable, than in a prison,
Where pleasure expires at the clank of the chain,
   And hopes are extinguished as soon as arisen ;

Far better an ocean of bed than of wave,
  Secure from the dangers of wild aerostatics,
I envy no seaman so close to his grave,
  While sick in a Boston hotel with rheumatics.

How many a Prussian now trembling in France
  With hunger and cold and unspeakable hard fare,
Would envy my bed, where no bayonet or lance
  Would conjure up all the wild horrors of warfare.
Oh, Christmas, what thousands of palls hast thou flung
  O'er hearts and o'er homes through this war's desolation?
Thy advent, once welcome to aged and young,
  Now brings only ruin, and woe, and starvation.
To count all the sorrows of Teuton and Frank
  This Christmas, surpasses all my mathematics,
But one thing is plain, my good angel I thank,
  That I'm sick in a Boston hotel with rheumatics.

I think of the thousands like me who recline
  In bed, but alas! with less hope of revival,
Who, friendless, unpitied, incurable pine,
  And think their best blessing Death's early arrival.
Ah! Christmas, what balm for those wretches hast thou?
  The memories thou bringest but heighten their anguish,
The joys that thou sheddest of yore are but now
  Dim phantoms before which they hopelessly languish—
For me, I but suffer some pain in my knees,
  Which yields to the soothings of homœopathics,
And calmly philosophize here at my ease,
  Laid up in a Boston hotel with rheumatics.

And were I at home! what is home to me now,
  Since those who endeared it are vanished for ever?
The father who sat at the board with the brow
  Of Jove when serenest, again shall sit never.
The mother whose face, like a garden of flowers,
  Gave out all its sweets to the sunshine of pleasure,
Sheds radiance no more on the festival hours,
  A sharp, sudden stroke reft my life of that treasure.

A sister and friend guard the homestead for me,
　　While Destiny flings me amongst the erratics;
Small difference then doth it make if I be
　　One sick in a Boston hotel with rheumatics.

Come, let us be jolly, whatever betide,
　　And fill up a bumper : let's call it Falernian.
It matters not what be the liquor supplied,
　　As long as we cannot procure the Hibernian.
Come, Mary and Pat, to your welfare here goes ;
　　Time flies ! see, already the day's disappearing !
The season comes round once a year, and who knows
　　The next we may spend in the dear land of Erin?
The thought is so pleasant, it makes me inclined
　　To try an experiment in acrobatics ;
This Christmas, at least, is the last that will find
　　Me sick in a Boston hotel with rheumatics.

During my illness I heard from the servants and visitors a great deal about the preparations which were being made to honour the Christmas festival. But I was very much surprised to learn that it is only of very late years that the solemnity has been observed at all, and even so late as twenty years ago, it was regarded no more than any other day in the year; and stranger still, that there were many persons in Boston and elsewhere who actually never heard of Christmas Day, or knew what it meant!

That the anniversary of the Nativity of Christ should be ignored amongst Christians while other anniversaries were remembered and respected, is very singular indeed, yet so it was. Twenty years ago, on the return of Christmas Day there was nothing to indicate that any extraordinary day had arrived. Business of all kinds went on as usual. There was no church service except in the few Catholic chapels that then existed, and no one spoke of Christmas Day. See what a change has taken place in a few years. Christmas

Day is now observed by all classes with as much strictness as it is in any part of the world. And not only are the churches filled, and all business suspended, but there is an unusual amount of feasting, and visiting and house decoration, and holiday-making everywhere, and this is increasing from one year to another. The newspapers state that no previous celebration of Christmas surpassed this one in festivity, and the community were congratulated upon their growing Christian spirit.

No allusion however was made to the means by which this great revolution was brought about, while everybody knows that it is entirely owing to the influence of the Irish. The Irish would not work on a Christmas Day—so great was their reverence from childhood for this festival, that no threat or privation could prevail on them to desecrate it by servile work. They sturdily resisted the solicitations of their employers, and the end of that was business had to be given up and the obligations of Christmas recognised. The despised race brought about this change; the weak ones of the world confounded the strong, and religion witnessed another triumph at the hands of a people to whom its interests are dearer than life itself.

Shortly after my last lecture, I received a letter of warm congratulation from a lady, "Miss Jannette L. Douglas," 209 Springfield Street, Boston, to which I replied on the eve of my illness, and which was soon succeeded by another. To the latter I replied soliciting the honour of a visit, as I was unwell. Miss Douglas came, and I immediately recognised a lady to whom I had been introduced to in the Victoria Hotel, Cork, about two years ago by my friend Professor Barry, since deceased. Miss Douglas is a fine looking lady—she had been travelling alone, as is the custom of American ladies, and she now informed me that, on that occasion she completed a tour through Great Britain, Ireland and France. Her admiration of Professor Barry was intense. She described him as the most finished gentleman she had ever met. And indeed she did not err, for the Professor's manners were most courtly, and his conversational powers unequalled. Her sorrow, when I informed her of his death was genuine indeed.

The lady had written the manuscript of a book which she is now preparing for the press, a journal of her tour, which I have no doubt, will be highly interesting, if I can form any opinion of her style from the correctness and elegance of her language in conversation, as well as from her powers of observation of men and things. I am to spend an evening at Miss Douglas's house when I am entirely convalescent.

I should have mentioned long since that I lectured at Portsmouth, New Hampshire, under the auspices of my friend the Rev. Canon Walsh, Pastor of that place, but with only trifling success, as the Catholic population is few, and not lecture-loving. The nett receipts were only fifty dollars. But my chief reason for going to Portsmouth was that I might enjoy the pleasure of meeting again that estimable clergyman, to whom I was introduced last summer in Montreal. His wit and humour, and hilarity were to me perfectly delightful, and his hospitality, which was of the genuine Irish pattern, made me feel quite at home. He had a few other guests, and his sister Miss Walsh, a very talented and interesting young lady.

From all I learn, the antipathy to the Catholic religion and the Irish population is very intense in this country. One instance of this amused me. A very estimable clergyman of Jamaica Plain was one day driving me in his carriage through a part of the country near his house. He pointed out to me a house on the road side, of not very portentous appearance, and a very stately mansion close by somewhat further from the road. The latter had been built before the former. An Irishman had dared to build a house within a few yards of an American; but what was to be done? The law afforded no solace to the wounded feelings of the Yankee, and as a last resource he erected a long and high wooden wall that would completely shut out from view the obnoxious domicile of the unoffending Patrick. I saw the wall of separation, and I could not help feeling disgusted to think that any man's hatred for another could carry him to such absurd and ridiculous lengths.

But Patrick goes steadily "marching on." Every year witnesses new triumphs of his nationality and religion, and there is every reason to hope that after a generation or two, both will be once for all in the ascendant.

In the city of Providence, and indeed, I believe, all through the broad island, there exists a law clearly aimed at Irishmen, that no "foreigner," no matter how long resident in the country, can vote for any *purpose* unless he have *real estate* to the value of 134 dollars. This law excludes from civil and municipal privileges many Irishmen, although it permits even niggers to enjoy them. Even a negro is preferable in the eyes of a Yankee to an Irishman.

According as I recovered from my illness I found it very necessary for me to go to some part of the country for change of air, for as long as I remained confined my appetite would not return. I bethought myself of the Rev. John McCarthy, of Watertown. I knew how kind and good he was, and I felt he was the proper person for me to stay with. As good luck would have it, who should drop in to visit me but the same good man, and he immediately invited me to his place. I promised to go on the following Friday, and he engaged to meet me at the station. When Friday came I left by the 12 train. The moment I entered the open air I felt it like a knife cutting my throat inside, and I coughed tremendously. I had no notion it was so cold, but it had snowed for some days previous and the streets were all white. This day I saw sleighs in operation for the first time; I had seen them before in coach-houses, but now I saw them passing through the streets over the snow, and heard the pleasant sound of the bells making the whole air musical. I was not long in reaching Watertown, which is only seven miles from Boston, and there Father McCarthy was ready for me with his sleigh and his wolf-skin rug—it is remarkable that the first day I ever saw a sleigh in action was the first day I rode in one. Father McCarthy suggested that we should take a good long drive before coming to the house, which was close at hand. I agreed. The whole country was covered thick with snow, and probably will be for several weeks, if not months. The air was biting cold, but bracing and healthy. I was snug in my magnificent Irish frieze coat, the envy and admiration of everyone who saw it; and the grand muffler made for me at home by the fairy fingers of Miss Bride Finnegan, encircled my neck and enveloped my ears, while two warm gloves without fingers, of which I had been made a present, kept my hands in a warm glow. We drove along—the horse, a splendid animal—and shot over the snow like a skiff, while the little bells tinkled a merry peal over the horse's back.

We met many other sleighs on the way, some driven by ladies, others by gentlemen; but ours was as good-looking, and our horse as spanking as any. The journey was very pleasant: but it was impossible to discern any beauty in the landscape, as all was enveloped in snow. Not a bird was to be seen anywhere. Father McCarthy told me that through the whole winter not one was visible, they all fled to southern and warmer climates, indeed, if they remained, a few weeks of starvation would have killed them all. It was amusing to see the various costumes worn by gentlemen driving in sleighs. Furs were the most abundant, and I saw one gentleman so enveloped from head to foot in skins that it would not have been difficult to mistake him for a wild beast, especially as there was a something ferocious in his aspect, quite in correspondence with the hirsuteness of his attire. Children derive great amusement from the snowy and frosty weather. They pull each other on small sleighs, which they call "sleds," and take a great deal of exercise in this manner. The atmosphere is by no means cold in this snowy weather, on the contrary, it is often mild and genial, and the bracing air quickens the spirits and makes one feel happy.

When we arrived at Father McCarthy's dinner was ready. The house, like most of the priests' houses I have seen in this country, is admirably furnished, and very elegantly kept. All the rooms are heated up to 70° Fahrenheit, summer heat, in fact; and it is so pleasant to step from the biting atmosphere of the ice and snow into such a temperature. This is one great point in which the Americans seem to be so much ahead of us—domestic comfort. They seem to make it the especial element of their happiness. Everyone appears to have a good house, and those who enjoy wealth, even in moderation, dwell in splendid mansions far superior in style and comfort to those of an equal position in Ireland. Almost all the houses, at least in the country, are built of wood— even the most magnificent palaces of merchant princes— but then they are all built in a beautiful style of architecture, are cooler than stone in summer, and warmer than stone in winter, and resist time and tempests just as well. Building in wood, too, seems to suit the genius of the American people exactly. They do not build for posterity. Each man appears to build for himself. As men do not pride themselves on their ancestry in this country, so neither do they seem to reck what may be the character or position of posterity. Architecture, then, is consulted only as to what it can do for the present day, and it supplies what is at once most elegant, cheap and commodious, and this applies to public as well as private buildings.

One of the finest houses I have ever been in, in America, was one which Father McCarthy took me to visit. It is the house of Mr. Adams, the chief of that firm known as the "Adams' Express Company." This company has its branches all over the United States. It is devoted to the transmission by express of all kinds of goods and parcels from one place to another. The principal (Adams) began life like so many remarkable Americans, without a cent, and is now one of the great millionaires of the country. Well, he has a splendid house, very close to Watertown, and large tracts of land, all round which he has fenced in by a low granite wall. Father McCarthy has a general entrée into the house, where there is a very fine gallery of paintings, and he drove me over to see the place. The paintings are very fine. I fancied for a moment that I was in some gallery on the continent of Europe, for the resemblance is perfect, and appears to have been studied. Many of those paintings are originals from European galleries, purchased at a great price, and others are very good copies. The whole is very interesting. The lady of the house hearing we were there came into the picture gallery and greeted Father McCarthy. He introduced me, and the lady hearing I was from Ireland, very courteously observed that " good pictures were no treat to me," which implied good paintings were rare in America. And so they are, I fancy, at least paintings which are the works of American artists. Mrs. Adams pointed out the pictures which are most admired, and gave the history of many—where they were got, what they cost, &c., &c. We bade her farewell, with thanks, and mounted to the top of the house where there is a Belvidere. The glass is stained, each pane a different colour from the next, and the landscape viewed through the various panes presents curious aspects. We saw the State House of Boston at a distance of seven miles, and the numerous little towns and villages all around that are so abundant all through Massachusetts.

The residence of another millionaire, Caleb Cushing, is in the immediate neighbourhood of Adams'; and the great attraction here, are the gardens on which he lavishes a great portion of his wealth, but as all these were now all covered with snow, and were only invisible green, we did not mind visiting them.

January 1st.—Father Shinnick came to-day from East Cambridge to dine, and in the evening some ladies and gentlemen came to see me, and we had a good musical treat, especially as Father McCarthy has a piano. All people in

America seem very fond of the Irish airs. Moore's Melodies are the great favourites. I do not know whether the Americans evince this love of our airs, probably not, but to me it is delightful to hear them—it makes me feel as if I were at home.

January 3rd.—I feel quite strong enough to return to town. Father McCarthy came with me ; I bid him good-bye at the Parker House. I engaged the Music Hall for Tuesday, the 24th inst., for the purpose of delivering my lecture on " The Chivalry of the Middle Ages." I met in the street Father Thomas Barry, of Rockport. It had been arranged between him and me that I was to preach and take up a collection in his church next Sunday, but he comes to tell me that the principal firm in the place had failed, and that hundreds of people were thrown out of employment, in consequence of which there was no use in my going. This was a disappointment, but there was no help for it.

I go by train to Lowell at 12 noon and make arrangements to lecture there on the 15th. I make the acquaintance of a leading Irish citizen there, a Mr. Patrick Dempsey, who receives me at his house, and gives me hospitality, and does all in his power to promote my interests. He drives me about and introduces me to several prominent men like himself, and I have considerable success. I sleep at Mr. Dempsey's. He is one of the best self-educated men I have found in his position of life. He is an extensive liquor dealer, and highly respected in Lowell.

On Thursday I go by train to Salem, distant about 20 miles from Lowell. Salem is on the sea, and is I think the oldest town in Massachusetts. It was the greatest stronghold of Puritanism in the State. There is a place here called Gallows Hill, where up to a comparatively late period, witches were hung and burned. Within a quarter of a century, all the Catholics in Salem were contained in one small church; they could easily be counted. Now they are six thousand, out of an entire population of 24,000, and increase from year to year. Farming and currying are the staple trade of Salem. Indeed the whole atmosphere is redolent of tan. As that trade was once prevalent in Cork, and then fell into decay, those who were thrown out of employment found, many of them, a good refuge in Salem. The Cork element is very strong here. I stayed with a Mr. Martin Egan, a tanner, from Blackpool, in Cork. He and his wife were very kind. I was treated with the most profuse and cordial hospitality by those good people. Mr. Egan took me to see several Cork friends, and others hearing of my arrival, called at his house to see me. I was quite at home here.

January 6th.—Celebrated Mass in one of the churches. Pastor, a young Irish priest, Father Gray; his curate, Father Healy, born at Muinteravsara, Co. Cork, dined with Mr. Egan, who drove me to Peabody. This is a large town, so close to Salem, that it is impossible for a stranger to discern any line of demarcation. It is the birthplace of the celebrated George Peabody, whose statue is in London, and in compliment to whom it takes its name, having been formerly known as Danvers. Mr. Egan took me to see Mrs. Foley, *née* Buckley, a cousin of mine (?), sister of Father Buckley, of Ballyclough, Co. Cork. She was very kind and insisted on the relationship. I was invited by so many to come again that I have resolved to lecture here. I hope it will be a success.

I leave Salem for Boston in order to be present at a great meeting to be held this evening in the Music Hall, to protest against the occupation of Rome by Victor Emmanuel. On reaching the hotel I got a great number of *Cork Examiners*, which were awaiting my arrival, and also a letter from Canon Maguire. I go to the great meeting, and justly indeed may it be called great. The Hall was crammed to suffocation and thousands had to remain outside who could not get admission. The Bishop was present. Mr. P. Donahoe in the chair. A great number of clergy also were there. The utmost enthusiasm prevailed. It was indeed, to my mind, the most genuine and thorough Catholic demonstration I ever witnessed. The Bishop's speech was excellent, eloquent, and exhaustive—he was received with a cordial welcome; the cheering was repeated over and over again. The next most popular speaker was my friend the Hon. P. A. Collins. Two things only were to be regretted. viz.,—that three of the speakers read their speeches, and that there was no programmes. There was no series of resolutions; each speaker said what he pleased on the whole subject, so that they were all harping on the one string, and many sentiments were repeated over and over again *ad nauseam*. But for spirit and ardour and Catholic earnestness, I never saw a better, nobler, or more effective demonstration.

January 8th.—In bed all day with rheumatism—shocking and constant pain in my knee. Dr. Salter called once more into requisition; servants very kind and attentive, as before; receive visits from many friends, which is cheering.

January 12th.—I feel better, get up and walk out. Here and there I get an opportunity of seeing my face in a looking glass, and the spectacle shocks and frightens me. I met Mr. Boyle O'Reilly and the Hon. P. A. Collins in Washington-street. They express the greatest alarm at the alteration in my appearance. I feel this is the best proof I could have of the bad effects of my illness. I come to my hotel, and address a letter to Father M'Carthy, of Watertown, where I am to deliver a lecture to-morrow evening, to say I cannot go. This is a great sacrifice, but I cannot help it. Doctor Salter comes; while he is present there is a knock at the door. "Come in," I cry. A boy comes in with some photographs of me from Mr. Black, my photographer, and the bill. I overhear the Doctor saying—"When I was a boy it was usual for boys, when coming into a gentleman's room, to take off their caps " (I observed the boy wore his), "but now-a-days boys have become too independent. Why do you not take off your cap, sir, in the presence of a clergyman?" The boy laughed outright, but never obeyed the Doctor. On the contrary, he seemed to have a great contempt for that worthy man, and to think that he had thrown away his speech. Yes; the system of democracy which pretends to bring men to a level brings some below it.

January 15*th.*—Am amused by an American gentleman, whom I met at the house of Mr. John Glanny, and who delivers himself of some very strange theological theories. After he had explained one opinion of his, he asked me what I thought of it. I said I could find no fault with it, except that it did not seem conformable with a certain passage in Job, which I quoted.

"Oh, but," quoth the gentleman, "I beg leave to differ with Mr. Job." His faith he summed up in the curious expression.

"I am a Catholic, but I reserve to myself the privilege of independent thought and investigation."

Every day something startling in theology turns up in America. A few days ago I saw a Rev. Mr. Alger, one of the great lights of Boston, advertised to preach the following Sunday. Subject—"What is to become of us hereafter?" a sequel to that gentleman's sermon of the previous Sunday, viz., "The Resurrection of the Body Refuted." A Rev. Mr. Morgan delivered a lecture lately, in Boston, on "Fast Young Men," which made quite a sensation, and he followed it up with another, on "Fast Young Men of Dry Goods Stores"—*i.e.*, in our phraseology, "Fast Young Men of the Drapers' Clerks class." These latter felt very indignant that their class should be thus ignominously pointed at, and called a meeting, in which they drew up a requisition to the Rev. Mr. Morgan, begging of him to lecture next on a subject which they thought a good counterpart to the "Fast Young Men"—viz., "Tough Old Sinners," of whom, no doubt, they deemed the said Rev. Morgan to be one of the most conspicuous.

I go to Lowell (twenty-four miles by train), and stay with Mr. Dempsey. He and Mrs. Dempsey and daughter (Etta) are very kind, and do all in their power to make me happy. On Sunday I am very sick, and eat nothing, or if I do, my stomach rejects it—am very weak and languid. Hear Mass and stay in the house all day. The success of my lecture is not likely to be great, as the priests are not disposed to publish it in their churches. One of them treated me in a very boorish manner, at my first interview with him, and he is still unrelenting. The Fates are dead against me of late. Miss Dempsey does all she can to amuse me. We play chess and draughts, and "Jack Straws" (an American game), and she shows me all the photographic and stereoscopic views in the house. She then brings me her autographic album, and wishes me to add my name to those of other "distinguished personages" who had already honoured its pages. This is a great trial to my modesty, which feeling suggests matter for the following lines, which I contributed to the young lady's album :—

"My autograph I here append,
  Although my modesty may be to blame;
But a deaf ear what man could lend
  When Etta asks him only for his name?"

The lecture came off successfully, as far as I was concerned; but otherwise, considering the audience, who numbered only 415, at twenty five cents a ticket. The nett proceeds amounted to only sixty-eight dollars, a great failure for so important a place. The lecture has knocked me up completely. I come home to Boston as quickly as possible, and go to bed.

January 21*st*.—I am wonderfully improved in my health since yesterday, and feel equal to anything. Went to Lawrence, an important city, perhaps twenty miles from Boston, on the invitation of Father William Orr, who had invited me to spend Sunday with him, and preach on that day, so that I might be known to the people, and make a good collection amongst them, this third Sunday of January. It was very kind. He acted an excellent part towards us, for which we are very grateful. Return to Boston, paid a few farewell visits, as we leave for New York next Saturday. Called to bid farewell to Bishop Williams, but found he was absent from home. Made other visits, and spent my last evening

P

in the Parker House, at least for some time. A deputation from East Boston waited on me, asking me to lecture there, and accept the total proceeds. I promised to come up from New York some weeks hence, when I shall fulfil a few other engagements also. A few friends called to bid adieu, and we spent a pleasant evening together.

CHAPTER IX.

THE EMPIRE CITY.

WE leave at 8.30 a.m. in a "Pullman Palace Car," quite a superb carriage, beautifully ornamented with mirrors, with compartments where two or three can lock themselves up comfortably, and enjoy each other's society, and sit or lounge on luxurious cushions. A young lady—Miss Mary Josephine O'Sullivan—Mr. John White's stepdaughter, is placed under my charge. She was never more than twenty miles from Boston, and is delighted at the idea of making her first visit to the great city of New York, where she is to be on a visit with some friends. The whole country is covered with snow. We go by Springfield and Newhaven, 209 miles. Miss O'Sullivan is provided with a basket containing a magnificent dinner, to which we did full justice in our little palace-car compartment. We had a very nice table, and every convenience. The Americans have a great notion of how to make themselves comfortable. The very carriage was so heated by steam that an overcoat or hat were quite unnecessary. A railway-rug is usually quite unnecessary in America. I use mine only as an additional blanket in bed.

We arrived in New York at 6 p.m. Have made up our minds to come to Sweeny's Hotel. A great number of Fenian prisoners, just released on conditions of exile, are there at present. Accordingly, we are transported thither. In passing I admire Broadway very much, and the sleighs, and the bells making music in the air. It is indeed a magnificent street. Sweeny's is a very fine hotel. From the roof hangs a grand Irish flag—a harp on a green ground. A great crowd of gazers throng the street, expecting to see the Exiles. As we enter, the great hall is filled with men.

While entering my name, a young gentleman steps over and addresses me. I recognise one of the Exiles, Charles Underwood O'Connell, looking wonderfully well, as if his imprisonment agreed with him. The last time I saw him was five years ago, in the dock in Cork, from which he saluted me. I gave him some Cork papers, with accounts of himself and his compatriots, for which he was very grateful. Next in the group I recognised General Thomas F. Burke, who made the splendid speech in Green-street Courthouse, Dublin, previous to the sentence dooming him to death. I was present at his trial. I introduced myself. He had heard of me. A splendid-looking fellow, and of a gentlemanly deportment. I also found Col. John O'Mahony, to whom I had been introduced last Summer. On the passage upstairs I found O'Donovan Rossa, whom I also recognised after a lapse of ten years. He remembered me, and introduced me to his wife, a very pretty and fashionably dressed young lady. Rossa also introduced me to Denis Dowling Mulcahy, and we had a good deal of conversation. In one of the evening papers, the *New York Evening Express*, the following appeared under the head of " The

Fenian Exiles: Programme for their Reception. *Inter alia* Rev. Father Buckley, of Cork, and a friend arrived at Sweeny's Hotel to-day, and have been presented to their fellow countrymen. They had a long and pleasant interview with the members of the Brotherhood."

This morning, *January* 31*st*, in the breakfast room, found all the Fenians breakfasting at one table—a real "Fenian Circle," as I called it when speaking with Rossa. Was introduced to Captain McClure, who distinguished himself at Kilclooney Wood.

We went off to see the Archbishop, and knowing how he persistently refuses his patronage to all persons coming on a mission such as ours, we apprehended that we too would be refused the privilege. We were ushered into a drawingroom and sent up our cards. The Archbishop soon presented himself and was extremely gracious in his manner. I explained the object of our visit. He replied that requests such as ours were the greatest difficulty he had to encounter. They were of daily occurrence, &c., &c., and it seemed to be a matter of trifling importance whether he granted permission or not, for priests whom he had refused had gone and collected in spite of him. I replied that we would be incapable of doing anything unbecoming the dignity of priests or gentlemen, when His Grace paid me the compliment of saying, "Indeed, Mr. Buckley, you need not tell me that." Finally, wonderful to relate, he granted us full permission to prosecute the object of our mission in New York, and wound up by saying that he should have us to dine on an early day. He also said he owed a great deal to Bishop Delaney, whose hospitality he had received, *et cetera*. This was joyful news for us.

We visited Mr. Eugene O'Sullivan, of Wall Street, who

entertained us at his house at Long Branch, last summer, and he is agreeably surprised to see us. In conversing with him, he confirmed what I had heard elsewhere, that in the Catholic Churches on Sundays you can observe that the vast majority of the congregation are persons who have emigrated from Ireland, but that very few are to be found who were born in this country of Irish parents. Does the Catholic religion then grow weaker in the breasts of the Irish-Americans from generation to generation? Father Charles McCready and Father O'Connell, of Chiselhurst spent the evening with me.

February 4th.—Dined with the Fenian Exiles this evening; it was quite a banquet. The gentleman who invited me was Charles U. O'Connell. When he saluted me from the dock five years ago, I little thought I would be dining with him in New York.

February 5th.—We paid several visits to-day. Amongst the other persons we visited Father Fecker, the founder of the Paulists, of whom I have made mention more than once already. On the subject of lectures he does not hold out to me much prospect of success. He says it is very hard to organize a lecture for a foreign object in New York, and suggests that I should engage myself as a lecturer to priests for some parochial charitable object, at a certain sum for each lecture. Father O'Connell, of Chislehurst, spent the evening with me and amused me a good deal by his views of America; like myself, he is surprised at the abundance of turkey consumed here. The commonest dish in America seems to be roast turkey. Fowl of all kind is general, but the turkey is the *piece de resistance*. And very good turkeys they rear, large and fat. At dinner there is seldom more than one joint, and in nine cases out of ten it is a roast turkey.

Nothing particular occurred until Thursday, February 9th, when we had the procession in honour of the Fenians. It was a very remarkable pageant, the whole city was astir all the morning, and crowds were assembling in front of our hotel to catch a view of the Exiles. They are fourteen in number, and O'Donovan Rossa is regarded as their head and representative. At 12.30 o'clock they were to leave the hotel for Tammany Hall. A little before that hour they assembled in a parlour upstairs. I joined them there. I was introduced to Colonel Roberts, one of those who had taken a very prominent part in the Fenian movement at its inception in this country. When all was ready Mr. Connolly invited me to join him in a carriage. I accepted the invitation. Our carriage was first, and contained besides me and Mr. C., O'Donovan Rossa and General Tom Burke. About ten other carriages followed. The enthusiasm of the people as the cortege moved slowly on was intense. Several men put their hands in through the carriage and shook hands with Rossa and Burke. One in a soldier's uniform cried, "Which is General Burke?" and when he was informed he seized the General's hand and looked at him most lovingly. "General," said he, "I am a soldier," and he kept loosing the General's hand and seizing it again for a long time, saying, "Burke, General, I love you." He was then made acquainted with Rossa, whose hand he shook, but Burke was his favourite, and he said so. It reminded me of the passage in *The Old Curiosity Shop*—"Short is good —but I cottons to Codlin."

We reached Tammany Hall in due time, and there was

a dense and uproarious crowd. The moment the Exiles appeared the cheers were simply deafening, and the enthusiasm indescribable. Richard O'Gorman took the chair, and made an oration. He speaks well, has a fine voice and good delivery. He welcomed the Exiles to America, and shook hands with them through Rossa. John Mitchel, whom I here saw for the first time, also spoke, addressing the Exiles as " Fellow Felons." There were cries for Burke and Rossa, and both spoke. Then the Hall was cleared and the procession formed. Union Square was close by, and there was a constant booming of cannon which were stationed there. I can give no idea of the crowd that blocked up the space here. The papers set down the whole crowd of on-lookers through the city as 300,000. I did not take part in the procession, but took up my place in a magnificent establishment in Broadway with my new friend, Father O'Connell. It was a great holiday for the Irish. The houses in many places had flags and other decorations. The heads of numerous horses were ornamented with green ribbons; people carried small green flags in their hands or rosettes in their coats. Many young ladies were dressed all in green. The men had green neckties. Banners with "God Save Ireland" hung out in many places. As the procession passed women screamed with joy, and waved their white handkerchiefs. It was a day of pride and jubilee. The spectacle of the procession was very imposing indeed. The police marched at the front of it, and at the rear several regiments, and patriotic societies with their bands joined. The Exiles were in open carriages, and had to keep constantly returning the salutations of the crowd. All traffic was stopped in the streets as the procession passed, and by that singular magic by which the police everywhere extort obedience, the people lined the pathways and left the whole centre clear. The processionists rode in carriages or walked. Civic authorities were there in full insignia. Numerous bands of boys marched clad in a peculiar and picturesque costume, and evidently boiling over with patriotism, though most of them never saw Ireland. There were several carriages containing coloured officers and soldiers who had fought in the war, and who shared in the procession as fellow victims of oppression with the Irish, now breathing the pure air of American freedom. They were received as they passed with striking manifestations of respect. The mayor reviewed the procession as it passed the City Hall, where the thunders of a smart cannonade typified the shouts of American welcome. Strange coincidence—almost at that moment Queen Victoria was opening the Session of Parliament, and proposing measures for securing peaceful relations between England and America. "While the cannon," says the paper, "in front of the City Hall, within a stone's throw of our office, were thundering their war-like welcome to the great passing Fenian procession, we were receiving despatches from London and from Washington, the whole purport of which is a new *entente cordiale* between England and the United States." It struck us as a most extraordinary concurrence of events, that while hearing this warlike thunder of the Fenian cannon, we should be reading those lightning despatches from the foggy Thames and the frozen Potomac—from President Grant and Queen Victoria. "Let us have peace." There were two rather remarkable carriages in the procession. One was a fantastically-fashioned barouche, drawn by six bay horses, of whom the four leaders were tandem, and all were decorated beautifully—banners gold-mounted and the reins white. This was the carriage of the celebrated Helmbold, the druggist, of "Buchu" notoriety. The other carriage was simply an Irish jaunting car, of which I am told there are only two in all New York. The music of the bands was bad, and the men did not seem to have the bold bearing or the elastic step of their brethren at home in the Green Isle. On the whole the procession was grand, and it clearly proved that the love of Ireland and the hatred of England is undying in the Irish breast all the world over.

To me nothing appeared so remarkable as the part the police took in the procession. In Ireland they are regarded as the enemies of the people, and dare not take part in any popular demonstration, but are rather ordered to look out for disorders and to repress them, if necessary, by the extreme rigour of the musket. There the police joined in the procession, and seemed proud of the honour. It is no wonder that Irishmen should love America, where they, once the victims of barbarous tyranny, breathe a free air, and bask in the sunshine of protection beneath the ægis of universal emancipation.

Dined to-day on board the "Tripoli," a Cunard steamer, at the invitation of the purser, Mr. Ambrose Shea, son of the late Mr. John Shea, once Mayor of Cork. We had a jolly snug little party; some of the officers of the ship dined with us.

February 10*th.*—Great exultation amongst the Irish about the success of yesterday's demonstration. The waiter who helped me at breakfast asked, how did I like it? I answered "It was splendid." He asked, "Did you ever see anything like it?" This "ever" vexes me. "Yes sir, we are a great people."

February 11th.—Father Maguire, of St. Paul's, Brooklyn, has asked me to preach in his church to-morrow, so I cross to Brooklyn by steamer. The ferryboat finds great difficulty in crossing on account of the immense quantities of ice in the river. In the middle of the day the ice was so compact that several people walked across. At the flow of the tide the ice increases; at the ebb, otherwise. It floats down from the Hudson and East Rivers.

February 12th.—I preach on "Christian Hope" at Mass; the snowiest morning I ever saw. How the people came to Mass astonishes me; yet there was a large congregation. By the way, every change of climate here is called a storm—if it rains or snows, it is a "storm"—I mean of course any change from good to bad.

Father O'Reilly, one of Father Maguire's assistants, tells us a funny thing. He had said early Mass, after which he is accosted in the vestry room by a man who is accompanied by a woman. The man has the appearance of a sailor. Man says, "Say, do you run this machine?"

"No," says Father O'Reilly.

"Then you're the foreman, I guess."

"No; what do you want?" asks the priest.

"What do I want? Why this lady and I want to get married right away."

The conversation turned on American institutions. All agreed in what has been already stated, that corruption rules everything. A man may murder another with impunity, if he has money enough to bribe the judge. The judge is elected by a political party. Rather than displease the party who elected him, he will yield to the mild influence of interposition, provided the certain number of dollars be rubbed to his judicial fist. Great freedom of religion—freedom to all. Hence the great number of churches, for every man may have a view of religion different from another, and start a theological theory, and open a church, and appoint a minister of his own. In one street in Brooklyn, perhaps a mile long, there are sixteen churches.

Went to the Cooper Institute to hear Mrs. O'Donovan Rossa read for the benefit of the widow of J. J. Geavny (a Cork Fenian) who died here by falling into a boiling vat of soap. A crammed and most enthusiastic house—General Tom Burke in the chair. The lady was beautifully dressed, green being the predominant colour. Every poem she read had, of course, a highly national complexion, and the telling points evoked furious rounds of applause. A lady from Cork whom I knew at home as Miss O'Brien (Mrs. Pollick) sang at the piano. A gentleman named Waters came forward and recited "Shamus O'Brien," but he ridiculed the Irish accent so unmercifully that he was hissed, and scouted off the stage. In one of the intervals there was loud cries for "Rossa." He at length came forward, and said he was not going to make a speech. "Deeds, not words" was his motto, but he would read a letter he had just received from a gentleman, addressed to his wife (Mrs. Rossa). The writer was Mr. Basford, and he presented a cheque for fifty dollars for the object of the meeting. Loud cheers for Basford, the modest, retiring, unselfish Basford. But lo! a gentleman steps forward, kisses hands to the audience. This is the modest Basford, advertising himself. He writes a letter, (1) presents his compliments, (2) presents his cheque, (3) presents himself. But modesty is a virtue unknown in Yankeedom. Behold another sample of it. There are loud cries of

"Roberts, Roberts!" This is the famous Colonel Roberts, once the head of a Fenian split of a split. I learn afterwards that the gallant Colonel had a lot of fellows paid to call on him. The air was filled with cries of "Roberts," and at last the Chairman came forward and asked was Colonel Roberts in the hall. The Colonel, who was at one of the doors modestly concealed, then marched up the whole length of the hall, appeared on the platform, took off his outside coat, and with a voice of thunder made a rattling speech on "Irish Nationality." He gave all the old claptrap, "these gallant heroes," "England's accursed tyranny," "Ireland's imperishable rights, founded on the principles of God's eternal justice," &c., &c., all well committed to memory. He paced the stage, and if England saw him then she would have trembled for her very existence. All this was a bid for the Irish vote! All got up by the astute Colonel himself. Curious engraftation on the programme of the evening, but puffing and advertising is the great Yankee notion. General Burke in returning thanks to every one, thanked Mr. Weber for the loan of his splendid piano. Good for Weber. Fenians, buy your pianos at Weber's! The gent who was hissed for "Shamus O'Brien" comes forward, one would think to apologise; but no, it was a mere little bit of trade:—
"Ladies and gentlemen, I beg to inform you that a full report of this evening's proceedings will appear in to-morrow evening's *Globe*," and so closed the proceedings. I adjourned to Mrs. Attridge's and, late for the cars, slept at Father Mooney's.

I go in the afternoon with Father Crowley to his place at Huntington, Long Island. We go by ferryboat to Hunter's point, and thence by rail two hours' ride, to Huntington. The ground is almost all covered with snow. Father Crowley pointed out to me as we passed along a very large tract of ground which the millionaire Stewart, New York, has purchased, and which he is laying out for the purpose of building a city on it. Big idea that; big idea. That reminds me of another American phrase, "We had a big time," *i.e.*, a very jolly time. Again :—"We had quite a time," may mean the same thing, or "we had a great row about something." "I intend to make a time about that," means I intend to make trouble about it. When parting with a friend at the door of one's house he says, "Good bye, you'll call again, won't you?" or "You'll call again when you're around?"

At Father Crowley's I had the great pleasure of meeting my dear friends, Helena and Caroline MacSweeny, who are living with him, and whom I had not met for the last ten years. Time, I am glad to say, had not diminished their amiability. They were very glad to see me, and we "had quite a time."

February 21st.—It snowed through the night, and we were all day confined to the house with the exception of a few hours after dinner, when Father Crowley and I drove out. The village is small and the place lonely. Now in winter it is desolate—in summer it must look well. No gas for 3,000 inhabitants. A very neat chapel is just finished, built by Father Crowley. He is a very good fellow. His driving costume was queer—a bearskin cap, chamois riding-gloves, a bearskin rug, he smoking a cigar the whole way. Ground very snowy and wet, and roads bad and sloppy. Queer names of places here, such as "Bull's Hollow," "Bread and Cheese Hollow," "Mutton Hollow," &c., &c. Had to stand a long catechising from the girls; had to give them news of a whole decade of years, for the place is remote from the world, and few write to them.

February 22nd.—Ash-Wednesday, Washington's birthday—a fast day and a feast. Business suspended through the States—shops closed, flags floating in the breeze, and bands playing through the streets. I came home at 3.30 p.m., and arrived at New York at 6. Letter from a friend telling me of the rumour at home that I have been appointed canon. It is only a rumour, but to me it is a matter of very great indifference. I would not give ten dollars for the honour. I spend the evening quietly at home. No new impressions gained, but old ones strengthened. Thus there is very little social enjoyment in America, and such as does exist is generally fast and wild, a violent outburst. The pervading idea everywhere is the dollar above and beyond all things.

I spent the evening at the house of a family named McCarthy, Third Avenue, all from Cork, nephews and niece of Mr. Charles McCarthy, Grand Parade, Cork. We enjoyed ourselves very much. On arriving home I heard that the celebrated Captain Mackey and wife had arrived. I sent word to them asking where and when I could have the pleasure of an interview. They replied, immediately in their sitting-room. Poor Mackey looks very much the worse for wear. He seems to be a very excellent character, mild, gentlemanly, religious, unassuming and warm-hearted. Mrs. Mackey was delighted to see me. She observes that I look not half as healthy as I did at home. I got some letters from her through Miss Cox; one from Miss Cox herself I read with great interest before retiring to rest.

February 23rd.—Stayed within doors all day preparing my

lecture for the Boston Theatre. Had a visit from Mr. B. Devlin, of Montreal, who came to invite me to lecture in that city in or about Patrick's Day. He wishes me to deliver an address on Patrick's Day to an Irish Society of which he is president. All right, I go from Boston after my lecture there on the 12th prox.

New York, and the United States generally, is a great place for slang. Various phrases without much meaning are soon picked up, and become quite common. At present there are two phrases afloat, viz.—"How is that for high?" and "you know how it is yourself." The former is used in this manner:—Suppose, for example, you tell a person that you have met some piece of good fortune, or that something has happened to flatter your pride, or to be a subject of congratulation, you exclaim, "How is that for high?" The second phrase is the burden of a popular song, and is very frequently used. Thus, when you are telling something to a person and you do not wish to tell it all, either because he understands it or because you don't care that the bystanders should learn all about it, you say, "You know how it is yourself." I do not know whether or not in the early part of this book I made mention of a song which was in the mouths of everyone on the whole continent of America last summer, it is called "Shoo fly." What the words signify, or pretend to signify, I could never learn; but meaning seemed to be a matter of no consideration. The burden of the song was simply unintelligible, but the air was pretty. Everyone had it—ladies played it on the piano, and boys whistled it in the streets. New fashions in dress, new articles of attire, were called by the name of "Shoo fly." There were "Shoo fly neckties," and "Shoo fly hats," and potatoes in hotels were dressed in a peculiar way and called in the bill of fare, "Shoo fly potatoes." Here is the whole song :—

>I feel, I feel, I feel,
>I feel like a morning star.
>I feel, I feel, I feel,
>I feel like a morning star.
>>Shoo fly don't bother me,
>>Shoo fly, don't bother me,
>>Shoo fly, don't bother me,
>>I belong to the Company G.
>
>There's music in the air,
>My mother said to me;
>There's music in the air,
>My mother said to me.
>>Shoo fly, don't bother me,
>>Shoo fly, don't bother me,
>>Shoo fly, don't bother me,
>>I belong to the Company G.

It was translated into French and German, and sung in those languages, and in many more, for aught I know.

The stranger in New York, and probably in other parts of America, is struck by the great number of military men in civil costume whom he meets every day. Nearly every second man is a general, a captain, a colonel, or a lieutenant. In the British Isles we associate the idea of an officer with what is generally understood as a gentleman—a person of good breeding, high education, fine person and easy manners. Here it is different. I have seen a colonel keeping a gin shop, and a major setting type. Passing Sweeny's hall I encounter a group of men dressed as artisans, one of whom knows me. He at once introduces me to the rest. One is captain, another major, a third colonel, and so on.

I find myself at once in the society of the *élite* of the American army. They are fine honest fellows, but their discourse is not of war or peace, or military operations. I have no doubt they are generous and brave, and as fitted for their parts as your " gentlemen," who do the strategy of England; but to one brought up to the English notions of military men, the contrast between the officers of the two countries is striking and somewhat amusing. I was in the *Irish Democrat* office yesterday, talking to Mr. Stephen Joseph Meany, the editor. He introduced me to a gentleman who sat at a table, and whom I took for sub-editor, though perhaps, for aught I know, he was only clerk; but whatever the gentleman was he was a major. Soon came in another gentleman, whom I recognised; he was a colonel. One cannot help being amused at seeing those military men looking so very civil, and engaged in the ordinary avocations of society, when he would rather expect to behold men of portly presence, *farouche* aspect, and that indescribable bearing which is generally understood as the *air militaire*.

The horrible habit of chewing tobacco is carried to great excess in America, and involves great filth. The first time I witnessed it was in the steamer coming from Queenstown. A fine handsome fellow from Alabama comes on deck while I was chatting with a Miss Badger, of Philadelphia, and he says to her—" Do you know anyone that has tobacco? I want some to chew. I have tried to write some important letters in the cabin, and I can't do it without a chew." I was disgusted, especially at the idea of a gentleman talking of such a thing to a lady; but that was nothing. Crossing the ferry in one of those large ferry boats that ply to Brooklyn, you pass through the ladies' cabin. Everything is clean, and

Q

the air is sweet; but pass through the "gents' cabin," and the atmosphere is disgusting, and the floor is an abomination. Man approaches very close to the brute. The heat of the stove and the fumes of tobacco make the air perfectly unendurable, while the floor reeks with the filthy expectorations of weed-loving gentlemen. Fortunately gentlemen who do not smoke enjoy the privilege of staying in the ladies' cabin if they are so disposed, and I for one always avail myself of that privilege. There is an article in a paper in which it is gravely, and hence I dare say, truly stated that it is no uncommon thing now to find receptacles for tobacco juice in pulpits and in the pews of churches of all denominations of the land, or if not so provided, those places are smeared with the filthy compound. Gentlemen take tobacco into their mouths, as men in Ireland take snuff into their noses. In the same article "Slang in the Pulpit," a preacher is represented as having said "Some time ago I knocked the bottom out of hell, and now I am going to hammer away at the sides." Another says, after laying down what he considered a wholesome maxim, "Stick a pin in that." Another on a similar occasion, "Put that in your pipe and smoke it." A third relating an anecdote broke off at a certain point and said, "You know how it is yourself."

Every evening some gentlemen visit me and spend an hour or two. The man that pleases me most is Stephen Joseph Meany. He is a person of very gentlemanly manners and appearance, scholarly and accomplished, and a very agreeable social companion. Other gentlemen come and proffer their services for the promotion of my lecture. I am very much struck by their kindness, one of them undertaking to write paragraphs for all the papers. Captain

Mackay comes and spends an hour with me this evening. He is a remarkable person, small in appearance, but high-souled as man could be; capable of bloody exploits, and a planner of daring "raids," yet almost monastic in his religious habits and style of living.

March 5th.—Come by train to Boston. Am visited by Mr. John White. Hear Mass at the Church of the Immaculate Conception. A very fine church and most respectable congregation, admirable music, and first-rate sermon from Father Fulton, S.J. I was very much pleased with the whole thing. I saw at Mass Doctor and Mrs. Salter. I met them coming out, and they introduced me to Doctor Marshal, an English convert of some considerable fame, an Oxford man, and author of a clever work entitled, *History of Christian Missions*, and a publication that caused great amusement a few years ago, viz.,—*The Comedy of Convocation.*

If there be one thing more admirable than another in this country, it is that no man is ashamed to labour, and no kind of labour is despised. Also that you may associate with any man, and bring any man into any company, and all are "gentlemen." You may sit down and eat and drink with the coachman who drives you, and introduce the gentleman to every one around. Men of wealth are always "boasting" how they began life with nothing. How they became shoe-blacks, or tailor's apprentices, or newsboys, and crept up into wealth. And somehow in society you discover no classes of rank. All men seem to commingle on a broad common ground. The conversation to be sure is not above the reach of the humblest intellect—but the manners of all are polite, and the poorest man is bold and independent, and speaks correctly and with force.

March 11th—Nothing particular. I kept myself as quiet as possible. The weather is delightful, and I walk every day in the common and public gardens, " the finest in the world, yes, sir !"

March 12th.—My lecture came off this evening in the Boston Theatre. The audience was immense and looked really magnificent. Twenty Cork ladies and gentlemen drove in an immense carriage with four horses from Salem to Boston to hear me, 15 miles. I had a great gathering in my room after the lecture—those twenty and some twenty more. Some witty things were said, for we Cork people are witty. The best was by John White. He has a great habit of saying "like a tiger;" it is an amplification, a superlative of his. We were speaking of niggers, and he said he met a nigger once who spoke Irish " like a tiger."

"And, John," said I, "did you ever hear a tiger speak Irish ?"

"To be sure I did."

"What kind of a tiger ? " I asked.

"Why, an Irish tiger, of course."

The lecture was for the Vincent de Paul Society, and must have realised a large sum.

I waited on Bishop Williams to thank him for his patronage of us and our cause. He was very agreeable and pleasing. Went to see some other friends and then came home. Had a visit from Mr. Ambrose Shea, purser of the " Batavia," with whom I dined, in his ship, at New York, February 9th. He has been twice across the Atlantic since. He was accompanied by Dr. Johnson of the same ship, and they invited me to come and see them to-morrow on board the vessel.

CHAPTER X.

"A PRIESTLY FENIAN."

March 15*th*.—Left Boston at 8 a.m. for Montreal, a distance of over 300 miles, a very long journey; it took fourteen hours. The day, however, was beautiful, and the scenery after the first hundred miles, and especially through Vermont, was charming. The soil for the most part appears to be thin and poor. There was little vegetation and no verdure. There were fine large rivers and mountains, many of which were wooded to a great height. I fancy in summer the scenery here is very fine. I had been introduced to a gentleman, Judge Woodbury, who sat with me for a few hours. He was in great glee over the result of the elections for New Hampshire the day before; the Democrats had obtained a large majority, an event that had not happened for the last sixteen years. The Judge was an ardent Democrat and himself a Senator for the State of Massachusetts. Wherever we went, whatever station we touched, the excitement was the same. Newsboys all flocked into the cars crying. "The *Monitor*," "All about the elections," or some other exclamations of the same kind. The people in the trains could talk of nothing else. The point of the thing was that it took everyone by surprise, Democrats themselves as well as Republicans. I as an outsider was very much amused by all this, and was sorry I could not take a livelier interest in it.

I was struck as we passed along by the strange names of some places. One station bore the name of Canaan, another of East Lebanon, relics of Puritan fervour, but we had no sooner passed the Canadian frontier than we were met by St. Alban's, St. Alexander, St. John, &c., a new style of nomenclature, indicating certainly a more Christian tone of feeling than Puritanism in those who named them.

St. Alban's is on the St. Lawrence, which I see for the second time to-day. Oh, the weary journey. The Grand Trunk Railway on which we get here is very rough and uncomfortable. I have heard the same before and can endorse it.

I reach Montreal at 9.50, and am located in my hotel at 10 p.m. Two gentlemen on the part of Mr. Devlin wait on me, Messrs. Doran and Egan. Where is Mr. Devlin himself? I have some supper in my room, and retire for the night.

In the United States there is constant hurry, activity, excitement—money-making always going on, every one trying to make the dollar. Nothing save the dollar is respected, and it is wonderful how many very rich men are everywhere. There is no street in which you will not find a man worth thousands, tens of thousands, a million of dollars. Nothing is so common as to hear a person say, " Do you see that man? That, man, sir, is worth a million and a half of dollars." Of another, " That man, sir, twenty years ago was a newsboy, a shoeblack, or filled some other low occupation, he was not worth a cent; now, sir, he is worth two millions of dollars."

Men of business habits—and that includes nearly all Americans—do not care how much time they spend at their business. One man, an Irishman, said to me of his employer:

"That man, sir, never stops thinking of his business—the only day he feels miserable is Sunday, because he must go to church, and cannot be in his store. Last summer he had a nice house at the seaside; his wife and family stayed there for some months, but nothing could induce him to spend one whole day there, except Sunday. He would go down every evening at 5 or 6 and be up again to business next day; yet, sir, there is no counting what that man is worth, he must be worth some millions of dollars, but he is as avaricious to make more as if he had not a cent." At a Masquerade Ball lately at St. Louis, a lady appeared dressed in the character of the "Almighty Dollar." The reader's imagination must supply the style of costume, but the lady illustrated the theology of the age and country.

March 16*th*.—Left St. Lawrence Hall and transferred myself and baggage to St. Patrick's, where I met again my old friends of last summer. The day was very wet, and strange to say it rained and froze at the same time. During a short time that I was out, I was obliged to raise my umbrella, and when I endeavoured to close it, I found it impossible, for the rain had been frozen on it, and made it quite rigid. This was a kind of thing I never saw before. I had a visit from Mr. Devlin. He seems warm about my speech to-morrow evening.

March 17*th*.—St. Patrick's Day. A very great day in Montreal. A very great day in every city in America. A very great day anywhere but in Ireland. Before I go down stairs, I am presented with a magnificent shamrock, the present of some unknown friend. There is to be a great procession, with bands and banners, consisting of several Irish societies. They are to meet at Mass in St. Patrick's church, and form there when Mass is over. Accordingly at 10 o'clock there are great symptons of preparations. The sound of music is heard, the well known anthem of " Patrick's Day" floats on the breeze, and the bandsmen in a variety of costumes, halt before the church gate to finish the tune. Crowds are assembled without, and evidently enjoy the gathering pageant. Within we have a considerable accession of clergy from various places, and their number is swelled by an accident. On Sunday next, the new Bishop of Quebec is to be consecrated, and many of the clergy from the West, bound thereto, halt there to join in the ceremonial of the day. Conspicuous amongst them are two bishops, the Most Rev. Dr. Pinsonnanet, Bishop of Hyacinthe, and Bishop Farrell of Hamilton. The students of the seminary, all clerical *elèves*, also are present. High Mass is about to be sung, Bishop Pinsonnanet is to sing it, a very handsome old gentleman with a fresh countenance, and grey hair. The church is thronged, and the bands enfilade up the nave playing the national air. This has a thrilling effect. The members of several Irish societies are present, each with a collar of velvet and gold. A messenger summons me from the sanctuary. I meet Mr. Devlin, who wishes to introduce me to the mayor, Mr. Coursal, who is decorated with the civic chain, and is a Catholic. When the church is full it contains about 8,000 persons, and it is crammed to-day. I had no idea there would be so magnificent an audience, and that the spectacle would be so splendid. The green banners give a grand aspect to the scene, and the shamrock decorates every breast. The Mass was beautifully sung, and the effect was greatly improved by a solo on the organ at the offertory of a pure Irish character—nothing less than the "Minstrel

Boy." The sermon was by Father Hogan, of St. Anne's. At the end of the Mass the procession began to form. The weather had been wet, and the ground is covered with hard snow since last December. Hence under foot it is all wet and slushy, and walking without slipping is a matter of considerable difficulty. But I must walk; so I accompany Father Dowd and Father Singer, who march in their soutanes, and have bearskin caps on their heads. I slipped once or twice, and this puts me on my guard. I take Father Dowd's arm, and even so, get on with great trouble. It was the most difficult three miles I ever walked, and the dirtiest. Such a state as my clothes were in! Oh, holy St. Patrick, what did I ever do, that you should treat me so? It was, nevertheless, a grand procession; the music was excellent, and in some places there were triumphal arches, with legends indicative of the blended feelings in the breast of religion and nationality. The spectators and gazers from windows enjoyed it as it passed along; but there was no shouting, no disorder. I asked if this procession gave offence to any party. No; on the contrary, all classes of people liked it, and would be greatly disappointed if it did not take place. I looked in vain for a drunken man. Strange to say, drunkenness is almost unknown in Montreal, and even in all Canada. This is very creditable to our people, and clearly proves that there is nothing in the national character incompatible with temperance.

In the evening there was a grand concert in St. Patrick's Hall, Mr. Devlin presiding. There must have been 2,000 people in the Hall. At the right of the chairman sat General Dart, U.S. Consul to Canada, and at the left was myself. I found that an address was to be delivered by the

Rev. M. B. Buckley, in the second part of the programme During the intermission, Gen. Dart was called on, and said a few words. Then my turn came. It was a difficult audience to address, Catholics and Protestants, Irish and Canadians—some in favour of British Government, others opposed to it. I was loud on Irish religion and patriotism, and "death" on English tyranny. I had my audience in the best of humour. After the speech I retired to get a drink of water, when a gentleman pressed my arm. I turned round, saw a handsome young fellow in full dress, and gazing at me with a pair of sparkling black eyes. "Turgeon," I exclaimed. He was no other than the young lawyer whom I met in the steamer "Georgia" from Quebec to Pictou last August. Our greeting was of the warmest description. He had come to the concert solely to meet me, having seen it announced that I was to deliver an address. We make an engagement for to-morrow and separate. After the concert there are refreshments for the *élite*. The people here are so like our own in their manners and habits, and so different from the people in the States. Considering everything, the day was a success for Montreal.

Sunday, March 19th.—Preached to-day in St. Patrick's church. After dinner the two brothers Burke waited on me with a carriage and pair of horses, and we had a very pleasant drive "round the mountain." The aspect of the day was very winteryish, and the air cold; but I was "wrapped snug from those biting pneumatics," and enjoyed the drive very much. On some parts of the road the snow was piled up four feet high at each side of the carriage, and must wait for the heat of summer to dissolve it. We returned by the St. Lawrence, which was frozen across the whole way from bank to bank, with ice three feet deep. It has not broken up yet, although I heard it had been. It appears that people do not desist any year from crossing it until some persons are drowned. I spent the evening with the Burkes and their two sisters. We talked a good deal of D'Arcy Magee. John Burke made me a present of a short sketch of his life, which I intend to read. The Irish in Canada are very content, pay little taxes, desire no change, at least the masses; it is only a class seek for annexation.

March 20*th*.—A flaming leader in this morning's *Gazette* headed "A Reverend Firebrand," blowing up my speech of St. Patrick's night in coarse and bitter language. The article is about a column and a half long. It accuses me of creating mischief by appealing to the bad passions of my fellow countrymen here by ripping up old national sores, such as my allusion to "700 years of wrong," *et cetera*. The article is very severe, and I am sorry that I should hurt the feelings of anyone in this city; but it admits that my speech pleased my audience. Passing through town I find myself the observed of all observers. It is not my frieze coat now that attracts attention, although that is remarkable enough, but there is quite a *furore* amongst the people, at least amongst the English part of them, in consequence of my speech, and I am the hero of the hour. It is the event, the "sensation" of the day. I have been called in the papers "a firebrand," "an incendiary," "a hare-brained agitator," and a great deal more of the same kind. It appears that several Protestant gentlemen left precipitately after my speech, and those who remained have been severely censured by their friends for so doing. The Catholics are most indignant that a Catholic priest should be assailed in this manner. When a Methodist or Swaddler comes and lectures here he may speak as much treason as he likes. Lately a Protestant clergyman of this city, in the course of a lecture rebuked England much more severely than I did, and yet there was no comment too laudatory for his harangue; but a priest is at once pounced upon by those lions of the Press, and his words and conduct are shown up to the contempt and scorn of the world. In fact I am informed that nothing has occurred in Montreal for a long time that has so much stirred up the strife of party as this. The *Gazette* exhorted my friends to drop me, to give me no further patronage, but my friends are not going to take the advice of the enemy.

The want of a Catholic paper is greatly felt in Montreal. There is a Catholic weekly, the *True Witness*. D'Arcy Magee also had a paper here, but it died after a year. His election to the Parliament of Canada withdrew his pen from the city, and the paper could not be conducted by another. Mr. Devlin made an attempt to start one, but failed; but now again they talk of it more vigorously than ever. There are several English dailies, many French-Canadians, one at least Scotch, and yet with a Catholic population of about 30,000 there is not a Catholic daily paper in Montreal. This evening the *Star* calls upon other papers to take the tone of the *Gazette*, and gives a letter from some correspondent who accuses me of justifying agrarian murder. This is too much. When your enemy forsakes the ground of legitimate argument and seeks to crush you by lies and calumnious inventions, he defeats himself and saves you the trouble of an encounter. From all this I conclude that party feeling runs very high here, that the same feeling of bitterness on account of religion prevails here as it does in Ireland, and that unfortunately the Irish lack that blessing of cohesion which would make them a compact body, a phalanx of strength, and thus a terror to their enemies.

At St. Patrick's there is a comic servant, Patrick, from Nenagh. He is general servant, and I meet him every morning when he helps me to breakfast. He is the purest Paddy I ever met, appearance, accent—all; but his peculiar phrases and style of speaking are most amusing. He says something new and strange every day. "Take an egg, sir," he says one morning, "that beefsteak is no good—take an egg, sir. I'll put one down for you, and the water is just in the humour."

" Patrick, this tea is not very strong," I say.

"No, sir," says Patrick, "'tis young yet, leave it grow."

Speaking of Father Toupin, one of the priests here, a wiry, active man, Patrick said, "Sir, he's as hardy as a wild-duck," and of a very thin young lady he remarked that she was "as thin as a saw." Last summer when I was here, my slumbers every morning were disturbed by a grating noise, at the unearthly hour of twilight, and long after. This noise was occasioned by an old man sawing logs of wood for firing just under my window. I spoke of the matter to Patrick, and he said, "The deuce take the old corncrake." I was vastly amused because the lively imagination of Patrick just struck off a good idea of the noise which I had in my own mind, but could not realize, as he did. After one of my sermons, Father Leclair said to him, "Well, Patrick, what do you think of Father Buckley?"

"Lave me alone, sir, he's a terror!"

His description of the cold of a Canadian winter was vivid, but I could not transcribe it, for it was conveyed more in gesture than words.

"And Patrick," said I, last summer, "I am told that the River St. Lawrence is quite frozen over in winter so that people can walk across it for months."

"To be sure, sir," says he, "there's not a word of lie in it, and I can tell you its no joke to freeze that river with the current that's running through it. It begins to freeze about Christmas, and the ice is thin for some days; but about New Year's Day there comes two or three days wicked, and there it is bound up as tight as a drum-head till Patrick's Day, and often longer."

One of the clergymen here told me an amusing anecdote. He was for some time travelling through a portion of the Western States of America, and one Sunday morning he celebrated Mass in the open air, for the benefit of some Irish navvies who were making a railroad in that "section." During the ceremony, whenever he turned towards the people he observed a tall Yankee standing against a tree, smoking his pipe, and seeming to take a great interest in the proceedings. When Mass was over, the Yankee came up to him, and said with the usual nasal twang:

"Friend, it takes considerable of a smart man to do a thing of that kind; I guess you could not do it again?"

"Oh! dear, yes," said the priest, "I will just do the same to-morrow morning, if you come you can see and judge for yourself." The Yankee's amazement was so great, and he gave vent to his feelings in the usual local expression of astonishment, "Waal, I do declare."

March 22*nd.*—Left Cork Harbour ten months ago this day. How quickly those ten months have fled.

Patrick is as usual amusing at breakfast. He pours out the tea with his left hand. "Paddy's left," says he, "is his bully hand," and when he places the butter on the table he says *le bare* (*beurre*), imitating the French which he hears so constantly spoken at table. When I was done breakfast he exclaimed, *Tout finit.* But in all these sayings of our Hibernian valet, the real humour consists not so much in the things said as in the way in which he says them.

I forgot to tell you of the strange circumstances of my meeting very frequently one gentleman, and only one who travelled with me across the Atlantic last summer. He is a young gentleman named "Tolley." We met him first at the pier of Toronto, next in St. John's, N.B., thirdly in Boston, which he left for some months and found us again on his return. Last Wednesday morning while I was seated at breakfast at the St. Lawrence Hall, Montreal, I was tapped on the shoulder, and on turning round saw my friend Mr. Tolley. We were both astonished at the circumstance, for it was singular that he and I alone should meet of all the passengers.

March 23rd.—I did not know until this morning the flattering epithets bestowed upon me at some loyal festive gathering of "true blues" assembled ere-yesterday to celebrate the wedding on that day of the Marquis of Lorne with the Princess Louisa in this good city of Montreal. A Reverend Dr. Burns called me a "priestly Fenian," and the other speakers intimated that now while a strenuous effort was being made to broach disloyalty, here was a becoming occasion for the display of the opposite feeling. My evening was spent with Mr. Donovan, the Corkman to whom Mr. Maguire alludes in his "Irish in America," as an instance of what may be done by an Irishman here who relies on his industry and temperance. Mr. Donovan is President of the

Temperance Societies of Montreal, a very worthy man indeed. He told me that only one member of their society could boast of having taken the pledge from Father Matthew, and that man is so superstitious that he is firmly persuaded that if he broke that pledge, God would strike him dead.

My host also amused me by telling me of an incident that occurred while he lived at Salem, Mass. It illustrates the absurd length to which fanatacism can carry men. Some stray prophet announced that the end of the world was to take place on a certain night, and that the elect were to be taken up to heaven. The "elect" believed, and actually gave away all their property, cleared out their houses of all their worldly goods, reserving only a decent dress in which to make their entrance to the Kingdom of Eternal Glory. Some of the ladies were dressed most gorgeously. It was quite a sight to witness the entrance to the church from which the elect were to be translated. They spent the night in prayer, sighs and groans, but they were not translated. Those who gave all away found themselves paupers next morning. One man who had been very rich consoled himself by saying the event could not be long postponed.

March 24th.—I go by appointment at one o'clock to dine with Doctor Kirwin. His wife is as pretty and smiling as ever, and his wife's mother, Mrs. Gunn, a fine old lady, is present. The only other guest besides myself is a M. le Comte de La Riviers, a real (Canadian) French Count, a young gentleman with all the style and bearing of an English officer, which I really thought he was at first sight. His black hair brushed and cut close was creased down the middle of his head, and he wore an exuberant moustache. The style of things and the tone of conversation as well as the accent of all parties, particularly of Mrs. Kirwin and the Count, brought me back from the democratic atmosphere of the United States, which I had been breathing for months, to the serener and loftier aerial surroundings of aristocratic life, and yet aristocracy is too full of airs, it seems too hollow, too affected to win admiration. Both phases of life-discipline, if I may so call it, have their faults. The principal of democracy is rational and good, but it is abused in the States. Every menial flouts his equality with you in your face, but then in all the studied speeches of the well-bred English or Canadian gentleman, in the precision of his movements and the accuracy of his dress, in the evidently forced chivalry by which he devotes himself to the ladies, and in a thousand other odds and ends by which he seems to study how to talk without tripping, there is too much of the artificial, too much to confine the soul and contract the heart, too much generally understood to be insincere, which takes from the dignity of mankind and makes friendship only a name indeed.

The Count went away early, and the Doctor took me into his drag and gave me a long drive along the St. Lawrence to Lachine, a drive I took last summer with the Burkes. The river however, presented a very different appearance now from that which it had last summer. It was thickly frozen over, and we saw people passing across. At one point it presented the appearance of an immense lake, five or six miles across, on any part of which a carriage might drive with safety. Only at this season no one knows when it may break up, and it would be too venturesome to try it. The rapids were frozen, and the ice there presented the same face of disruption and confusion as the rapids themselves. It seemed as if the tumbling waters had been caught and frozen at some one moment by an irresistible power of cold, and retained in their arrest, the aspect of conflict and agony which they had when seized. It is snowing as we ride along, and the whole scene is as wild and wintry as could be imagined. We drive back and I reach home about four o'clock.

The *Gazette* this morning has an article, a letter from a country reader, headed " Rev. Mr. Buckley and St. Patrick's Society," in which it speaks of me as " Priest Buckley," and hopes that the insult offered through me to the other societies present at my speech, will not be considered as expiated by the castigation of me the chief culprit, but that the St. Patrick's Society who brought me here, will apologize to all the rest, and thus give reason to hope that the like will never occur again.

Sunday.—Preach to-day for Father Hogan. Fine church, and splendid congregation (Griffinstown). Have a nice drive with Father Leclair, to Hochelaga, the eastern bank of the St. Lawrence, which is all frozen over hard, white and thick. Opposite, about three miles distant, is the village of Longuiel, and I see horses drawing sleighs across the river, foot-passengers and skaters. There is a regular road across the river from Montreal to Longuiel. It has been there all the winter, and seems covered over with straw and other refuse. Return by the Wharf, where I miss the busy aspect of the shipping which I found here last summer. Not a small boat is to be seen. This stoppage of navigation all through the winter and spring is a great drawback to the prosperity of Montreal. It becomes an inland city for half the year. Dine to-day with the Burkes, at Michael's house. They are very good and kind. Miss Burke presents me with a very handsome pair of slippers which she wrought for me.

March 24*th*.—The ground is all covered with snow, but the sun shines out gaily. After dinner, at 11.30 o'clock, I walk out and call at Turgeon's offices. He soon appears, and we have a chat. I then propose a drive in the country. Dr. Kirwin, who keeps livery stables, told me that I might at any time order a horse and carriage at his place. I accordingly go and order a carriage to call at M. Turgeon's office at 3.15 o'clock. It came punctually, and we drive along, Turgeon acting as charioteer. He intends to take me to see the Ottawa river, which is about five miles from Montreal. The afternoon is very cold, but I am wrapped in my Irish frieze, and he is still more snugly enveloped in a coat made of the skin and fur of some wild animal. We had just passed a toll-gate about a hundred yards when one of our shafts lost a screw and nut, and became useless for travel. We turned back, and the toll-keeper, an Irishman, soon got us over our difficulty. I doubt if any man is so ready in an emergency, or so inventive of the means for mending it. The toll-man cast his eyes about and saw some wire in a neighbouring fence. He instantly cuts off some of this wire and, with it, connects the shaft to the beam to which it had been screwed, and, in fact, "fixes it up" as strong as ever. Offering him many thanks, which he duly acknowledges to "your reverence," we pursue our journey. We pass by a great number of waggons, all driven by French-Canadians, with whom Turgeon familiarly chats in their own tongue. They appear to be very polite and extremely respectful to him, not that they all know him, but that they seem to have a great deal of that respect for aristocracy which exists among the Irish peasants, and which is a relic of the feudal system. They clear the road where he is to pass, or they halt till our carriage passes. I thought within myself how slow a Yankee waggoner would be to afford us so much accommodation. Those peasants were wrapped in all kinds of clothes and furs to protect them against the cold, but the most singular and picturesque costume was that which many men wore, and which I cannot better describe than by saying simply that it was the habit of a trappist, bound round the waist with a sash, and with the hood stretching up to a point on the head.

Turgeon told me that the Canadian peasantry are very simple in their manners and habits, and intense bigots in matters of religion, being all Catholics, and having little or no toleration for any other religion. Seldom does one of them become addicted to habits of intoxication, and when such one appears he is despised and avoided. They drink when they come to town, but seldom to excess. Their houses are clean and their diet simple. Seldom do they rise to the luxury of a roast turkey. Pork is the meat they most commonly use. Bread, butter, eggs, beans, molasses, &c., are the staple food. They make little money, and are very unambitious. The art of cooking, which is so well understood in France, they seem to have lost. They jog on through life having little, but content with their lot. Turgeon is a "rouge," a pure democrat, and yet I upbraid him with the pleasure he seems to take in the simple homage which those pay to his superior rank. He admits the superiority, but says there must be grades in all society, and adds that he wants a state of things which will afford all men the opportunity of reaching that rank in life which they ambition and for which they are adapted. The only aristocracy to which homage should be paid is to the aristocracy of intellect.

The day is fearfully cold, but our great coats and buffalo-robe make it less biting. At length we reach the restaurant of M. La Jeunesse, where Turgeon appears quite at home. He rattles away in French to the host, and shows me over the house. It is crowded on Sundays, for this is a favourite drive. We walk to the river and view it from a large wooden arched bridge which crosses it here. A broad river covered with ice, except one part where a tremendous current flows. The scene is very fine although it is wintry and cold. Turgeon's birth-place is some three or four miles farther on across the river, Terrebonne (Terra Bona—Ban-tir), and he is anxious I should see it, but not to-day, it is too late.

We return to town in our carriage. The Mountain (Mount Royal is covered with snow, so are the fields in some places), and the domes and spires of the city lie in front. The whole scene is bathed in a flood of red sunset-light and looks charming. And the Canadian peasants returning homewards with their peaked cowls give a romantic picturesqueness to the tableau.

March 28*th*.—I dine to-day with Father Campion, of St. Bridget's; and preach for him in the evening. There are 30,000 Catholics (Irish), in Montreal, and only three Irish priests !!! The Irish are never content with any priest except one of their own, and they go so far in this desire that they prefer a priest from their own part of the country to any other. Anecdote on this subject:—In Boston a woman's husband dies. She is Southern Irish. People ask her had her husband the benefit of a priest in his last moments. She replies "He had and he had'nt."

"What do you mean?" say the neighbours.

"It was one of them Far-Down priests he had," she said, thus conveying that a far-down, that is a Northern priest, could not enter fully into the feelings of her Cork husband.

March 27*th*.—I am in Father Egan's room. The boy comes and says to him "Sir, there is a lady down stairs wishes to speak to you."

"This lady," says Father Egan, "is most probably a servant girl, very few ladies come to see me."

"And," said I, "Is it the same here as in the States—is every woman called a lady?"

"That," he said, "greatly depends—if the person wears a feather she is a lady, if a muffler, she is only a woman. For some few weeks here in the winter there were no ladies. The cold weather banished feathers and introduced mufflers and clumsy head-dresses. Then every person who called here was, with the boy, only a 'woman.' But when the cold disappeared for a short time, none but ladies called. On ordinary occasions, if a male visitor wears a moustache, he is a 'gentleman,' but should he lack that characteristic of facial adornment, he is only a 'man.'"

At 8 o'clock this evening my lecture came off. The Hall was literally crammed, nor had the deep and still falling snow any effect on the numbers. There must have been 2,500 persons present. A magnificent band—the band of St. Patrick's Society diversified the entertainment; they played several airs, all Irish. The proceedings lasted two hours and the audience appeared in the best of humour. The Presidents of the several societies were seated on the platform in the insignia of their office, namely, a collar of velvet and gold. Mr. Devlin was chairman. He made a long speech, alluding to the excitement caused during the past week, by the comments of a portion of the press on my speech of Patrick's Night, and making proper explanations. I delivered my lecture first, and then made a speech of explanation. The audience were in roars of laughter the whole time. I never met a better humoured crowd of people. All admitted it was about the pleasantest evening they ever spent in that hall. My friend Turgeon was on the platform. The whole thing was a grand success.

March 28*th*.—My lecture and the proceedings of last night are the great topic of the newspapers this morning. There are no editorial comments yet. In the afternoon the *Star* has a leader, but a very mild one.

I visit Mrs. Sadlier, of New York, at the Ottawa Hall. The Irish citizens of Montreal are to give me a banquet this evening. I make other visits, and at 7.30 the dinner comes off at the Ottawa Hall. I was glad to find from statements made during the evening that the Irish are equal to any others in Montreal in wealth and prosperity, and that no less than 10,000 of them have deposit receipts in the bank. From all quarters I have heard of their sobriety. Father Dowd assured me for five years he had not seen a drunken person. I can add that they are very kind, generous, and social, and all seem pleased that this little "tempest in a tea-pot" should take place, because it bands the Irish together, and gives them common cause of battle against their enemies.

March 29*th*.—The *Gazette* is out this morning with a leader headed "Irrepressible," in which it deals pretty severely with me, reiterating its charge of Fenianism, and refusing to accept any explanation except as glosses made in a spirit of cowardice and insincerity. The *Herald* has a full report of Mr. Devlin's speech and mine. The *Witness* in the evening is caustic and bitter. There is as much religious bigotry here as in Belfast. It is worse in Toronto, but it is more remarkable in a city where the majority are Catholic, in a city which some have rather inconsiderately designated as the "Rome of America."

March 30th.—This morning the proceeds of the lecture were handed to me by Mr. Donovan. I went at once and turned them into a Bill of Exchange at the Ontario Bank, of which Mr. Stamers is the manager. The newspapers are quiet to-day.

I pay a few visits and prepare to leave the city. Some of my friends meet me at the terminus. We part. I cross the St. Lawrence, over the Victoria Bridge, and the huge river is still frozen hard and thick. I go from a region of cold to one of genial warmth, and from one people to another very different. A young gentleman with glasses and a very scholarly air, introduces himself (Mr. George Isles). He offers me Mark Twain's "Innocents Abroad," which I read and enjoy very much. It lessens the tedium of a very long journey. The country all around is very flat, and presents a pleasant cultivated aspect, and the trees everywhere give the scene a charming picturesqueness. We reach St. Albans, and Mr. Isles directs my attention to the large number of emigrants we brought, and whom the carriages are now disgorging. The word emigrants is associated in my mind with the Irish, and I was startled by the expression of my companion. But these are only emigrants from Canada—French-Canadians on their way to the factories of Massachusetts, to which they flock at this season, but return home in the summer, for they are a very home-loving people, so are the Irish, perhaps still more.

We take refreshments at St. Albans. Mr. Isles branches off, and I take the Vermont Central Route. As I am to travel all night, I am to have my first experience of the sleeping-car. At the cry of "All aboard," I step into the sleeping-car. The conductor is at the door, cold and indifferent. I say, like one who knows all about sleeping-cars, " I want a berth, please." Perhaps this was a mistake —it looked like confounding trains and steamers. From his impassive features I could not see whether he detected any greenness about me. He only said, " All right, step in there," pointing to a place behind a curtain. I wondered did this conductor ever smile, or did he ever say an unnecessary word? Is he always the conductor? Does he ever sing or be social? Has he a wife, and does he take his children on his knee and pet them? He seemed to me to be the incarnation of office. So is it with most American conductors. One would think that they had accepted the position in a pure spirit of condescension, and that the position ought to be very grateful to them for so doing.

I sit on a kind of narrow bed. It faces the stove, and so I am very warm. I take off my hat and coat. Mark Twain is no use, for it is dark, and in this berth there is no place for a lamp. What shall I do? Is this the bed, where is the pillow, where are the bed clothes, or are there any? Ask the conductor? Oh, no! He probably would not answer me. I lean against the panel and doze, and then I feel very sleepy. At last I make a pillow of my outside coat, and lie down awaiting the issue. I don't know how long I may have been asleep, but I was waked by a question.

"Time to wind up, eh?" I opened my eyes, and saw the rigid conductor. "Oh! yes," I said, "where shall I go?" He pointed and I obeyed. I sat in the next berth, and he pulled from another, a bed, bed-clothes and pillows, and "fixed" mine. When he gave me the signal to return, I found my bed had been increased to twice its width, and was very snug and comfortable. But just fancy the magnificent conductor making it for me. It was an indescribable condecension. I retired and slept very well indeed. While the train was in motion I slept, but its stopping always woke me. We passed through Burlington, the chief city of Vermont, and next morning at 5.30 reached Troy, which must be somewhere about 150 miles from New York. The accommodation for washing in sleeping-cars is not *recherché*, and there was no hair comb or brush, so that I did not feel very clean when I stepped on the platform of Troy. Here is a splendid refreshment room considering the point of size—but of what kind are the refreshments? I sat at a small table, and a nigger almost as *nonchalant* as the conductor, attended me. "Tea and eggs," I said. When they did arrive, after a considerable delay, the first egg proved to be rotten. I appealed to the nigger, but he said it wasn't so bad, that it was about the best to be got, and most people did not object to eggs in such a condition. I replied, I only envied the stomachs of such people. The tea was some abominable decoction of hay and heath, and other indefinable herbs. I ordered coffee for the next cup, but the tea was nectar in comparison, the bread was damp, and the butter, like the egg, far advanced in decomposition. The only genuine article of the breakfast was the payment of some extravagant number of cents. But I only heave a sigh for old Ireland, and change cars for New York. We steam away through a long street of Troy, as if a railway train was as innocent as a wheelbarrow. We kill no one, however. The people are scarcely out of bed yet. Soon we move by the pleasant banks of the Hudson—it is a charming morning. The Canadian cold is gone, but I find traces of snow thus far south.

March 31*st.*—After a few miles we see Albany sitting on the river, a truly charming spectacle, with its church spire and fine houses, all neat and fresh as if turned out only yesterday. I admire the Hudson immensely, and it looked lovely this morning—its broad waters, a noble tide, glistening in the beams of the early sun; with far beyond the long bold range of the Catskill mountains, all sprinkled with snow, making a magnificent back ground to the landscape. I feel nervous as we approach the bridge where occurred the terrible railway accident of the 9th of February, known as the New Hamburg disaster, when, at night, by collision with a petroleum train, some carriages were precipitated into the frozen river, some 25 people were drowned, the bridge was burnt, and all America was shocked for a moment. We reach it at length, it has been newly built, we crawl over it at snail-pace, and I see the charred timbers of the old bridge sticking up gloomily from the placid waters. When we are over, I feel very comfortable and fear no farther danger.

Queer names of places here "Catskill," "Pigskill," "Fish-kill," and "Poughkeepsie," the three latter being names of towns on the Hudson. It was on this line I first noticed the nuisance of newsvendors, and vendors of all kinds in railway carriages. While you are quietly reading, you are startled by a book or a paper, or a package of "hop corn," or a prize candy package cast into your lap, or into the book you are reading. You must inspect those things, and if you buy them, why you give the money when the man comes round, or if not he takes back his wares. It never ceases, when they have left one series of things in the laps of the passengers they go over the same process with something new.

CHAPTER XI.

NEW YORK IN SUMMER.

I REACH New York about twelve o'clock, and proceed to Sweeny's hotel. The change of temperature from Canada is what strikes me most.

April 6th.—I have been for some time suffering from a kind of asthmatic affection—an incapacity to walk without puffing, and a certain strange stiffness about my knees, and want of muscular power in my legs. I see I must look to it; it comes from want of exercise. Happy thought—take a good long walk every morning. Told Charles U. O'Connell about it. He knocks this morning at my door at seven o'clock; I am just getting up. Lovely morning, a little raw, but good for exercise. Charley proposes we begin the walking; so we start along Broadway, stepping into Trinity Church (Protestant) on the way to look at it. A fine church, with a splendid stained glass window. We are sorry we cannot say our prayers: we can only think them. We march along until we come to the Battery, Castle Garden, and all that. Before reaching those places, however, we find ourselves in a handsome round square, where there is an iron railing enclosing a green plot, where there are some high trees. The upright iron bars of this railing were, while the English ruled here, surmounted by heads of George III., but during the revolution the heads were torn off by the Americans, and made into shot to turn on the English. It is easy to see the signs of the wrenching. The place where the British Consul lives is close by, and is distinguished by two lions couchant, one at each side of the doorway. We got on board the ferry-boat for Staten Island. I had a most delightful trip across the spacious basin within the harbour. It reminds me somewhat of Queenstown, and if not as gay in summer time, is far more active. All kinds of craft are plying about with truly Yankee smartness. Little tug-boats particularly, which, like all small agents, even in humanity, strive to make up for diminutiveness by an affectation of gigantic energy. There are two Trans-Atlantic steamers, Guion and a Cunard, both apparently in quarantine, for smallpox prevails here just now. The sun makes the water dazzle, and I long to tread the deck of one of those vessels, and sail out the harbour's mouth, straining my eyes for the rugged coast, and the green fields, and the dear old hills of my native land.

April 7th.— Don't feel so well to-day. Nevertheless, Charles O'Connell and I take our morning excursion. We cross over in a ferry-boat to Hoboken. The morning is cold and rough, with a dry east wind. What is Hoboken? A collection of houses verging into another collection called Jersey City. We walk through till we come to Jersey. Here we go on board the "Oceana," the last Trans-Atlantic steamer built — built in Belfast — first of a new line, the "White Star." She is a splendid vessel, 432 feet long by,

I think, 42 beam, most gorgeously fitted up. Before we went out I should have said we had a tumbler each of boiled milk; but, alas! it was not milk. What was it? What was it like? I know not; but one thing I am certain of—it was not milk. This is too bad. That when a man pays his honest money, he will not get an honest article. But what can you expect in a country where it is notorious that a fortune has been made by a dealer in wooden nutmegs, and that a man saved his bacon by the sale of wooden hams. Nothing is genuine here. How so many escape poisoning is to me mysterious.

I preach this evening at St. Paul's church. Brooklyn is a fine city, with, probably, half a million of inhabitants. It is always on the increase. The number of houses built within the past twelve months in Brooklyn exceeds fifteen thousand; and yet there are men living who remember when there was not a stone on a stone in this great city. When Archbishop M'Closky, of New York, was preaching a few years ago, at the laying of the foundation stone of the new Brooklyn Cathedral, he used words to this effect:— "Well I remember when there was not a stone or a brick house in all Brooklyn—where I was brought up in my childhood, when only a few wooden shanties skirted the water's edge, and when I, a little boy, was accustomed to walk with my little Irish mother along the sand on a Sunday morning, and went by a small ferry-boat across to New York, to Barclay-street church, almost the only one then in that great city, to hear Mass. Little indeed did I then think that this great Brooklyn would be the third city of the Union, and that that little Irish boy would fill the proud position in which He whose ways are unsearchable has placed me."

April 8th.—The most sudden and extraordinary change of weather I ever experienced; from a harsh east wind to the boiling heat of summer. It has taken everyone by surprise. The thermometer rose in the afternoon to 81°. All the evidence of summer became suddenly manifest—the butter melted at table, everyone was seized with a craving for bitter beer, or sherry-cobbler and ice beverages of all kinds. Men threw off their coats, and children swarmed out of doors like ants, some very lightly clad, and some simply statuesque. The sun asserted itself, the pavement glowed beneath the feet, the imagination bore men away to the seaside to Staten Island, and Longbranch, and nature longed for a cool bath in the swelling salt-sea waves. Brows glowed with heat and pearls of perspiration rose on the forehead, handkerchiefs were plied with unusual vigour, and as if summer were impatient of postponement, there was one veritable case of sun-stroke—a man named Elishah Divan. Neither the prophetic influence of his first name, nor the Oriental magic of the second, saved him from the fatal stroke of that fire-king, whose rays glow hardly more fiercely in his own torrid realms of the east.

Crossing from Brooklyn, where I slept last night, I beheld with gladness, such only as that with which summer lights up the heart, the sparkling waters, as it were, dancing with a suddenly inspired ecstacy for the return of the gay and joyful time, and to my vivid fancy, the sloops and schooners, with their white sails wafting them swiftly through the waves, appeared like birds of passage, returning from cooler zones to the brighter and more genial azure of their own.

April 9th.—Easter Sunday. The heat to-day is intense—as hot as anyone could desire. A cool breeze would be a luxury, yet it is not that fearful heat of a New York summer which renders people utterly incapable of doing anything—it is pleasant and comfortable; but much walking would make it disagreeable. The streets are very gay and bright. People wear their holiday costume, and now and then a young girl appears in blue dress trimmed with white, and with white satin shoes, and mayhap a bouquet. Some fair child, who has just emerged from some church where she was a processionist, or had been to receive holy communion. The sight of so much beauty and innocence in this worldly-minded city on this great holiday has a peculiar charm. And *apropos* of the religion of New York, I may remark in passing that there is a great deal of religion here, especially amongst our people. The priests are always hard at work and are really most zealous. The churches are crowded on Sundays; but what I have observed most is the spirit of religion that animates most individuals whom I meet in private life. I have met a great number of men of whom it might be said that they were Christians in the true sense of the word—anxious to do good for themselves and others, deploring the temptations to which they were exposed—particularly temptations to drink, and making, aye, and keeping, stern resolutions to resist them. Indeed in one word, I may say that I found as much true religion in New York of a solid unostentatious character as ever I met at home. I have no doubt that many neglect their religious duties altogether and perhaps lose their faith; but of what Catholic land is not that true? I know nothing of the religious feelings of those who are not Catholics, but there is no doubt that New Yorkers as a class are great church-goers. The *Herald* every day plumes itself more and more of being the great moral teacher of America, the great religious apostle of the press. People say it does good in that way, I know not what kind of good; but I know that if a "gentleman in search of religion" wanted to build up a theory of faith—to fashion a creed for himself out of the preachings of the *Herald*, he would find he had created a monster more hideous than Frankenstein—a union of anomalies which no mind could grasp—no intellect reconcile *monstrum horrendum informe ingens cui lumen ademptum*. I dine to-day with Mrs. Attridge. The spectacle of the streets where the Germans most do congregate, particularly Avenue B, and the streets off it, are very gay to-day, because to-morrow is to be celebrated the "Peace Jubilee," namely, a general rejoicing for the termination of the late war between Germany and France. In this celebration the Germans alone are to participate, and it is said that it is to be one of the grandest public spectacles ever witnessed in the United States; that the great object of the Germans is not so much to congratulate their country on a return of peace, or to exult in a triumph over their French neighbours, but to show to the whole world their strength as a great component part of American nationality, that in the distribution of power their claims may not be overlooked. The only other element with which they have to contend in the ostentatiousness of power is the Irish. These latter put out all their strength last Patrick's Day. On that occasion the procession was conducted on a scale of magnificence unprecedented in the history of the Irish; but it is said that the Germans will far outstrip all previous displays no matter by whom made. As I pass along Avenue B, the spectacle is indeed pretty. From every window, nay, from almost every pane of glass floats a banner. Tens of thousands of flags decorates the houses, some immense in size, others ordinarily large, the rest dwindling down to the size of a piece of paper. The only flags observable are the German (black, white and red), some few Bavarian, and the American "Star-Spangled Banner." "The Deutchers" are all out in holiday costume, and assume an air of unusual importance, as if New York were theirs for the next twenty-four hours. And no one seems to interfere with these delicious feelings of self-complacency on their part. Indeed that is one of the things which a stranger, and particularly an Irishman, observes most in this city—every nationality celebrates its own festival, whatever the occasion may be, without offending others. The Germans look on and admire the Irish processions, the Irish are equally generous to the Germans—the only nationality whom the celebration of this "Peace Jubilee" could hurt would be the French; but though 40,000 strong, they will keep quiet, and to give the Germans their due they make no allusion to France in the matter, but think only of the — peace! Again, I remark the immense number of children in this German quarter. To almost every house there are steps, and those steps are crowded with little boys and girls making a terrible din, while the old folks sit admiringly outside the door, Mein Herr generally smoking his *meerschaum*, and the Frau Gemahlin reposing with her hands folded and calmly resting on that amplitude of sub-pectoral development which seems peculiar to the ladies of Deutschland.

April 10th.—Easter Monday. Surely never did a brighter or lovelier dawn usher in a day so favourable for a public demonstration than that which called forth from their slumbers this morning the children of the Vaterland. I was awakened at six o'clock by the booming of cannon announcing that the hour had arrived for the great event to begin. There is something catching in the joy of a great multitude— it creates a corresponding emotion in the breasts of those who have no other reason to be sympathetic. I felt a sensation of gladness as I looked out into the street and saw the German houses around me all "brilliant and bright," with flags and laural festoonings and inscriptions in the German tongue. Gladness was, as it were, in the air. The streets appeared to be more than usually crowded, and the passing people were chatty and hilarious. The bells ringing on the necks of the horses drawing the street-cars seemed to chaunt a strain of jubilation, and the little flaglets fixed in their foreheads gave the idea that even the brute creation rejoiced with the exulting Germans. Now and then through the dense mass of ordinary citizens, would pass some German in the costume of a Prussian soldier, or a bandsman, or a member of some society, with an appropriate badge cr decoration betokening the coming gala. Later on huge waggons gaily festooned and inscribed, pass along drawn by six or eight horses, occupied by men of the various trades, and bearing the emblems of their craft, all proceeding to Tompkins Square, Avenue B, which is the general rendezvous, the starting and finishing point of the procession.

At eleven o'clock I also betake myself to Tompkins Square, or rather to Father Mooney's house which commands it. There is no language of mine by which I could convey the beauty of the spectacle all through the German quarter. The thousands of flags of yesterday seem to have multiplied a thousand fold, and myriads of Chinese lanterns are hung out in preparation for the illuminations in the evening.

The hot sun shines over all, the air is filled with the music of gathering bands, the streets echo to the sound of treading horses, bearing the processionists to the ground. The hum of a hundred thousand voices increases the babel. In the midst of the enormous square, from which the iron railings exclude the public, is an immense platform, capable of holding three thousand persons, all wreathed and ornamented with Chinese lanterns and the mingled flags of Germany and America in boundless profusion. Every window in the square has its crowded spectators gazing on the bright and busy scene from amidst a forest of flags, while the very roof-tops all around (square flat roofs) are swarming with men and women, shaded by umbrellas from the scorching heat of the sun. The procession forms, and those thousands of spectators, from window and roof, from basement and attic, all wave their white handkerchiefs in admiration of the scene. Here is a splendid band, then follows a long train of horsemen in military costume, then comes the enormous waggons thick with their foliage, in the midst of which the bakers bake their bread, the smiths ply their sledges on the anvil, the butchers surround a mimic ox prepared for the work of slaughter, or the rosy god, Bacchus, in correct mythological "fixings," sits aside on a large barrel and swills veritable draughts of lager beer; next come footmen, keeping the step in true military style, bearing wands and banners; then comes open carriages with their aristocratic freights; the inevitable Helmsbold is there with his magnificent six-horse tandem, but it is all vain for me to attempt a description of this procession, which is admitted on all hands to be the grandest public demonstration ever made in America— a public spectacle unparalleled in the annals of the United States. One of the German papers, afterwards alluding to the procession, described it as the greatest that ever appeared in the world. It was twelve miles long. The number of decorated carriages was 250, and it was computed that the number of processionists was 50,000. It was regarded as a great triumph for the American-Germans, and was a model to all other nationalities for the various qualities that distinguished it—the lavishness of expenditure, the unanimity of tone, the universality of participation, the propriety of conduct, the moderation of feeling, the artistic taste and effect of the whole *mise en scene* were creditable in the highest degree.

The Irish seem to feel they are beneath the Germans in this kind of thing—and why are they so? Because the *respectable* portion of their people regard Patrick's Day procession as vulgar and unworthy of their patronage or attendance, while the Germans high and low combine to make this pageant what it is, succeed, and are applauded and envied. Great expense is necessary to carry out a great procession such as this, and the Germans subscribed in abundance, but the rich Irish, though wealthier than their German compeers, lack the public spirit to make this sacrifice.

How shall I describe the illuminations in the evening? It is vain. Tompkins-square was the great attraction. The houses all round were brilliant with Chinese lanterns; the platform was brilliantly lighted up, and 400 voices chaunted hymns of jubilee; electric lights and lime lights turned night into day; fireworks were going on in all quarters; rockets mimicked the stars; hundreds of thousands promenaded the streets. All through the city, wherever a German habitation stood, were decorations and illuminations. Every *Bier-Halle* swarmed with lovers of lager, and of the whole demonstration it can be safely said that it was one of the most magnificent spectacles ever witnessed in any great city —one of the grandest demonstrations by which a wealthy, a patriotic and a united people sought to prove that they were entitled to the respect and honour of the country they had adopted as their own.

April 11*th.*—Mark the vicissitudes of the American climate. The hot broiling weather is gone, and a cold, harsh, dust-making March wind has set in again. This is another day for two coats. I spend the greater part of the day in my hotel paying up arrears of correspondence long due. In the evening I go with John Attridge to the Academy of Music, where the 71st Regiment have a ball. Previous to the ball there is a military drill. Twelve candidates compete for three prizes—a silver-mounted musket, a medal and a cup. The drilling is rather monotonous, and it lasted a good while. The whole spectacle, however, was very fine. The hall is a very grand building—half-theatre, half hall— with galleries and boxes. The pit was all hidden from view, covered over with a flooring placed for the purpose of dancing, and easily removable. A great number of officers were present, and they looked *like* officers—*i.e.*, gentlemen, like ours at home, and very unlike the colonels and captains I have met in undress. Perhaps if the latter were dressed *en militaire* they would look as soldierly; but take men as you find them. The evolutions appeared to my unpractised eye very well performed; but, strange to say, the two whom I thought best were not amongst the rewarded. These two were the only ones whose exercises were applauded by the audience, which I regarded as a flattery to my own judgment; but we were, it would appear, all wrong. Three were selected for the prizes whom no one seemed to admire very much. No doubt we were all wrong. The moment the drilling was over, the floor was thronged with dancers. It was the first public ball I ever saw. The dresses struck me as very beautiful, but the ladies as the reverse. Out of about two hundred ladies there was not six who came up to my standard of beauty, while some were hideously ugly. The ugly ones appeared the best dressed, as if they endeavoured to supply by art what Nature denied. Poor creatures,

"They strove to bless
In all the glaring impotence of dress."

Fashion, it would appear, has introduced in New York a a habit of powdering ladies' hair, a good refuge for the grey, and to them a great saving of powder. They also powder their faces. One lady was a perfect fright—old, scraggy, gaudily attired, but with her long, profuse, and doubtless false hair, all powdered steel grey, and her face as if it had been dashed with flour—she will not look half so hideous when she is a corpse. Then she will look at least natural. Balls are a study to a philosophic mind—to mine, of course, only in proportion to its philosophic depth. But why do people dance? Is it that they may be seen and admired? Dancing is not necessary for this; promenading would do as well, and better. Those dancers to-night looked like moving statues; they interchanged no smiles, no words; they looked cold. Nay, it would seem to a stranger as if they felt that smiles or interchange of sentiment would be vulgar, or bad taste. They simply danced, and then promenaded, and strove to look self-possessed and severe. Probably if I were a dancer I would see the pleasure, but being only a spectator, I am, of course, a cynic. Well, I hope so, I heartily hope those butterflies enjoyed themselves. They certainly looked very pretty from a distance; the tableau was charming, and I trust they will all feel better to-morrow morning.

The notorious Colonel James Fisk, junior, better known as "Jim Fisk," was here, in full regimentals, a good-looking man, but I thought sensual-looking, perhaps because I know that he is sensual. All the world knows it, and "Jim" makes no effort to conceal it. He is the most notorious man (excepting, perhaps, Train) in the United States; but Train is "played out," while Fisk is yet in the ring, and likely to be. He is proud of being the biggest *roué*, the most successful swindler, the least God-fearing, and the richest man in America. He speculates in everything, and everything thrives with him. He is in the papers every day, for something or another. He seems to enjoy an immunity from the perversity of his excesses, because he is wealthy, and America is a slave to Mammon, and to all Mammon's hierarchy. Fisk is the best living type of an American, his motto being, "*Rem, rem, quocunque modo, rem.*" He is at the top of Fortune's wheel to-day. To-morrow his coat may be trailing in the dust—to-day his friends swarm around him and do him homage—to-morrow, if he fall, the homage-giving group will be scattered to the winds. But this is the old, old story, and my philosophy is growing common-place. I have seen Jim Fisk, I go home contented.

April 12th.—A curious thing about shops in New York, and more or less with other cities I have seen here is the strange mode of advertising. I was aware before now, that tobacco sellers generally hung out a sign in the shape of a man smoking. Here is every variety of such statuesque symbols of trade. They abound at tobacco stores. In one place, it is a statue of a red Indian with a bunch of cigars in his hand. He is duly accoutred with feathers, tomahawk, and apron. In another place, a squaw does duty, but a squaw with an amount of beauty, and symmetrical grace or form which we associate only with the Caucasian race, some tobacco sellers have before their doors on a pedestal, a life-size form of a charming young lady attired as "the girl of the period," with extravagant chignon, a preposterous grecian bend, short dress, close laced high heeled boots, smoking a cigar. Whatever be the artistic excellence of these figures in a sculptural point of view, they are all painted most gorgeously, and with a perfectly rainbow like variety of colouring. Outside some shops it is a Bashaw with a turban, and loose trousers pulling a long pipe. Outside another it is a nigger decked out with striped pantaloons, white hat, and frilled shirt, smoking a cigar. In some places it is a soldier, in full costume, with a box of cigars in one hand and the other pointing to the "store" where those unparalleled Havanas or Partigas may be had. By the way the word cigar is generally spelt "segar" in New York.

Other trades beside the tobacco dealers have what I call their statuesque symbols. On Broadway outside an umbrella store, is on a pedestal, the full length statue of a man holding a blue umbrella in his hand open over his head, on a wet day. You envy the fellow, he succeeds so well in keeping himself dry. On Broadway also stretching out into the street from the very top of a house is a gigantic figure a bear, to imply that bear-grease, and other ointments may be had below. Shoe and boot makers usually have an enormous colossal boot, quite a "seven leaguer," placed on a pedestal at the kerb-stone in front of their houses: but indeed the variety of such symbols are endless. I go to see Mr. and Mrs. Williams off by the "Scotia" for Europe. An immense number of passengers go. Mr. Stephen Meany is also present. Mr. Florence, the actor, is going and his wife. To the latter he introduces me, she is an actress, a stout young lady with an exuberance of yellow hair. I could not help saying to Mr. Meany—This transatlantic navigation is a very wonderful *institution*—the noise, bustle, baggage, carriage, beauty, ugliness, age, youth, flash and plainness, aristocracy and shoddy; the tears and smiles and kisses, and waving white handkerchiefs all around the tender as she bears her living freight to the big ship out in the harbour.

Now and then, in newspapers, you see advertisements that amuse you, because they are so unintelligible to you, although to the initiated no doubt they are full of interest. I cut out the following lately, which appeared to be emphatically American, or at least not European. "Local items— Green turtle soup and stakes at the Terrapin, little neck clams always on hand. Clam chowder for lunch this day." I should like to know what an Englishman would guess the "Terrapin" to be, what are his notions of Neck Clams, especially little ones, and what sensations would be excited in his stomach by the expectation of lunching on Clam Chowder?

I see by a paper of this day's date that the number of thieves in New York has been computed to reach 30,000.

Funny little fellows those New York shoeblacks. They abound in London, and are generally found in places most frequented. The shoeblack looks at your boots as you pass and if he observes that they are soiled, he cries at you interrogatively, "Shine?" Now a stranger would have no notion what he means by this monosyllabic enquiry, but the initiated knows that he means "your boots are soiled, shall I make them shine?" Indeed contraction of expression is cultivated everywhere in America, and one remarkable illustration of it is found in the way people designate the streets in ordinary conversation. They generally leave out the word street; for example, instead of saying "Summer Street," they will say "Summer," or corner of "Summer," and "Washington," "19 Court," and so on.

Went this evening by the Broadway Stage. The "Stage" is just the same as our omnibus, and here it runs only along Broadway and some adjacent avenues; the horse-car goes through most of the other streets. I cannot help being astonished at the cleverness of the stage drivers. Remark: there are hundreds of stages and stage drivers. He sits on the box outside. He must have his eye out constantly for persons wishing to ride by his stage; he counts the number as they enter, pulls the door after them by a string fixed to the place where he sits; receives the money through a hole in the stage. Should a passenger delay payment he warns him by a bell to pay up. The money, which is nearly always paper, requires sometimes to be changed, he manipulates and changes with surprising dexterity, although in cold weather he wears gloves, and clumsy ones, and this he does by night as well as by day, and all the while guides his pair of horses through the immense and bewildering throng of carriages, waggons and other stages that crowd this perhaps the most carriage-driven street in all the world.

I find myself lapsing into that American expression, "in all the world." Last year I laughed at a gentleman who, in what I considered a spirit of national *amour propre*, pronounced Broadway the finest street "in all the world." I am beginning to veer round to his opinion—perhaps because, my long absence from other great cities diminishes my powers of comparison; I cannot say, but surely this evening passing along Broadway I fancied that no street could surpass it for beauty, long, straight, broad, thronged full of life and bustle, "brilliant and bright," with thousands of human beings passing along, with its magnificent houses, most of them five and six storeys high, some even higher, all lit up, some with plain gas, others with coloured lights of every design that fancy could suggest; the theatres illuminated as if for some great festival, a dazzling lime light beaming from the roof of one and lighting up the whole street for miles at either side; a running glance into the restaurants and refreshment rooms as we pass—a long vista of tables daintily laid out for supper, and a countless number of ladies and gentlemen regaling themselves amidst a firmament of lights, in a word, an aggregation of all that speaks of wealth, grandeur, beauty, bustle, life, elegance, taste and magnificence, all this is to be found in Broadway.

On our way home I remarked a curious machine that I had not seen before. It was a huge waggon drawn by two horses, which might be called a union of brush and a box. As the machine passed, the brush, a circular one, revolved quickly and swept all the dirt of the street into the box. It ought to be called the "Mammoth Chiffonier." It made the cleanest sweep of the streets I ever saw or thought possible.

April 15*th*.—Am unwell to-day, and remain confined to my room until 3.45 p.m., when I go by steamer to Huntington, Long Island. The voyage lasted two hours and a half, and as the evening was fine it was very pleasant. The scenery along Long Island Sound is very beautiful, and an abundance of sailing craft added to the charm. We passed by Blackwell's Island, which I described in the early part of this work. Curious blunder of Charles Dickens in his *American Notes* concerning this island. He speaks of it as Long Island or Rhode Island, he could not tell which—in point of fact it was neither—and how he could have mixed up the three islands, Long, Rhode and Blackwell, is strange and it implies a peculiar ignorance of American geography.

We passed through "Hell Gate," a kind of dangerous rocky passage. At the Huntington Pier Father Crowley met me with his horse and "wagon," and drew me to his house. The Miss Sweeny's were glad to see me. Spent the evening quietly in doors.

April 16*th*.—Sunday. Celebrated Mass and preached to a very small congregation. In this church there is Mass only every alternate Sunday. Father Crowley, the only priest, has to go off 20 miles every other Sunday to a second church. This was the Sunday for no Mass in Huntington, but he sent abroad word that a strange priest had come and would say Mass. The congregation were wonderfully well dressed considering they were only villagers, and Irish. The day was charming, and we had an exquisitely charming ride—visited a large empty house which the Jesuits have just bought with forty acres of land, for the ridiculously small sum of ten thousand dollars. The situation is wonderfully fine, on an eminence commanding a vast prospect of land and water.

In the neighbourhood are some breastworks thrown up by the English in the time of the War of Independence. We visited the landlord, Mr. Lloyd, a gentleman of English descent, and very English airs, a man of education and elegant manners, but strangely aristocratic. I say strangely, for how a man can preserve aristocratic airs in this country is to me difficult of comprehension.

I was amused driving through some woodland here, to see the antics of the squirrels among the trees, it was the first time I saw squirrels in a state of nature.

April 21*st.*—Fell very unwell, my heart flutters at the least exercise, simple walking gives me a violent palpitation. Nothing remains to me but to rest.

I am introduced to the celebrated John Mitchel in his office, Nassau Street. He is editor of the *Irish Citizen.* I claim more than ordinary regard from the fact that I was a friend of his dear friend Father John Trenyon of Templederry. Mr. Mitchel is a prematurely old, broken down man. The conversation turned on patriotism, politics, &c., and he ventilated some very strong revolutionary principles. He alluded to my book, "Father O'Leary," which he had read, and reviewed it in his paper. Of Father O'Leary he was no admirer. He deprecated his loyalty to the British throne. "No good Irishman," he said, "could be loyal under any circumstances to English rule."

I receive two engagements to-day to lecture at terms— one hundred dollars each lecture. One at the Athenæum, in Brooklyn, for the orphans under the charge of the Sisters of Mercy, the other at Camden City, N.J., for Father Byrne, P.P. I accept both.

I rise to-day much better than any day for the past week.

Last evening and this morning I read a small book—a life of Stephen J. Meany, now my friend. He is to my mind a gentleman, scholar, and true patriot. I admire the man more than ever.

April 25th.—Preached at St. Andrew's Church, after which went by invitation to the consecration of the Church of St. Rose of Lima (Father McKenna,) Cannon Street. The Archbishop (McCloskey,) Bishop Loughlin of Brooklyn, and Bishop Mullen of Erie were present, also about fifty clergy. Vast and most respectable congregation. Sermon by Father Hecker.

The Catholic faith seems to be very strong in New York, if one were to judge by the number of new and splendid churches being erected, or by the devotional aspect of the crowds who fill them. After the ceremony a grand banquet was prepared in the old church building, at which, besides the bishops and clergy, several lay gentlemen sat. After the usual toasts were proposed, the Archbishop did me the very high honour of proposing mine in connection with the name of my bishop, Dr. Delany, of whose hospitality he spoke in terms of the warmest eulogy.

In the evening I attended a lecture in the Church of St. Stephen's (Dr. McGlynn,) I think the finest church in New York.

April 26th.—My home-sickness continues very bad. It is like a disease. I now understand why the love of home is called a sickness. I spend the day moping about, finding fault with everything, and I last seek a balm for my troubled mind by writing a long letter to my friend, Father William Murphy, in which I state my whole case. Ridiculous idea to tell my complaint to a physician 3,000 miles away.

April 27th.—My home-sickness is greatly abated, almost gone—strange vicissitudes of my mind—I cannot account for it. I would willingly recall my letter to Father Murphy, but let it go, the disease will return again, and the letter will do for the next attack just as well. In the early morning the stranger whose slumbers are not broken by the milkman's cry of "milk" must have a very tranquil conscience, or very stolid ears. It is the most unearthly hideous cry I ever heard. A murdered victim in his last agony could scarcely rival the misery of it. I was hearing it for weeks before I could tell what it was. Its bitterness is enough to curdle the milk in the cans.

April 30th.—Travelled this evening to Camden, New Jersey, distant from New York about 100 miles. Camden holds the same relation to Philadelphia as Cambridge does to Boston, or Brooklyn to New York; in short, it is at the other side of the river. The day was pleasant and the scenery beautiful. Our road lay through the State of New Jersey, and we passed through some very important towns and cities, such as, Newark, Elizabeth, New Brunswick and Fenton. The aspect of the country reminded me much of England, as seen on the Great Western Railway from Bristol to London—low, well-cultivated, verdant, and with abundance of trees. Everything looked charming. New Jersey is a very agricultural State, but parts of it are very sandy. It is said that on occasions of great hurricanes whole farms are swept away, but on the return of the wind they are brought back again.

The Delaware river lies along the railway, a magnificent river rising in the State of New York, about 500 miles long, and joining the sea about 100 miles below Philadelphia. I reach Camden at 8.30 p.m. It is dark; I am driven to the house of the pastor, Father Byrne, who has engaged me to lecture to-morrow evening for 100 dollars, at the solicitation of his assistant, Father Hogan, once of Brisbane, whom I met in Ireland. Father Byrne I met the first time. He is a young man, thirty-three years of age, and six feet six inches high, very muscular, and very zealous.

Sunday.—I go across to Philadelphia by ferry-boat. The big city lies on the water, just like any other American city, a long, low range of red brick houses, with church spires at intervals. I am alone, and know no one here, save one, a Father Kirwan, whom I met in Cork last year. He lives at a place called Port Richmond, an extremity of the city, which, distant as it is, I find out, and him too. My visit was merely one of courtesy. I had an opportunity of seeing the city, though not much of it. It is a splendid city, very large, embracing an area of 127 square miles! of course not all built up, but intended to be, and paying city taxation within those limits. Thus, said to be the largest city in the world, population, 750,000, founded by William Penn— "City of Brotherly Love"—full of Quakers, hence methodical, quiet, not Catholic, though, probably, the Catholic population is 200,000, perhaps more. Germans are very abundant; the first man I met was a German. Philadelphia, always quiet, is almost a desert on a Sunday. No cars, that I could see, except the horse-cars, being out. I think I saw one or two carriages, but I am almost sure they were either going to or coming from church. The streets are, for the most part, rectangular. Method is the great feature of Philadelphia, the Quaker City.

I reach Camden; I am warned by Father Byrne that a

T

number of gentlemen, members of the local Father Mathew's Temperance Society, are at present in the church, and wish me to receive an address from them. This is embarrassing, but I go through it. A Mr. Hennessy reads the address; it is very flattering, and of course I shall preserve it. In the evening I deliver my lecture on "The Bible," in the church, to a very large and respectable audience.

Monday.—Father Byrne has arranged a pic-nic for me on the river at a place called Redbank, about ten miles away. He keeps four splendid horses, and is a lover of the noble brute. A pair come round to the door for him and me. We drive to Redbank, which we reach at twelve o'clock. There is a regatta on the river, which is so broad here that it resembles a great lake. Not far from this, and quite in sight of the spot where, in the war between the Americans and English, a man-of-war belonging to the latter was sunk by guns fired from this spot. The ship was the "Augusta," one of the largest in the navy at that time. She has been recently got up, and now floats in the dock at Philadelphia. "Ben Heritage," the farmer at whose house we put up our horses, pointed out to me one of the cannons employed in the sinking of the "Augusta." A stone monument on this spot commemorates the valour of a Lieutenant Green who here defeated 2,000 Hessians with only 400 men in the same campaign.

Soon after us arrive Father Hogan and Father Wiseman, the latter parish priest of Gloucester, a town within three miles at that side of Camden. Also came Miss Anne King, niece of Father Byrne, and some other very young ladies all of whom are very useful in laying the dinner on the green sward at a point commanding a lovely view of the great river. There are about forty yachts spread over the lake-like surface of the Delaware, many of which are racing and the rest spectators of the contest. There are steamers also conveying hundreds of sight-seers down from Philadelphia and following the course of the yachts. We had "a good time."

We return homeward in the same order, Father Byrne and I together. He shows the mettle of his horses this time, leaving all other charioteers "nowhere" on the road. There exists in America a great love of competition in all things, but most of all in speed. Steamers race on the great rivers, nay, on the ocean, and accidents frequently occur; lives are lost, too, but no matter, the question is who had the glory and honour of "beating the other?" One man has a splendid pair of black horses, and when he perceives Father Byrne is following he puts on all steam. No use. Father Byrne flies past him like a storm-wind. But the other pursues, and as he approaches we perceive that he has torn the mouth of one of his horses. Every attempt he made to get before us was signally frustrated by the superior skill and mettle on our side. At length when it was quite clear that he was defeated, Father Byrne pulled aside and let him pass.

Tuesday.—Day excessively hot. Go across to Philadelphia with Father Hogan, who takes me into a hatter's and makes me a present of a Panama hat, which I don at once. He wears one, too. Nobody minds a priest wearing such a hat here in the streets. I take him to see Mr. Moorhead, the gentleman whose acquaintance I made on board the "China" coming out last year. We reach the house indicated in the directory, 1612 Walnut Street—by the way, many of the streets of Philadelphia are named after fruits—

e.g., "Walnut," "Chestnut," "Pine," "Vine," and many more I cannot call to mind. But unfortunately Mr. Moorhead has left this house and gone to reside far out in the suburbs. What fault could he have found with this house? I think the finest in the whole street, built of cut granite, with a Grecian portico and steps. It was furnished in the most sumptuous and elegant style, and we could see even some marble statuary within apparently of great size and beauty. Coming home we see hundreds of Quakers going to meeting at their house in Arch Street. They meet very frequently this month. Their costume is the same here as at home, plain and clean. We spend the evening at the Cassidys—very nice elegant people—consisting of Mrs. and Miss Cassidy, her daughter, Mrs. Jenks, Mr. Jenks, the husband of the latter lady. Our conversation was more or less literary, philosophical, &c.

May 1st.—Eleven months in America. I call on the Rev. Dr. M'Glynn of St. Stephen. He invites me to preach next Sunday. Spend the evening with Father O'Farrell (jun.) of St. Peter's, Barclay Street, a fine young gentleman. We had company and spent a pleasant evening.

The great topic of New York at present is this—A few evenings ago (Sunday, April 23rd), a Mr. Putman a merchant, of Pearl Street, New York, was riding in a street car, escorting to church two ladies, mother and daughter. A young man named Foster enters the car, and acts with impropriety towards the young lady. The gentleman comes to the rescue, and, of course, offends Foster. The latter says "wait till I get you out." Accordingly when the party got out, so does Foster. Seizing a car-hook attached to the vehicle, he breaks the gentleman's skull. The latter dies. Foster is arrested, and, query, will he be hanged? The papers all cry out for his hanging, so does the public, and so are things done here, that it is mooted—he *will be got off by influence !*—political influence : *Nous verrons*—If Foster is not hanged, I will regard it as the most flagrant injustice ever offered to a community. We must watch the case.

May 2nd.—This evening walking in one of the streets, I see walking on before me a number of young men whom it was impossible to mistake for anything but Irish peasants, and I also fancied that they had just arrived.

"Boys," said I, addressing one with a pipe in his mouth, "how long are you out here?"

"'This minute, your riverence, we arrived," said he. "Put the pipe out of your mouth," said one of his companions in Irish. "Don't mind your pipe" said I, in the same tongue. They gazed in astonishment, and then ensued a conversation in the Celtic, from which I gathered that they were from Tuam.

"And how is Archbishop McHale?" said I.

"Well as he ought to be," was the reply. I hope these poor fellows will escape the many dangers that beset "greenhorns" in this country.

The names of the streets here are painted on the gas-lamp at the corners, and very seldom on houses. Strangers are here some time before they find it out—it is very useful at night.

Manhood suffrage by ballot is the great pride of America—but in New York it is a humbug. Votes are bought and sold with unblushing coolness, and many candidates for office who obtain majorities are counted out by bribed scrutators. A thousand evils accrue from this, for example, there is no rule of fare for cab-drivers here, they can charge what they please. Why do not the municipal authorities fix a tariff? Because the cab-drivers are a large section of the community, and at an election their votes and those of their friends could turn the scale against any obnoxious candidate. Favours are granted to the clergy and other influential persons, for the bare solicitation. Let a man be sentenced to imprisonment for a grave crime—a priest by properly manipulating the matter can get an order for his release.

May 4th.—Was introduced to-day to Mr. John Savage, whose name in Ireland and America has been mixed up for the last twenty years with Young Irelandism, Fenianism, &c. He is what is known as a "gentleman." He invited me to his place, and I shall go. My lecture this evening on "Curran," was a success as things go here.

May 5th.—Received this morning, a handsome tribute of praise of my lecture from Mr. Sweeny, proprietor of the hotel in the shape of a cheque for One Hundred Dollars. Dine this evening at Fifth Avenue. This is the most aristocratic quarter in all New York. While surveying the magnificent apartments, furniture, &c. I thought of the pride which some of our aristocrats at home feel over their houses. But, on the other hand, a thing very amusing here is the remarkable contrasts between the style of the houses and the style of their occupants. In many cases, no doubt not in all, most of those who are wealthy were once poor and uneducated, ignorant of fashion—what are called the "shoddy aristocracy." When they became rich, they purchased a great mansion on Madison or Fifth Avenue. They gave a commission to an upholsterer to furnish according to improved taste, regardless of expense. Similar commissions were given to the bookseller, the painter, the chinaware man, and thus the great houses were fitted up in right regal style: the human birds once accustomed to the wild freedom of poverty, now plumed themselves, and strutted about in their gilded cages, peeping out with their bright, sharp proud eyes at their former associates abroad, as if they would say "why can't you get a pretty cage like this?" Plebeian specimen of the *ormis*, "avaunt! I pity thee; I live on Fifth Avenue, chirp, chirp, chirp." But it is a vulgar chirp, and savours much of West Cork and Kerry, and the mountainous region of Sligo. No matter—you get a good dinner, at the right hour, at seven or half-past, and the wines are excellent, so are the "segars," the real Habanas, or the genuine Henry Clays, and you wind up with a good game of billiards at a table worthy of a club. And then next day, you are able to tell your friends that you were sorry you could not have called last evening, but really you could not accomplish it, you had to dine with a friend on *Fifth Avenue*. Should the person you address thus live "down town," he feels suddenly elated by the apology, for it is a high honour to him to have on the list of his friends, one who actually dined the previous evening on Fifth Avenue, and who seems to regard the circumstance as quite an ordinary event in his life. There is not a more aristocracy-loving people on the face of the earth than your American *democracy*.

May 19th.—Spend this evening with Mr. and Mrs, Lyons, Greenwich Street—very litttle aristocracy here; but a vast deal of genuine good nature, and warm hospitality. We were about fifteen, and we were all Cork people. There was a Mrs. Flynn, formerly of Nicholas Street, Cork. I remember the name well, and I remember the lady's mother; once a friend of my mother's. This lady remembers me a child. Her daughter, Miss Flynn, is also here, so are a whole family of the Draddys, of Quaker Road, out here for the last thirty years—a mother and three sons. At home they were stone-cutters; here they are "sculptors"—a most respectable family indeed. We had a very pleasant evening; some capital singing, and agreeable dancing. The old lady, Mrs. Draddy, danced as gaily as if she were only fifteen. I could not help feeling, when I saw the air of respectability that marked these young men—their thoroughly gentlemanly behaviour, and whole bearing—when I saw the happiness of the woman—I could not help feeling that things would have been very different with them if they had remained at home in Ireland. The stone-cutters would be very little regarded—the iron that cut the stone would enter their souls; and their manly airs inspired by the aegis of American freedom would be the downcast bearing of men crushed by a diabolical legislation.

May 20*th.*—Mr. Connolly had fixed on this day for taking me to the "Islands" to visit the "Institutions." We went to Bellevue Hospital—a splendid one. Mr. Everett, formerly of Skibbereen, was with us. Leaving this we took the steamer, accompanied by Mr. Nicholson, Commissioner of Charities, and proceeded to Kandall's Island. Great respect shown the Comptroller and his friends everywhere. Flags flying from the buildings on the islands—Foundling Asylums, Orphanage for boys and girls. The boys turned out in military array with mimic guns, and marching with a band. They drilled before us under the guidance of their drill-master—and one stepped forward on the part of the rest, and delivered an address to us. We saw all the asylums—

the idiots were an interesting though painful study—one boy particularly was dreadful to look at—the smallest head I ever saw—no forehead—long nose—receding chin—no expression in the eyes—whole body stunted—he looked very like a monkey.

The "Soldiers' Home" was interesting—lame, infirm, poor broken down soldiers, supported by the State.

The "Inebriate Asylum" for drunken men and women, came next. The treatment is simple—hard cases are gradually weaned. About four days is sufficient to administer stimulants before final abstinence—then good plain food and exercise for a few months—but many relapse. In Blackwells Island are asylums for all kinds of human infirmity. Saw here a woman 107 years old. Democratic idea realized—Mr. Nicholson sees a young woman in bed and asks of the nurse "What is the matter with that young lady?" The diseases are all beautifully classified here, so that the hospital for the sick is rather an aggregation of hospitals. There is a large room in this Island made in the shape of an isolated house, which might be called the calisthenic department. A lunatic man plays the piano, while, at the direction of a sane young woman, other women, for the most part paralytics, epileptics and lunatics, exercise themselves, to the time of the music, at dumb-bells, poles, etc.; this develops the muscles, and promotes health generally. In fact, these institutions are magnificent; the buildings are of the first style of architecture. No expense is spared. Light, air, room, cleanliness, good diet, fostering care, benevolence, religion, the ministrations of the Sisters of Mercy—these are the great features of management one discovers here. Hence, as far as nature permits, you discover in every department health, content, happiness, ease and plenty; disease is dispelled, and where that is impossible, the patient enjoys an existence as long protracted as art or science can confer.

Having completed our inspection, we sat down to dinner, provided for us by Mr. Warden Keane, an old gentleman seventy-two years of age, but displaying all the elasticity of forty. He was clad all in white, from his head to his heels, a humble man, but a democrat. Mr. Connolly was very kind and gracious to him, and Keane was equally condescending to the comptroller—beautiful equality. Keane would help us at table—he turned himself into head-waiter; but, as you took the plate from his hands, you could not forbear saying, "Thank you, sir." There was no degradation in his helping you—he felt there was not, and you felt it too. In this spirit he once or twice struck the comptroller on the shoulder while we were at dinner, and starting back, exclaimed, "Well, Richard, you're looking splendid." I thought, as I gazed on the complacency of Richard under this operation, how differently an English millionaire would have treated such a familiarity on the part of a menial; but this is a glorious country, where "a man's a man." We go again on board the "Minnahannock," and get back to the city, delighted with the day's enjoyment.

This evening, standing in the hall of the hotel, I converse for a few moments with General Halpin. We shake hands, and rush out into the street to catch a car. In a moment there is a cry, a rush, and a crowd; the General has fallen, and is under the wheels of the car. I almost know he is dead, so evident does it appear; but, thank heaven, he is not. He is got out, and on examination it is found that he only has sustained a nervous shock, while a small bone in his shoulder is broken.

I go to Father M'Carthy, Forty-second Street, where I am to preach to-morrow. His servant, Mary Ryan, knew me at home. She was servant at the Mercy Hospital when I was chaplain there.

Sunday.—The heat was so intense that I scarcely closed my eyes all night. I was frequently forced to rise and pace about the room. Preached at 10.30 Mass, after which an old man comes round who knew me at Ballyneen long ago. I remembered him; his name was Donovan. The poor fellow was in tears the whole time he was speaking to me. Father M'Carthy, who was a spectator of the scene, was deeply moved. The day is fearfully hot. I spend the greatest portion of it with Father M'Carthy and his curate, Father Brophy.

About three o'clock I come home. At five the sky darkens, a fierce wind suddenly rises, clouds of dust rush through the streets. The people fly, anticipating a storm; gay dresses are fastest in the race. It is really fearful to look at, it is so violent, dark and sullen, and seems so to prognosticate something worse. I look through my window at the flying crowds—they laugh and shout at the fun of the thing. Such is the pride of human nature, that when we are really in distress we laugh to pretend that we are indifferent. Then begins the rain; the huge drops fall heavy, one by one. Oh, the cool sensation of the wind and rain, after the heat it is delicious.

I have to go hear a lecture to-night in Father M'Alea's church, Twenty-fifth Street. I go through the gloom, damp and desolation in the cars, into which some young women come, who have folded up in handkerchiefs their saturated skirts, and appear in their white petticoats, dripping flowers, blooming still, but blooming damp and bespattered. Father M'Alea is an old gentleman—a fine old fellow with long grey locks, and a good deal of the Nestor in his reminiscental style of conversation. He is in America for the last fifty-two years, and is always promising to revisit the land of his birth. It is not likely that he'll ever do it. The lecture is well attended.

My friend Mr. Healy comes round—he was at my sermon to-day, too, with Madamoiselle Contan. He takes me to the Grand Hotel, Broadway, where we have coffee. A young lad, perhaps 22 years old, attends us. He speaks English perfectly, and yet he is French, Dupret, born in France. Asks me do I speak Irish? I say yes. He then speaks Irish, and does it very tolerably. And yet he was never in Ireland, except for a few days, when a vessel in which he was sailing put into Sligo through stress of weather. He was quite a *litterateur*, a philological phenomenon. "I could manage the Irish very well," he said, "but the articles and prepositions bother me." Rather cool for a waiter. But this is a great country. N.B.—A cant phrase I never heard before—"Cutting up shines"—somewhat like our "running a rig," is applied best to a man who unexpectedly pursues a course of conduct for which the public are not prepared, *e.g.*, Dr. Dollinger, Père Hyacinthe, &c.

Go down this evening by previous arrangement by steamer to Huntington, L.I., in order to spend two days with Father Crowley. He comes to town just before we start, and accompanies us. I described the trip before. We enjoy the Sound immensely. The scenery exquisite. Reach his house at 6.30 p.m. Helena and Caroline are delighted to see me. They have tea ready, after which we all sit on hammocks fixed to the trees outside the house, and loll there in the moonshine, enjoying the cool, refreshing air, and charmed with the rural silence and solitude, compared with the din and bustle of New York. We sang old songs, and my memory, with those two ladies beside me, goes back to that pleasantest episode in my life, the days I spent at Coolmountain.

May 31st.—Rain, heavy rain, but very refreshing, and most welcome to the parched earth, which swallows it up as quickly as it falls. A young gentleman, George C. O'Donohoe, calls; he is from Brooklyn, he lounges about with us the whole day. We were to have a day's fishing, but the rain has put a stop to it.

Rev. Dr. Farrelly, of Jamaica, L.I., calls and dines, so does Augustus O'Donohoe, brother of George aforesaid. The rain lightens, but it scarcely ceases all through the day, so that we can only lounge about. A little variety is caused by the fact, as announced in the papers, that in the village to-day, at 1 p.m., a gentleman (Mr. Rocknell), a celebrated horse-tamer or trainer, is to appear and illustrate his science, with a view to getting pupils at five dollars a head. He was to take out restive, unmanageable horses and make them "cut up all sort o' shines" in the public street. I doubted it, having come to the conclusion lately that there is nothing at all wonderful in the world; wonders exist only in man's imagination. Like the hero of the comedy, "*L'Homme Blasé,*" I have tried everything, and "there's nothing in it." But we go down to the village. There is a crowd, and a man is haranguing them from a carriage, to which a pair of horses are attached. It appears he had just driven those horses "all round," and that he made them do all kinds of obediences. But the burden of his speech is not only that he can train any horse, but that he can teach others to do the same; let them come, then, and put down their names; the charge is only five dollars. He has a bit here—a bit mounted by himself—"the bit of bits," as he modestly called it, and also a book on the horse, written by himself. The bit and book can be had for *two dollars*. In all this there seemed a good deal of the charlatan. When a number of names had been booked he commenced another performance. This consisted in bringing forth a pure milk-white steed, his own property, and placing him in a ring formed of a rope held by the people all round. This steed he made do all kinds of things—walk, dance, snort, yawn, fetch a handkerchief, nod assent, smile with satisfaction, and frown with fury—point its forefoot or hindfoot as ordered, put out its tongue, and do a variety of other things. It was curious and amusing, but not wonderful, as I have seen horses do exactly the same in a circus. Another horse he produced, and a greyhound. The latter he made jump on the horse's back, and stand or sit while the horse galloped round. Nothing very wonderful here, except that the poor dog seemed to be in agony between the fear of the whip on the one hand, and the fear of a toss on the other. But no savage horse was experimented on, no volunteer brute. I only beheld a piece of task-work, done, I suppose, the same way every day in the year by the same performer; yet it was a diversion to us in a small village on a rainy day.

June 1st.—The fun is all over and depression succeeds.

We rise sleepy at five—breakfast in moody silence—bid farewell—go off in a tumble-down old stage—get on board the steamer. The morning is misty, but it soon brightens up, and reveals the glories of the scenery. We pass through Hell Gate, which, by the way, is about being blasted, and reach the city about 9.30 o'clock. Spent the evening with a Mr. O'Mahony, of Clinton Avenue, Brooklyn. Mr. O'Mahony is a Cork man, and I was informed that he wished to know me, and give me a contribution for the Cork Cathedral. I found him and his wife living in a magnificent house in a fashionable quarter—a house splendidly and elegantly furnished. Why will people speak with contempt of the Irish? They only want fair play for the exercise of their talents and industry. If they gain wealth they know how to purchase with it the rational enjoyments of life, and to adapt themselves to an exalted position as well as people of any other nationality of the world. Mr. O'Mahony has a splendid library, and if I am to judge by his conversation, he makes good use of it. He thought I might be induced to remain for the night, and proposed that we should go across to Mr. M'Conville's, a friend over the way, who keeps a billiard table. But I compromised matters; I said I would come to-morrow evening, and that we could play billiards as long as we pleased, and that I would sleep at the Chateau O'Mahony.

June 2nd.—Very warm day. I divert myself writing a description of the "Cork River," which I shall probably have published in one of the papers here. In the evening I go to Brooklyn to Mr. O'Mahony and sup with him and Mrs. O'Mahony. At 8 o'clock we go across to Mr. M'Conville's. Mr. M'Conville is a self-made Irishman, very wealthy, living in a palatial residence on Clinton Avenue. A smart man, as is evinced by his success in life. Here are a Mr. O'Rorke and a Mr. Hennessy, the latter a Cork man, both well to do in the world. Mr. Hennessy is a Commissioner of Education. We play billiards. The game is different from the English. There are four balls and no side pockets. To pocket yourself scores against you. What we call a "Cannon," they call a "Carvin." What we call a "Fluke," they call a "Scratch." The general principle of the game, however, is the same as ours. I have been struck on more occasions than this by the temperance of those with whom I came in contact. Here abstinence seems to be the rule, or if not abstinence, at least moderation. The cigar appears to be the common luxury. I am happy to say that amongst the clergy, as far as my experience goes, temperance appears to be the rule. Indeed, after one year I am able to say that I have not met in society any gentleman, lay or clerical, the worse for drink. The impressions on this matter which I had before coming here have been erased. Calumny and prejudice injure countries as well as individuals.

N.B.—Nothing is more remarkable in this country than the literary mediocrity of the newspapers. Perhaps the least entitled to respect is the leading journal, the *Herald*. In its articles and in its correspondence—in fact all through it—there is a coarseness, a vulgarity, a cant, a recklessness of style, debasing to literature. This remark applies more or less to the other organs, especially the smaller ones, such as the *Sun*, *Star* and *Globe*. In all there is a disposition to treat all kinds of subjects, even the most grave and solemn, in a spirit of levity—every feeling is sacrificed for a joke. In treating matters of the most serious nature, there is a play on words. The writer never ascends to dignity, or if he does, he jumps down again into absurdity. Even when enforcing morality he appears to scoff at it, thus, the *Herald*, while correcting those who ignore eternal punishment, describes it as "perpetual roasting," clearly proving that he ridicules the idea which he pretends to preach. In this general condemnation of the Press literature of New York, I do not include the *Times*, *Tribune* or (very pointedly) the *World*. The last mentioned paper is slightly tainted with the common vice, but not much. The *Times* and *Tribune* are dignified. But in almost all is one patent vulgarity, and that is a desire for alliteration in headings. I subjoin a few headings of this kind— "Personal Prattle," "Literary Lispings," "Cream of the Courts," "Feminine Fancies," "Poor Paris," "Suburban Scraps," "Brooklyn Briefs," "Literary Locals," "Lectures," &c., and in allusion to a terrible mine accident, in which some twenty lives were lost, at a place called Pittston, "Pittston Pitt." I shall note down others as I go along. Enough for the present.

"Shining," *i.e.*, shoe-blacking, is not a bad business. One of those boys tell me they earn about two dollars a day. A number of them swarm around our hotel all day, way laying the guests as they come in or out, and shouting "Shine?" Their costume is by no means elegant, and is of peculiar frailty, generally weakest at the knees, and cleanliness is no characteristic of the craft. There seems to exist a strong spirit of fraternity amongst them, as is evinced by mutual accommodation of trade materials, and also, strange as it may sound, by an exchange of books and newspapers. But I very much fear that the class of literature to which those hangers on of Crispin devote themselves, is not of a very *recherché* or improving character, and that it dwells more on the exploits of "Jack Sheppard" and "Captain Kidd," than those of "Julius Cæsar" or "Rollo, the Dane." However, a love of reading is commendable in the shoeblack, and the boy who "shined" me this morning was amused when I reminded him, in reference to the book he had just laid aside, that "he was equally diligent in polishing his own intellect as he was in brightening the understandings of mankind." All the glory and pride of his profession was awakened in him. He felt that to be a shoe-black was indeed to be something, and that what had been said of him could not have been applied without the very bitterest sarcasm to Ulysses S. Grant, President though he is of the United States.

June 13th.—Drove in a carriage and "double team" with Father Mooney, to Jerome Park, to the races, a distance from town of some twelve miles. The day was fine, but the wind made the dust unpleasant. We passed by the great new cathedral which I had not seen for a year; it is advancing rapidly, and is truly magnificent—white marble—but it appears to me to be too short—350 feet long. It will be a splendid church, but I do not see how it can ever be called a grand cathedral, comparing it with those of Europe. We drove through the Central Park, which is truly grand—everything looked so fresh and bright to me who had not had a drive for several months. There was a great lack of enthusiasm at these races, nothing like what we have at home, although in this instance the style was not trotting, but "jockey riding" and hurdle as well as flat races. The "people" were not there, but fashion was there in full fling, and on our return home the equipages that passed us by were gorgeous, many of them, while all were elegant. There was the inevitable Helmbold and his six horses, there also was the irrepressible Jim Fisk—there was the demi-monde and its attachès—boisterous, rollicking, and gaudy. The racing was poor compared with ours—the contest for precedence coming home was remarkable, fast trotters, once over " nothing in it."

Spent the evening with a family named Walter—the father Irish—came out poor—has made a fortune. The old story, he cannot see why every Irishman should not come to America. He could not live in Ireland now—would not be happy there no matter how wealthy he might be. When I tell him I could not live in America, he stares and wonders. He loves Ireland to be sure, and longs for her freedom, *et cetera*, but as a place to live in, he regards it as one might regard Labuan or Honolulu. The two things that Irish people in America have against Ireland are: first, the difficulty of making a fortune or a living there; and secondly, the grinding oppression of the law, as compared with the large freedom and equality that exist in this great continent. Equality; a very good thing, but like all other theories, sometimes awkward in practice. For example: in the Comptroller's office, are gentlemen with salaries ranging from two thousand to ten thousand dollars a year. Now these salaries enable all those gentlemen to live in a manner quite in keeping with the name of gentlemen; and I must say, having met them all, that they are equal in respectability to most persons I have met at the other side of the Atlantic. Nevertheless, the very door-keeper, a man named Reardon, addresses Mr. Lyons as "Stephen," and sometimes with the still closer familiarity of the diminutive "Steeve"—while this very evening a young shoe-black who turns in to clean the boots of the gentlemen before going home, when asked by "Major O'Rorke," another official, to clean his boots, says "Right away, I have to shine Mike's first," Mike being Mr. Michael Maloney. This is equality with a vengeance.

Charley O'Connell told me last evening that Dr. Byrne had invited him and me to the Jerome Park races for to-day. I accept the invitation. Charley meets me at 10.30, and Dr. Byrne joins us soon after. We proceed by car to Twenty-first Street, where we are introduced by Dr. Byrne to his friend Mr. Moore, and Mr. Connolly, a common friend, turns in by appointment. We proceed to the races in two open carriages with a pair of horses each—both magnificent turn-outs; Mr. Moore, Charley and I in one car, Mr. Connolly, Dr. Byrne, and two young Connellys in the other. Mr. Moore is a rich man, an Irishman, who is the first of his countrymen that sought to make a living by the manufacture of Weiss-Bier—a beverage theretofore exclusively brewed by Germans. Wherever I go to-day I see something indicating the success of my countrymen here, either in good or evil.

Rain had fallen in the morning, and the roads were in splendid condition. The Park was superb. We stopped at a restaurant *en route*, and while the horses were being refreshed, Mr. Moore pointed out three men to me, and told me the middle man was Joe Coburn (Irish), the most celebrated pugilist in America. Joe is a decent-looking fellow, and as much like a gentleman as most other "gentlemen" here. He and his companions go off in a "light wagon with a double team," or what we would call a "carriage and pair." Passing through the Park we observed the statue of Professor Morse, erected a few days ago (I should have said unveiled). Professor Morse, they say, invented the electric telegraph, and still lives, thus affording one of the rare instances of a man having a statue erected to him during his lifetime. The statue is bronze, and it was executed by an Irishman named Power. The course is reached; we go on the grand stand, where we recognise many friends, who swarm round us, and form "quite a party." The events of the day are very interesting, the horses very well bred, the racing good jockey-racing, all flat. Here again my countrymen distinguished themselves. Three Irishmen won—men with the very Hibernian names of Coffee, Kelly and Shea. Indeed whenever an Irishman's horse went out he came in the winner. Mr. Moore, whom I instructed to point out all the celebrities to me as they turned up, next directed my attention to "Reddy, the blacksmith," who might be called "the hardest case of a rowdy" in New York. Reddy is famous for many daring exploits, the last of which was the killing, in a drinking saloon, of a bigger rowdy than himself—namely, Jimmy Hagerty. The murderer was acquitted for two reasons: first, because he was acting in self-defence—the other, because "he has immense *political influence.*" Reddy is an Irishman; he is a low, square-built, hard-featured man with a white coat, Panama hat, put on recklessly, and a thick red moustache. Several fellows who owe him a grudge are watching for the opportunity of doing for him, and they will, thus saving the hangman a great deal of bother, and the public a great deal of maudlin cant.

When the races were over, the first man that started for home was Jim Fisk. Mr. Moore also pointed to me

Mr. Vanderbilt, the richest man in America. He is an old, slight gentleman, with white hair, whiskers and neckcloth, and wearing spectacles. Thus, in one day I saw the richest man in America, the first *roué*, the first pugilist, and the first rowdy. All are equally looked after, all are equally celebrated. We spent a very pleasant day. No expense was spared, and the journey was delightful, in every sense of the word.

The Archbishop was administering confirmation to-day in St. James's church, and I was invited to dinner. It was a very stylish entertainment, and was supplied by Delmonicos. The Archbishop, though apparently grave, yet has a good fund of humour in his composition, and tells very good anecdotes; but if I were a bishop, I too would be very anecdotal. It only requires to have a good supply of stories, and to get an audience. I have the stories, and if ever I become a bishop, people will listen through respect. One point only do I wish to note here. The Archbishop said that the failing population of native Americans, though often ascribed to crime, must be also attributed, in a great measure, to the effeminacy and delicacy produced in both sexes, and particularly women, by the heating of houses in winter. I have not the slightest doubt of it. He told how being on one occasion on a visit, in Paris, at the house of a vicomte, it being mid-winter, he sat at the fire, and could scarcely warm himself. He observed the two daughters of the vicomte at a distance near the window, and he invited them to share the warmth of the fire; but their noble father forbade them, saying, " There are only two fires allowed in this house at any time—one in the kitchen and one in this parlour; the latter has been prepared solely for your lordship. My sons do not need a fire, for they can warm themselves by out-door exercise. My daughters must abstain from the luxury of warmth, for they are to be the mothers of soldiers."

In Ireland, and Europe generally, bishops are addressed " My Lord," or what is equivalent to it in the other languages. Not so in America. There you say, " Yes, Bishop," " No, Archbishop," simply. Bishop M'Closkey amused us by telling how when he went to Ireland first, on meeting with a bishop, the " My Lord " stuck in his democratic throat, and could only be got up at a second attempt.

June 24*th.*—My foot being sore I remained at home through the day. In the evening my friend Healy called, and so did C. W. O'C., the latter provided with a written order for the admission of myself and friends to the balcony of the City Hall, to witness the procession of the Saengerbund. And what is the Saengerbund? The Germans we know are proverbially a musical people, and in America there are almost in all important cities affiliated choral societies leagued in a band of union, and assuming the name of the Saengerbund. The coming week there is to be a great Saengerfest, and this evening the proceedings are to be opened. The representatives of the various choral societies of this continent have arrived, and have arranged to march 2,000 strong before the City Hall at 8 o'clock, when they will be received and welcomed by the mayor. On that occasion there is to be a grand choral performance in the open air by the 2,000 members of the Saengerbund, and it is to witness this spectacle, and to hear this magnificent concert that I and my friends have resolved. The various houses in New York where Germans reside have been made festive with innumerable flags and filial decorations arranged with that promptitude and taste in which the children of the Fatherland are justly distinguished at home and abroad. From several windows banners are hung out with such inscriptions as "Willkommen, Sängerbrüder," &c., &c.

The citizens generally of every nationality, except the French, laud the enterprise, the taste, the patriotism, and peacefulness of the German character. They are a very law-abiding people, and the mingled flags of Germany and America flaunting from their windows and housetops attest their blended feelings of patriotic attachment to the country they have relinquished, and to that which they have adopted. It is to be regretted that the Irish do not emulate their spirits of unanimity in national undertakings. Were they to do so, there is no power in America that could resist their influence, but where most of their enthusiasm should be aroused they sink into apathy, or only make a show that reveals their weakness, when it might show forth their magnitude and strength.

About 8 o'clock we three proceed to the City Hall, where only a very select few are admitted, but our order has a talismanic influence on the sturdy janitor. We are ushered upstairs to a splendid suite of apartments where I had been last year—large rooms ornamented with the pictures of America's great men. Here is arranged a supper table, and the "big bugs" gradually arrive. From the prevalence of the German tongue, I know that few except Germans are present. But Mayor Hall recognises me, and invites me to drink some Rheinwein, which I do. He and I hobnob, much to the surprise of the by-standers. I introduce O'Connell and

Healy to His Worship—I should have said "His Honor." The sound of instrumental music reminds us that the fraternity of song are mustering their forces below. Through an open window we enter on the balcony overlooking the City Hall Park (what a misnomer is "park," by the way). It is misting slightly, but the rain does not damp the spirits of the irrepressible "Dutchman" (a name given to all here who have any connection with Teutonism). On the balcony a gentleman makes a calcium light which illumines the whole park. 2,000 Chinese lanterns hanging from poles are held in the hands of the Sängerbünd. Below the Mayor and other gentlemen stand on an improvised dais with scarlet carpet and swathed in banners, all tastefully illumined with Chinese lanterns. Ten thousand people must be around, for it is a rare attraction. The rain increases. My friend, Healy, remarks that, "Heretofore in America the rain was RARE, but now it *was overdone.*" I told him that his wit must be boiling over. A sketcher from an illustrated paper was taking down the scene from a spot near us. "But *l'homme propose et Dieu dispose.*" Down faster and faster came the rain—the lightning flashed, and the thunder rolled, and the huge drops fell heavier and heavier. At last it descended with such fury that no human enthusiasm could withstand it. Ten minutes produced the most wonderful change in the scene. Where thousands of lights gleamed, now all was darkness, and the Chinese lanterns lay in saturated fragments on the ground. Where ten thousand people, men and women, stood in breathless expectation of festive song, now not a trace of humanity was visible. Only a huge cannon pealed forth its thunder, and lit up the darkness with its sudden flashes. Men, women, light and song—all melted away, like the feverish phantoms of a dream, like the "baseless fabric of a vision."

Sunday, June 25th.—Lovely day. A new church is to be consecrated to-day by the Archbishop, at Mott Haven, on the Harlem River. The curate of Mott Haven at present is the Rev. B. ——, whose father taught him and me Latin grammar together much more than "twenty golden years ago." Twenty-two years have elapsed since I met him. I resolved to fulfil the romantic desire of seeing him to-day. By arrangement I call on Mr. Healy at his lodgings, Fifth Avenue, and proceed with him to Mott Haven. This place is reached many ways, but we go by the Third Avenue cars, and reach Harlem on one side of the river. We cross the Harlem bridge on foot, and find ourselves at Mott Haven. We reach the house of the pastor, Father Hughes, and I soon catch sight of B——. I recognise him at once, and ask, "Did you ever see me before?" He replies rather gruffly that he does not know. I tell him who I am, and the announcement does not seem to move him much. In a word, it seemed to make no difference to him whether I was an utter stranger or an old school-fellow; but I reposed in the consciousness of having gratified a worthy feeling of my own.

The Americans are a great paper-reading people. "What paper in New York has the largest circulation?" asked somebody. "Of course *The Sun*—it goes round the earth every twenty-four hours—the largest circulation in the world." Newspaper gentlemen have a great many cant phrases. "Piling up the agonies" means heaping Pelion on Ossa, of horrible description.

June 27th.—Lovely morning, charming country. We

drive, *i.e.*, Father Crowley, Charley, "Gus" and I, in two carriages, to a place called Westhills, the highest point in Long Island, and most probably the first American land I ever saw. It commands a splendid view, reaching from the Connecticut shore all round the Atlantic, as far as the "palisades" of the Hudson. The scenery at our feet of the surrounding country is very beautiful. Indeed Huntington has been styled the "Garden of Long Island." Splendid cedars grow quite commonly here, even along the road-ways, also locusts, a tree somewhat resembling acacia, wild cherry trees, pines, oaks, &c. There is said to be a tulip tree here seven feet in diameter. I have not seen it, and shall be dubious till I do. Indian corn is cultivated all round, and the ripe fields of maize resemble our full grown wheat crop. The roads might be better—dusty in summer, slushy in winter. The land is mostly undulating, and there is a great deal of wood. The country villas are all beautiful. No two styles are alike, and there is a freshness and gaiety about them, and such an array of flowers, as indicates extreme neatness and taste. They look charming on the slopes of the landscape, lawn before and protecting fields behind. There is no poverty here, no begging. The farmers all own their land in fee. There is a solitary policeman in the town. The nigger population is large. There is an air of comfort everywhere.

June 30*th*.—Am much better, though not quite well. Have a visit from C. W. O'C. He speaks of a friend, Major Haverty, who informed him that of the book-buying portion of the public six-tenths are Cork people. This is creditable to the literary taste of my fellow citizens. Charley takes me out and makes me accept a present of a pair of French crystal spectacles, purchased in Broadway for six dollars. They are excellent glasses. He and I soon afterwards experienced an attempt at cheating us, which fortunately proved unsuccessful. Charley was thinking of buying a Panama hat. Now Panama hats are very expensive, but there are cheap ones, too, and an uninitiated purchaser does not well see the difference. We went into a shop whose speciality was straw hats. Charley took up a Panama.

"What is the price?" he asked.

"Twenty dollars," was the reply.

The young man who made the answer then disappeared, and another man came on the scene, probably the "boss" of the establishment.

"Well, sir, don't that hat suit you?"

"It is too dear," says Charley.

"Dear!" he cried. "Sir, I can give you that hat for four dollars less than any other man can give it."

"That may be," says Charley, "but I can't afford to give twenty dollars for it."

"Twenty dollars?" said the man. "Why, sir, the price is only six dollars." We then informed the man that the other had demanded twenty.

"Oh," cried this one, "he doesn't know anything about it."

We sought the first to confront him with the second, but he was not to be found. We then clearly saw that the first fellow had tried a swindle on our ignorance and credulity, and the second seeing the failure of the scheme was glad to sell the hat at its real value. But Charley was disgusted, and we made no investment then.

I went this evening with Mr. Williams, whom I had met

at Mr. Barry's last Sunday evening. Mr. Barry also was with us, and another young gentleman, an Englishman, named Anderson. We dined at the table d'hôte. It was a boarding-house. What nuisances those boarding-houses are. The company are mixed — ladies and gentlemen — all strangers to each other, while the lady of the house presides and carves the joint or joints as the case may be. Silence for the most part prevails. In the present instance, however, it was rudely broken by a gentleman with a very Yankee air and voice, crying out to the servant, "Don't remove that plate. You should know better. When a gentleman has dined he lays the knife and fork parallel on his plate. Mine were not parallel, but at a very obtuse angle. Again" (pointing to his tea-cup) " when I have done with my tea I place the spoon in the saucer; when not done I leave it in the cup." These words, uttered with great force and precision, made us all smile. He soon left the table, and we all fell a-chatting like old familiar friends. I fancy that on occasions of such miscellaneous gatherings at table—whether in boarding-houses or hotels—any man who would set everyone talking would be not only clever, but a very benevolent member of society, for everyone is anxious that the spell should be broken, but nobody knows how to break it.

After dinner we four sat and had cigars on a piazza. It was agreed that America was before England, nay Europe, in many things, particularly hotels—the fires department—peculiar made-up drinks—enterprise of all kinds—employing men on their merits and not on the recommendation of friends " interest" as it is called—insurances (every American insures his property, one third part of Englishmen don't).

Newspapers—at least the *Herald*, which, despite an opinion I have elsewhere expressed, is superior to the London *Times* in the immense machinery by which it is worked, and in every other respect, except the material, paper, and the elegance of style.

A number of young "gentlemen" are here, lately come out from Cork looking for employment. Of five that I know, one only succeeded, the rest are several weeks here and can get absolutely nothing to do. What a mistake those young men's parents make; they have educated their children for the professions; the professions are over-stocked; the superfluity come out here. They have education—it is not wanted. What is wanted here is *work*. These young men are now ready to do any kind of work in order to keep body and soul together. Here work is honourable—at home it is degrading. How absurd. Try to enforce these lessons at home.

To-day I leave by steamer at 3.50 for Haverstraw on the Hudson. Lovely evening—magnificent scenery—wide river, at one side perpendicular cliffs, called the palisades; at the other sloping wooded lawns with gorgeous residences varying ever in style—all elegant, many palatial. Mount St. Vincent is a splendid red-brick Convent of Mercy, immense in length, elegant in style, charming situation over the river. In front of it is a stone castle belonging to the nuns, built by Edwin Forrest the great actor, for his residence, but given by him to the nuns. We passed Yonkers, a lovely town on the river; splendid country seats all round—Tarrytown the same—Irvington, close to which is the house of Washington Irving—Sing-Sing, the place of the great State Prison of New York. Then came Haverstraw—a great brick-making place, at the foot of very steep wooded cliffs. Lovely country all around. Warren Village is the real name of the town; Haverstraw is the name of the "ploughland," one-fourth of Rockland County. Close by is Rockland Lake, where the choicest ice is found for the use of the New Yorkers. The village, however is now called Haverstraw--the greatest brick-making place in the State.

July 23rd.—George, Gus, and I go on board a sloop laden with bricks, and cross Long Island Sound, thirty-five miles, to Bridgeport. The voyage with a good breeze would only take three hours, but there is no wind, and so we take very much longer. Bridgeport is a nice town. The surburbs are very beautiful. It is the birthplace of Tom Thumb, whose family, excepting himself, were all of more than the average size. The celebrated Barnum lives here, when he is at home, which is seldom. One of the finest houses in the suburbs here is that of Wilson or Wheeler, I cannot say which, one of the great sewing-machine firm. The great charm of the villas here is the wonderful variety of their styles, as well as their extraordinary beauty of design. They are mostly frame houses, and their beauty is much enhanced by abundant foliage and well-kept gardens.

At ten o'clock we leave by the Nangatuck railroad for Waterbury, of which my old friend and class-mate, Tom Hendricken, now "Doctor," is pastor. The distance from Bridgeport is eighty-six miles—scenery pretty, hills and rivers; several villages and small towns on the way. Dr. Hendricken is not at home. Hard, as I have not seen him for eighteen years. He is on retreat at Worcester; but his servant treats us with a hospitality that augurs well for his own. Waterbury is a manufacturing town, with 14,000 inhabitants.

We go off again by rail, thirty-six miles, for Newhaven, one of the finest cities of New England, on the Sound. It is much unlike American cities generally—a good deal of brick and stone, somewhat like an English town. Here is our hotel, the Newhaven Hotel, a very fine one, and right before it, buried in trees, and surrounded by grass plots, is Yale College, one of the most celebrated in all America. We spend a pleasant evening.

July 26*th.*—After breakfast we walk through the grounds of Yale College, a large aggregate of detached buildings, without any pretensions to style. It was vacation, and there was nothing to be seen. We hire a carriage, and drive around for two hours; but it is wet, and we have to change from a landau to a brougham. The scenery of the suburbs is like that of Bridgeport—very beautiful; but the houses are more frequently of stone than of wood. No place looks well in rain, and so with Newhaven. It was dreary and damp, but evidently a wealthy and important city.

At 5.45 we go off by rail to Hartford, the chief city of Connecticut, distance also thirty-six miles, where we arrive by express in one hour. We stroll through the town, and admire it very much; but we are weary and *ennuyés*, and so we retire early.

July 27*th.*—Breakfast at 8.30, after which we hire an open carriage, and drive for some hours all through and around Hartford. The same characteristics of scenery as elsewhere. Charming suburbs, fine villas, many trees, and perfect horticulture. We see the Deaf and Dumb Asylum, the Lunatic Asylum, and Trinity College, and the magnificent residence of Colt, whose name is associated with the famous revolvers. This is one of the finest houses I have seen in this country, charmingly situated, with splendid scenery all around—the Connecticut River beneath, and the ground adjacent laid out in the very highest style of artistic taste. We also see Colt's Revolver Factory, a huge pile of buildings, where hundreds of men are employed. In the neighbourhood, and quite in the country, is one of the loveliest little Gothic churches I ever saw, built of brown stone. It was built out of the private purse of Mrs. Holt, at a cost of 250,000 dollars. Evidently no expense was spared on the exterior, and the driver assured us that the interior was beyond all conception, magnificent. Strange, that money made by the manufacture of instruments for taking human life should be devoted to the erection of an edifice intended to promote the glory of God!

After a very pleasant drive we take the train back to Bridgeport. Here we stop at the Atlantic Hotel. We expected to find the sloop preparing for a return trip to Huntington, but there was no sign of it.

July 28th.—Up early; we strained our eyes looking for the sloop, but there was no sloop. We were therefore obliged to come to New York (fifty-three miles) by train. This evening coming down in the boat I had a good specimen of the democracy of this country. A young nigger boy, about fourteen years old, employed by the ship, was going around, crying out "ice cream," at ten cents a plate. He asked me would I have some, but I said "no; but there is a man below with peaches. Would you, like a good boy, fetch me up a quart of them?" He looked, smiled, and coolly replied:

"You are poor enough to be your own servant."

Politeness is a rare thing to find in America. On

another occasion in the same boat, a drunken man came and sat beside me. He tried to draw me into conversation, but I said, "Now, my dear friend, I am not disposed to talk. Would you kindly go and sit somewhere else?"

"This is a free country," he replied.

"Then," said I, "I shall avail myself of that freedom, and I shall sit elsewhere."

There is a nice letter from Rev. Dr. Hendricken, regretting his absence on the day I called, and expressing the warmest affection for his old friend and class-mate. A few days afterwards comes a newspaper in which it is stated that the State of Connecticut is to be severed from that of Rhode Island, with which it has been hitherto united as part of one diocese, and become a distinct diocese in itself, with Dr. McFarland as bishop, and that of the three names which have been sent off to the Pope for the new episcopate of Rhode Island, Dr. Hendricken stands first.

July 29th and following days were spent in one dull monotony, so that it is quite impossible for me to adhere any longer, at least for the present, to the resolution I formed at the beginning of the year, and to which I have thus far steadily adhered, of noting down specially the events of every day. Where there are no events there is nothing to record. The weather is intensely hot. I can only read, write, drive, lounge, bathe, and keep off musquitoes and flies which are a horrible bore. I have got a letter from my bishop, in which he hints that he wishes me to desist from going to "Frisco" until he hears from his brother to whom he has written on the subject. I have been shocked on reading in the *Examiner* of the death of my friend, Mr.

Eugene Shine, who gave me an entertainment last year at the St. Nicholas Hotel. R.I.P.

August 15th.—A great clam-bake takes place to-day on the shore about a mile from Huntington. And what is a clam-bake? Well, there is a small fish, called a clam, of which I have already spoken, and it seems to be considered by Americans a great delicacy. On certain occasions, duly advertised, the public assemble at a certain spot, generally picturesque, where thousands of clams are previously provided by persons who make the matter a pecuniary speculation. Those thousands of clams are gathered into one immense heap, under which wood has been piled, and they are covered over with rods, twigs, and branches of trees. The wood is set fire to, and the clams are roasted. The public, which at a clam-bake as at other gatherings, is miscellaneous, embracing every sex, age, and condition, assemble and spend the day. The whole thing assumes a holiday aspect. Families bring their basket with cold provisions, not daring to trust to the monotonous and precarious clam. Long tables are arranged on the grounds from which the speculators aforesaid vend various descriptions of potation, generally mild; proceeding in strength from the vapidity of ginger-pop to the very resistible force of Lager bier. The performance is varied by several concerted and casual operations, the latter left to the humour of the crowd, and jolly or otherwise, according to circumstances. The Huntington Clam-bake was looked forward to as one of the great annual events of the place, an event so important that the local papers—the *Suffolk (Co.) Bulletin* and the *Huntington Independent* [?]—made allusion to its forthcoming some weeks before the event, and intensified allusion in the direct ratio of its proximity. In the issue immediately preceding the great event, the eye of the reader wandered down column after column of the paper, and his eagerness for something new was ever disappointed by ingeniously varied allusions to the great clam-bake of the 15th. Thus: "Prepare, prepare—the day is at hand. At Bouton's Point, on the 15th comes off the great Clam-bake." Again, "The event of the period—the great Clam-bake of the 15th. Secure your tickets in time; only one dollar entrance to the grounds. See Mr. Atkins at once." "What!" you exclaim, as your eye runs down the columns of the paper, "is it nothing but clam-bake?" You turn over to the third page or to the fourth as caprice suggests, and while you peruse an account of the meeting of some local board, or amuse yourself amongst literary excerpts from standard periodicals of the day, your eye is suddenly arrested by a short interposed paragraph about "St. Clambake, whose festival falls on the 15th, and which is to be celebrated at Bouton's Point." Where every visitor is expected to "*offishiate*" on that *auspicious* occasion, etc.; or "Beauties of Huntington! They will be all at the Clam-bake on Tuesday." "Terpsichore! who will refuse to witness thy performances on Tuesday next at the great Huntington Clam-bake!" and thus *ad* the *infinitum* of the fatigued imagination of a newspaper editor who is a great and particular friend of Mr. Atkins, and the party Mr. Atkins represents. Of course I must go to the Clam-bake—one of "our institootions."

CHAPTER XII.

A TRIP IN LEATHERSTOCKING'S LAND.

August 17*th*.—I received a letter yesterday from Sarah McAuliffe, dated Catskill, saying that she and party, *i.e.*, Mrs. Attridge and John, were about to leave for Cooperstown, the residence of Father Devitt, their particular friend with whom they would spend some days, and expressing a hope that I would be able to join them there. Accordingly this morning I rise early and proceed by stage to the pier (they call a pier a "dock" in America), distant about three miles. Here I take the steamboat, the "O. R. Martin," and accomplish 35 miles more of the journey, reaching New York at 9.30 a.m. Thence I proceed to Albany by express rail, leaving at 10.30 and reaching at 2.45, distance 142 miles. The route lay along the Hudson river, whose beauties I am never tired of admiring. From Albany I proceed by "cars" to Cooperstown, distant 91 miles, through the Susquehannah Valley, a region of great loveliness, embracing every feature of scenic beauty—undulating grounds, vast tracts of foliage, smiling well cultivated fields, now "rich with golden grain." The spiral river now so tiny that it only "bickers down the valley," now spreading into copious volume, while at intervals of every seven or eight miles, some charming village, such as Richardville, decorates the scene, reposing in the valley beneath, and from its white walled houses throwing back the reflected brightness of the August sun. This railroad extends from Albany to Binghampton, but at a certain junction I deflect from Cooperstown, distant 16 miles. I reach the town just about twelve hours after I had left Huntington, having traversed in that space of time by land and water a distance of 271 miles, and accomplished it perfectly at my ease, either inhaling the fresh morning breeze from the deck of a steamboat, or lounging on the luxurious cushions of a Pullman's Palace Car. On arriving, the porter of the "Cooper House," the great hotel of Cooperstown, accosts me, and finding what I wanted he, with that genuine courtesy so peculiar to an Irishman when dealing with a priest, undertakes to conduct me to Father Devitt's house, but requests that meanwhile I would stay for a few moments at the hotel while he was superintending the stowing away of some luggage just arrived. I assent. The hotel is close by, and I sit on a sofa in the large hall. Here is unusual bustle, as if some great festive event were coming off. The sofa of which I speak stood in the midst of a long broad corridor running the whole length of the hotel, and confronting a large square hall which forms the entrance. The floor of the corridor is carpeted and the walls all around are adorned with pictures. Into the corridor several doors open, through which are constantly emerging groups of ladies and gentlemen, all attired in ball costume, while the sounds of soft music are heard not far off. The gay groups parade up and down the corridor, chatting, laughing, and displaying their bright plumage in the glaring light of many lamps and chandeliers, while some fascinating damsels decoy their beaux to a table in the hall where are spread for sale a vast variety of bouquets (always pronounced "boquéts," accent on second syllable), "dearly bought for ladies." I fancy a great ball is about to go forward, for in addition to the ladies and gentlemen, groups of children, boys and girls, very gaily dressed, play and run around, making the air still more musical by their shouts and ringing laughter. It is a bright scene, and one which, though no participator in its enjoyment, I can heartily admire, for why should we not be happy while we may? and why not bask in the sunshine of pleasure, and languish in the perfume of sweet flowers as long as the pleasure is innocent and as long as the sweet flowers bloom?

I rise and view the pictures on the walls. Here is a splendid photograph of an old gentleman with very regular well-defined features, an eye of wonderful sharpness, and a forehead worthy of a Plato. Who is he? I cannot help inquiring, and find that he is William Cullen Bryant, the celebrated living American poet. Here are portraits of others, even of less note than Bryant, probably well known to the visitors of the Cooper House, but as far as my experience goes, undistinguished in the annals of world-wide fame. The pictures of scenery are very beautiful—one is "Leatherstocking's Cave," another "Leatherstocking Falls," a third "Cooper's Monument," a fourth "Otsego Lake," etcetera.

I find that I am in a region of great natural beauty, whose created charms are rendered still more bewitching by the vivid imagination and the stirring romances of James Fennimore Cooper, with whose name and whose works we have been familiar from our earliest boyhood. More we shall see as we go on; but here is the porter now done his work, who comes to conduct me to Father Devitt's house. We walk while he takes my valise on his shoulder. It is nearly quite dark, but just as we pass under the gable of the hotel a light streams out through the windows, and I see in its glare a party of ladies and gentlemen passing close by me. One gentleman appears to be a priest, by his costume. I say to myself that Father Devitt cannot be far off. I see another gentleman of similar appearance. Then comes a lady who might pass for Mrs. Attridge, but I am not sure of her. At length comes another lady, there is no mistaking this one: it is Sarah. "Hallo," I cry. They all turn round and seem surprised and confounded. John Attridge comes over to me and exclaims, "By Jove, 'tis Father Buckley!" I will not attempt to picture the astonishment of the whole party, who never dreamed of me at the moment, and to whom I appeared as an apparition suddenly dropped from heaven, or elsewhere. The air was filled with their exclamations of surprise and delight, but when I informed them of the long journey I had made in that one day, they regarded me as some great general of old might have been regarded, who had achieved a forced march with extraordinary activity, and stood at the enemy's gates when they deemed him hundreds of miles away. We go back to Father Devitt's house, and spend a pleasant evening. I should have mentioned that the porter told me that the festive proceedings at the Cooper House were nothing special this evening, but that almost every evening there was a "hop" of some kind or other.

August 18*th.*—After breakfast we all proceeded on foot to the lake Otsego, which I humorously dubbed "Hot Sago." Here we take a yacht and go forth for a day's sailing. The wind is pretty high, and our helmsman is a young lad named Joe, who is on a visit with Father Devitt. I do not feel comfortable at the idea of entrusting our lives to the care of so very youthful a pilot, although he has acquired much experience of boating off the Coast of Staten Island as Father Devitt informs me. Nevertheless we set sail, and are prepared for the consequence, or rather do not calculate too nervously on them. A lovely lake is this Otsego, nine miles long, by an average of three miles broad, the water so green that one might fancy it was rather salt or that it reflected the vernal hue of the surrounding foliage, for foliage abounds on every side. On one hand, the left, the land slopes upwards gently from the lake, and is mostly laid out in demesne from the midst of which peep out charming houses fantastically shaped, picturesque country residences of city millionaires or local magnates, embedded in leafy solitudes. On the other hand, the land rises all along into the attitude of a hill or mountain, and is one vast range of forest, reminding me of the wooded Tornies that spring from and frown down upon the lovely Loch Lene, the lower lake of Killarney. At one point of this mountainous wooded range we discern the necropolis of Cooperstown, the city of the dead, indicated by the white tombstones looking down upon us from amidst the surrounding trees ; and in the midst of our pleasure, like the page behind the king's triumphal car in the Roman procession of old, reminding us that we are mortal. As we sail gaily before the brisk breeze and our view of the scene is enlarged, we see hills rise behind hills in the distance ; eminences robed in the "forest primeval," whither, doubtless the foot of man has not yet reached. A gay little steamer sounds forth its shrill whistle from the pier, warning the world that "it" is about to start for the remotest point of the lake, and awakening the thousand slumbering echoes of the mountains. As she steams past us we perceive that her name inscribed on the paddle-box is "Natty Bumppo," and that she is called after one of Cooper's celebrated heroes of romance. Everything breathes of Cooper in this romantic region. Amongst the monuments in the cemetery we distinguish the marble pillar raised to his memory by public subscription, and further on is the precipitous frontage of rock beneath which is "Leatherstocking's Cave," and to which tourists ascend by a wooden staircase constructed for the purpose.

But the wind grows stronger and stronger as we reach the centre of the lake, and the waves rise, and the boat scuds on like a bird, and her rudder indicates, by its rushing noise in the water, that we are careering at a tremendous rate. We deem it imprudent to go farther, lest the gale may increase or the direction of the wind change, and for my part, I do not feel comfortable in the hands of the young pilot, "Joe," who seems somewhat disconcerted at the responsibility which the increasing storm has placed on his shoulders. By general consent we turn, but the sail flapping in the wind, and the frequent lurching of the boat in the trough of the waves, fill us all with alarm. It is pretty clear that Joe is not equal to the occasion. The ladies screamed, and I confess I felt miserable. Some minutes of this terrible apprehension passed, and we heeded not the spray rushing over the gunwale, deluging the boat and drenching us thoroughly. At length we get all right, and steer for the nearest point of land, which fortunately we reach in safety. We bathe, and dine, and lounge about on the grass, and in the sunshine, in sheltered spots where no breeze blows, and beguile the time in a thousand ways, but chiefly in talking of the long, long past, on the home of our birth, and most of all—for that is what now strikes us most —on the lovely scenery of Lake Otsego. Some few hours after we prepare to return. The wind has gone down, and we can scarcely advance a yard. We tack, but make no headway. We then take the oars, and get on slowly, for the boat is large, and the oars are small. Thus the evening creeps on, and we are within two miles of the shore. Suddenly a fresh gale springs up behind us, the sail is set, and in five minutes we reach the pier.

August 17th.—The weather is very beautiful, and we are tempted to go again upon the lake. The temperature here is very mild. Cooperstown is situated at a height of 1,200 feet above the level of the sea, which makes it constantly cool, while the refreshing breeze from the lake adds its quota of mildness to the air. It is needless to say that the town is called after the Cooper family—not, however, after the novelist, but his father, Judge Cooper, who came and settled here in the year 1785. Since that time eighty-six years have elapsed, and yet the town cannot boast of more than 2,000 inhabitants; and yet there are several hotels, but they are unoccupied except in summer, when thousands of fashionable visitors throng to enjoy the luxuries which Nature has here scattered around with so profuse a hand. Judge Cooper was an important personage in his day. He came here from Burlington, in New Jersey, in the capacity of Chief Magistrate, and owner of property around the lake. On his arrival here, in the double capacity of judge and landlord, in the year mentioned, the inhabitants of the little village, thirty-five in number, came forth to welcome "the lord of the manor," and paid him that *quasi* feudal homage which has since grown not obsolete, but odious even to the memory of America's fierce Democracy. Here Judge Cooper was visited by George Washington in 1789, and in 1795 by another distinguished hero of that age—no other than the famous Prince Talleyrand. By what strange impulse of the mind does one indulge in a dreamy pleasure standing on the spot and gazing on the scenes where the great men of the past stood and gazed as we do? I know not; but this pleasure I felt as I stood on the borders of Otsego Lake, and fancied that, perhaps, on this very foot of ground George Washington developed to Judge Cooper his military schemes, or Talleyrand cracked some witticisms for his Worship's amusement.

We go on the lake and row to the spot from which tourists ascend to Lakewood Cemetery, to which I have already alluded. Here we debark and ascend. The cemetery slopes up to the very summit of the hill, and is formed by a succession of terraces, between which the tombs and graves are placed. A perfect forest of trees encloses and enshrouds it. The first monument that meets our eye is that of which I have made mention, the marble monument of Cooper. On the base are carved the words "Fennimore Cooper." The pillar is ornamented with carvings indicating the implements of savage warfare, and the top is surmounted by a statue of Chingachgook armed *cap-a-pie* with feathers and scalps, with tomahawk and mocassins. This is not the grave of Cooper; we shall visit that in due time. Having "done" the cemetery, which is one of the prettiest I ever saw, we take the boat once more, and chat over the strange saying of an enthusiastic tourist who was here lately, and who was such an admirer of Cooper and his tales that he said his greatest ambition would be to be drowned in that lake and buried in that cemetery. We row for the Susquehannah River, which rises in the lake, and pursues a course of 400 miles before it reaches the ocean. It is narrow at the source, but we admire it very much. We take to fishing for perch, and have no success for some time, until at length one of the ladies, with a scream of surprise at her own success, hauls up a finny creature about the size of a sardine. Her triumph stops there, however; and indeed I believe she had more to boast of than any of us. Thus we passed the evening, and returned brimful of the delight which is the inevitable creation of innocent enjoyment.

August 20th.—Sunday. I celebrate Mass, and preach. The congregation was small, but much larger than was anticipated, for there was to be no Mass, only for my unexpected arrival. Mass is celebrated here only every second Sunday, as Father Devitt has to attend another church at Richfield Springs, and a third at Cherry Valley, both very distant from Cooperstown. The rumour was spread abroad that Mass would be said at the usual hour on Sunday, and it must have been spread to some purpose, for about 250 people were present, and that was a good number, considering that the church would scarcely hold more than 500. The Mass was a *Missa Cantata.* The organ was played by a young widow lady, Mrs. Tilton, and the soprano, I was told, was a very pretty young lady named Tanner. I gave Benediction in the evening at eight o'clock, and preached again. About fifty Americans were present on this occasion. Father Devitt informed me they come every Sunday evening, when he preaches on something doctrinal. A large congregation were present.

August 21st.—All up at five this morning, because we

have to make a long journey to the celebrated Sharon Springs, via Cherry Valley. The latter place is fourteen miles from Cooperstown. We start at six o'clock. The morning is damp and misty, and the scenery is not very distinctly visible. Our vehicle is a barouche, and our charioteer a "coloured gemman." Our road lies over the mountain, on the right hand of the lake, by the cemetery. Through the foliage we catch glimpses of the water below. The view all along the road is very charming, but its effect was sadly marred by the persistent mist which hung all day over the landscape. This was particularly unfortunate at Cherry Valley, which, even veiled as it was, and displaying only a few glimpses of its beauty, was still delightful to behold. Our imaginations supplied the charms which our eyes were forbidden to reach. This region, which might well pass for the Happy Valley, was once the scene of an Indian raid made on the white inhabitants, who were massacred without mercy, sometime in the last century. Strange impulse of corrupt nature, which teaches it to defile with human blood and guilt the loveliest scenes in God's creation. Witness the ruthless massacre of Glencoe, perpetrated by so-called civilized men!

From Cherry Valley we go by train to Sharon, distant seven miles. On this railroad are some wooden structures running through ravines over which the train passes, and which are constructed with a reckless disregard of human life. Some day, ere long, a terrible accident will occur here, and then some more solid structure will be substituted for the present one. We reach Sharon and are at first somewhat disappointed, for there is nothing to be seen but some detached houses and a few shabby hotels. But we go on farther, or rather deeper; for it is all one long descent into a valley, buried in high wooded hills. When we have got down to the lowest flat we find ouselves in Sharon—one long street with enormous hotels on each side, and a very dirty, slushy roadway. These hotels are all supplied with piazzas, and on these piazzas lounge and sit ladies and gentlemen chatting: the latter in the invariable white hat and tweed clothes—the former in the *degagée* morning costume, or the more elegant afternoon attire, but all with the most fantastic *coiffure* which a diseased imagination could invent, or which Beauty could possibly desire for the purposes of suicide.

We stopped at the first hotel we met—the "Mansion House." No one was visible. We walked into a room—it was untenanted, and there was a most unpleasant sensation of warmth about it, as if it were artificially heated, although the month was August. We left precipitately and went further. We fixed on the United States Hotel, left our things there, and ordered dinner for one o'clock. Meanwhile we go and have a sulphur bath, previous to which we drink sulphur-water, which has, to my mind, the taste of a hard-boiled, cold, rotten egg. All these watering places are about the same—the same in America as in Europe. Sharon is a Wiesbaden, and Saratago a Homburg. Sharon, however, is nearly "played out." Its waters are losing their strength, or are surpassed in strength by others. Hence, the hotel-keepers lay it on pretty heavily, being reckless with despair.

We dine—the little morsels of chicken or beef-steak to which we were helped would remind one of the limited rations on board a famishing ship, or in a besieged city.

But what right have we to complain? We fear to order wine, and so we call for ale. "Yes, sir," says the waitress, and she fetches it after a quarter of an hour. But now, she brings on a tray about six or seven wine-glasses, which she helps around, and then proceeds to fill them with ale from what we call a tankard. Good gracious! what notion of ale have they at Sharon Springs? Do they regard it as some precious wine which must be doled out sparingly and drunk in sips, like Tokay or Marcobruner? like Assmanshauser or Liebfraumilch? We scoff at the idea and scout the wine-glasses from the table. The astonished waitress at last gathers what we want. She removes the wine-glasses and fetches bumpers. But what is the matter now? Is it ale, or muddy wine? Where is the foam, and where is the sparkle that speaks poetry to the heart, in a glass of Allsopp or Bass? Alas! we stood with our lips on the brink of liquid bliss, and as with the wretched Tantalus, the bright stream passed away for ever. But what is it? we taste and put it away again—in this region of sulphur, we wish it to the region of brimstone. It is only a coloured fluid, utterly tasteless and almost solid with infused dust. It is said that everyone must eat a peck of dust before he dies. Let him drink the ale of the United States Hotel of Sharon, and the task will be accomplished in a few weeks.

August 22nd.—A telegram comes to Father Devitt from a place called Exter, some nine or ten miles away, saying that he is wanted to see a sick young woman there. We combine business and pleasure. We start in a barouche for Richfield Springs—we can take the sick call on our return, and we must be home at six, as a couple are to be married in the church at that hour. Away with us then, along the lake for the whole nine miles of its length. There is no mist to-day, but all is bright and beautiful. What more can the eye of man desire? The placid waters of a vast lake—the lofty mountains—the dense forests—the bright sunshine of summer. Every passing cloud gives some new aspect to the scene. Some miles down from the head of the lake, we observe apparently only a few feet under water, a large grassy exposure, as if a field overflowed by a flood. This, Father Devitt tells us, is called the " Sunken Island," and there is a legend which accounts for the phenomenon. A certain Indian respected by his tribe, dwelt in times of old on this island when it projected from the lake. It was an island of peculiar beauty and fertility. He had acquired by some means a wonderful knowledge of pharmaceutics and was celebrated all round the country for his medical skill. No power could resist the power of his art. Like Lucifer, he grew haughty and defiant, he compared himself to the Deity, and proclaimed his independence of his Creator. Then came the retribution. One morning those who wandered by the lake sought for the island but could discern no trace of it. It had been swallowed up during the night, and nothing remained to tell that it ever existed, save the green grass waving, as it waves now, a few feet below the waters of the lake.

Having passed Otsego Lake we find ourselves in the open country; but even here the hand of Nature has constructed other lakes, smaller than Otsego, but very pretty. We observe three very close to each other other. At length we drive through Richfield, a bright, cheery, and fashionable village; very elegant, in the midst of a well-cultivated and picturesque country. The hotels are here on a very large

Y

scale, and with their white walls, and green blinds, and the gay costume of the ladies lounging on the piazzas, look very pretty and gay. I always speak of the *dresses* of the ladies, not of themselves; for those whom I have seen in those fashionable watering places are for the most part ugly as sin—shrivelled, parched, skinny and gaunt; and whatever other adjective you please that implies dryness and coldness. When one sees creatures like these trying to look youthful, pretty, and coquettish; with costly silks and cosmetics, and artificial hair, teeth, and for aught I know, artificial eyes and limbs, it is a shocking spectacle, and makes one almost sigh that the Darwinian theory is not true, as then those female apes would at least have remained natural. I beg pardon of all good-looking, simple, unaffected ladies for my severe strictures on any members of a sex to whose refining and civilizing influence we men owe so much.

We take a sulphur bath, first drinking the sulphur water, which is superior to that of Sharon; by which I mean it tastes more strongly of rotten egg. I pay one dollar to a man for two baths—when I come out the man hands me back the dollar:—"Sir," said he, very respectfully, "when you came I did not know who or what you were. I have since learned all about you. Please take your money back. I am proud to have a priest from the old country taking a bath here, and you are welcome to one every day on the same terms." He was an Irishman from Sligo. I find the Irish the same all over America—attached to home, to religion, and its ministers; affectionate, warm-hearted, not covetous for the dollar like their indigenous neighbours, but generous and unselfish where a noble motive can inspire them. There is a pretty Catholic church here, but very small. Father Devitt says Mass here every second Sunday; but the congregation mostly consists of visitors to Richfield, visitors from New York and other great cities. Richfield Sulphur Springs were discovered some thirty years ago, but came into repute only within the last few years. It is "bound" to be a big place.

We return, and Father Devitt intends taking in the sick call in his way. Our road lies by a beautiful lake "Schuyler," a few miles from Richfield, six miles long by about three broad, almost as beautiful as Otsego, but that the surrounding hills are not so high. There is a pretty wooded island in one portion of it, and crowds of small boats convey pleasure-seekers over its surface. We reach a small village called "Foot o' the Lake," and diverge into a narrow road by which we are to go to the sick woman's house. Three miles brings us to the place, and those were a very unpleasant three miles, inasmuch as our carriage wheels often ran within a few inches of a precipice, and in other places there were a few broken planks thrown across streams by way of bridges, which were so badly put together that the horses leaped them rather than trust their legs to such a treacherous footing. Here is the house—a poor cabin—the occupants are Irish. The sick person is a very handsome girl of 18, married scarcely a year. Her husband, a mere boy, loafs around, and her mother is her nurse. The hectic flush and expressionless eyes seem to denote consumption. Mrs. Attridge and Sarah are very attentive and consoling; they recommend some nourishment; but it comes out there is not a cent in the house. They give the poor woman some dollars.

We leave for home; it is now half-past six o'clock, and

the marriage couple are probably waiting in the church at Cooperstown. We have twelve miles to travel, and cannot reach before nine. I cannot describe the journey back, as it was dark. I can only say the road was very hilly, and we were more or less nervous, not knowing it well. When we got home we found the church crowded with people, especially Yankees, who came to see the marriage ceremony performed; but alas! there was no account of the bridegroom. He never came, and what was stranger still, is that it is the second time he has thus deceived a woman in the same church. So passed this day.

August 26th.—Morning wet; proper time and state of the atmosphere to visit Cooper's grave. He is interred within the precincts of the Episcopal Church, which was the one he frequented. By the way, for 2,000 inhabitants there are six churches in Cooperstown, *all* of different religious character, *all* leading votaries to heaven their own way. I hope we will all meet at the same place, though reaching it by different roads, always provided the place be agreeable for all eternity. The Episcopal Church is within the village, or shall we say town? I dare say we had better say town, especially as it publishes two newspapers—the *Otsego Republican* and the *Freeman's Journal*. I want to know is there a village in America that has not its newspaper? I have often been proud of Skibbereen and its *Eagle*, and blushed for Dunmanway which could not rise to the dignity of a *Democrat*, or other exponent of public opinion. Shame on you Bandon! Hide thy diminished head. O Kinsale! there are cities of ten houses in America with their newspapers, cities not one fiftieth your age, while for the centuries that have passed over your old effete heads you have done verily nought for the glory of literature, you for sworn children of the wise Minerva.

I stroll out in the damp morning and proceed to Cooper's grave. Attached to the church, and overshadowed by the thick foliage of dripping trees, is the graveyard, of which a large section is cut off and paled in for the Coopers and their relations, the Pomeroys. Two large horizontal slabs raised on brick some two feet over the ground indicate the burial place of James Fenimore Cooper and his wife. On one stone are inscribed a cross, and beneath it the words, "James Fenimore Cooper, born Sep. 15, 1789; died Sep. 14, 1851." No more. I did not note the inscription on his wife's tomb, but I did note that she survived him two years, and that her name was De Lancey. Cooper was brought by his father when only three years old to Cooperstown from Burlington, in New Jersey, where he was born; and even in his boyhood traces of Indian life were still visible about the banks of Lake Otsego. Although the Indians as a tribe had left the head waters of the Susquehanna before the settlement of Cooperstown, yet numbers of them still lingered about the old camping grounds, and stragglers from the Delawares and the Mohawks were occasionally seen hovering about the shores of Lake Otsego, with traces of war-paint upon them. True, they had buried the hatchet with the close of the war for independence, yet the story of their bloody deeds, and their wild and untamed looks, as yet hardly changed by contact with civilization, was sufficient to arouse the vivid imagination of Cooper in his boyish days. His lively brain was filled with half-forgotten legends and tales of the Indians, which the presence of their native woods and the occasional smoke of the wigwam, served to heighten and intensify, until it gave birth, in after years, to that wonderful series of Indian romances which have charmed young and old of all countries for nearly half a century, and rescued from oblivion the chivalrous and the heroic in the "noble red man." The monument of Cooper's father is here also, and somewhat like his own in shape, but more worn by time.

An immense number of other stones, all perpendicular, and of marble, indicate the final resting-place of Cooper's family and friends, Pomeroy being the only name that varies the monotony of Cooper. Several infants, children of Cooper, lie buried here. The thought of "Sic transit" irresistibly steals over the mind. Alas! what is human greatness, which ends in a little earth—in damp solitude and everlasting silence? We pass out of the churchyard and see the house where live, at an advanced age, two sisters of the novelist, and close by we see the spot where stood his dwelling-place, named the "Hall," of which, since it was destroyed by fire, no trace now remains.

We go again on the lake and fish. What a bore the poor fish must think us. But thunder, lightning and rain again drive us prematurely home. We talk a good deal about ghosts this evening, and I grow nervous. They say the house is haunted. Whether it is or not I heard shuffling of feet and knocking at my door to-night after twelve. The knocking was several times repeated, and I cried, "Come in," frequently; but the shy spirit did not obey. Are ghosts timid?

August 27th.—Sunday; awful storm, and equally awful heat; thermometer at 80° all day; never ceasing rain from morning till night. Mass and sermon by me. After Mass a number of men interview me at the house, five from Co. Cork, two from Waterford. They are all farmers, and live about seven miles from Cooperstown. The great rain and wind did not hinder them from coming to Mass on Sunday. They have purchased their farms "out and out," and have got plenty of time to pay up the purchase-money. They do not fear a landlord's frown, or an agent's threat; they are independent. We had a long chat about the "old country," and I told much that interested them highly. Another sermon at benediction in the evening. Yankees, as usual, present in good numbers.

August 28th.—Last day's boating on the lake. I do not know what is the charm about Cooperstown. It seems as if it were a retreat—a place isolated, shut in from the whole world, where one could be happy for ever. What a place for a monastery would be the bank of this lovely, lonely lake, and how the glorious works of Nature around would raise the heart to Nature's God.

We take tea at Miss Tanner's very pretty house, "Butternut Cottage," so called from a large tree in the lawn called a butternut. Her father and mother are nice people. Miss Tanner had told me that after tea she would take me "up a tree." But she was literal, and proceeded to fulfil her promise. The large butternut tree to which I have alluded stood in the lawn. It was very old and wide-spreading. The trunk extended up about twelve feet from the ground, and then thick branches shot out from it. Within the branches a flooring was made with seats all around, the backs of which extended from branch to branch. In the centre was a table, and the elevation was reached by a rude staircase. Here we sat, and chatted and joked over the novelty of our situation. The sun had just set, and the full moon shone through the foliage of the trees all around, while in another direction we saw the calm surface of the lake almost at our feet reflecting the full moonbeam. The whole scene was lovely, but I was not permitted to enjoy it long. At 8 o'clock I delivered my lecture on "The Bible" in the church. A small gathering of people was there, conspicuous amongst whom was the Presbyterian clergyman who took copious notes as I went along.

I should have mentioned when speaking of the Leatherstocking Falls that I had no loss in not seeing them. They were a mere tiny driblet, as the weather was so dry. At their best they are not much; but they enjoy a fictitious importance from the romance cast around them by the vivid imagination, and highly-coloured descriptions of Fenimore Cooper.

CHAPTER XIII.

CONCLUSION.

August 29th.—Sarah and I leave Cooperstown at 9.25 a.m., for New York, *via* Albany. We leave with regret; for we enjoyed the place immensely—but no human pleasure lasts long. We enjoy the Hudson exceedingly; reach Mrs. Attridge's at 8 o'clock and retire early.

August 30th.—Fearfully bitten by mosquitos last night. See Father Crowley off for Ireland by the "Minnesota"—"*Bon voyage!*" Come down to Huntington by train, and spend several days in the dull routine of do-nothing-ness.

I find that the author of "Home, sweet Home," was J. Howard Payne, a native of East Hampton, Long Island, a small village towards the end of the island, within Say Harbour.

To anyone ignorant of law affairs in New York, the following extract, which I have taken from a paper of August 27th last, will explain all :—

"In the city of New York there are upwards of eight thousand men who follow, at a more or less respectable distance, the profession of the law for a livelihood. In other countries, such as France and England, the legal profession is looked up to, not only by the lay community, but by the members of all the other learned professions, as one requiring and peculiarly adapted for the display of the highest possible degree of learning, culture, knowledge of the world and human nature, deep thought and study, and general ability. In England and in France the highest prizes in the field of statesmanship have, as a rule, always been carried off by lawyers ; and so far above divinity and physic has the law been regarded in public estimation that many a parent of moderate means who might have made his son a clergyman or a physician without leaning very heavily on his purse, has been known to exhaust his resources and reduce himself to the very verge of ruin in a too often unsuccessful endeavour to make his boy a counsellor. In this country, too, the most coveted positions in the arena of public life have been, and still are, in the majority of cases, filled by members of the legal profession ; but the time has long since gone by when the law was regarded by the general public as the most desirable of all the professions. The cause of this is very plain. Every calling or avocation is respectable and desirable only in proportion to its comparative exclusiveness, that is, to the difficulty, time, labour, expense, and unborn talent involved in the pursuit and acquisition of it. A long course of study, involving considerable expense, a liberal general education, and a fair share of natural ability were all necessary heretofore to the completion of a 'Limb of the Law.' But how has it been of late years? There is scarcely one intelligent reader who does not know an ignorant and stupid fool with his name over the door of a lawyer's office, whose whole qualifications for his successful admission to the Bar have been acquired by three weeks' reading of Blackstone, as many years' drinking of bad whiskey, and a little influence with the judge. A diploma of this kind is so easily obtained that hundreds 'of jocose youths of various occupations, who never dreamed of entering on the practice of law have had themselves admitted to the Bar for the fun of the thing.

"These, however, are the more harmless class of our legal luminaries. Another source of supply for the law offices is the unhealthy and alarming dislike entertained by American tradesmen and mechanics towards bringing up their children to the trade by which they themselves have been enabled to pass through life on an independent competence. We are undoubtedly becoming wofully snobbish in this country already, and nobody is so badly bitten with this same snobbishness as the average mechanic. He is ashamed of being only a 'working man.' He is dazzled by the shiny coat which the briefless barrister and the poorly paid clerk have to pinch from their stomachs to put on their backs, and he determines that his boy, instead of being 'a poor drudge,' as he calls it, must be qualified for a gentleman. So the foolish man wastes his surplus earnings on young hopeful, who is put through a cursory 'course of study,' is called to the Bar, and in due time finds himself a full-fledged counsellor, attorney, and barrister-at-law, with nothing to do and nothing to eat. It has been already stated that there are now over 8,000 practising lawyers in this metropolis, that is out of every hundred of our population one man is a lawyer. Leaving out the women and children this gives us one lawyer to every twenty grown men, so that admitting that every man in New York goes to law with another man at least once a year, each lawyer can have only twenty cases per annum at an average to live upon. Now, inasmuch as some of our eminent lawyers monopolise some hundreds of these cases, it is plain that many of the lesser lights of the

Bar are left without any case at all. Still they must live somehow, and the question how so many lawyers do live in New York has oftener been asked than answered. . . . The unsavoury history, haunts and practises of the 'Tombs Shyster,' that nondescript animal and social pest, are well known to every reader of the *Herald*. The public are not wholly unaware of the existence of a class of disreputable men who prowl along the docks in search of sailors with grievances, and who persuade poor mercantile Jack into empowering them to institute suits in his behalf against the owners and masters of vessels on board of which he has been ill-used, and afterwards compromise Jack's case for some sum of which the plaintiff never sees a cent, though he has already 'come down' to his philanthropic counsel with a retainer equal to the whole amount of the wages he has just received. There are inumerable other ways by which needy and conscienceless lawyers manage to 'make out the case.'"

N.B.—A "Shyster" is a lawyer such as described, who hangs about the Tombs' Court trying to net miserable dupes who may employ them. Some time ago there was a legal firm on Broadway, "Ketchem and Cheetham." The double entendre was too much for the public—the brotherhood were fairly laughed into a severance of their partnership.

Poets are rare in America. I believe Longfellow, Bryant and Whittier are the best; Saxe is the Tom Hood of American Literature. There is one named Walt Whitman, and how he has the audacity to claim the laurels of a poet, or how any reader is stupid enough to grant the claim, is one mystery out of the myriads by which we are surrounded in this world. A writer named Bret Harte has lately appeared on the literary stage as a poet. His book is small, and the pieces, all fugitive, are very brief. Some of them are written in American slang, some are indelicate, there may be four out of the entire lot fit to stand an examination. One has made him a name somehow, it is called the "Heathen Chinee." It is of the slang class, and illustrates the cheating propensities of the Chinese immigrants to this country. But in truth there's nothing in it, yet Harte has, as it were, founded a new school of American poetry, and has his disciples. Another named Hay has appeared, and his collection is remarkable for nothing but cant, profanity, and indecency. And, *en passant*, it may be remarked that Americans, to my mind, are the most profane, blasphemous people in the world. The lightness with which the name of God and of religion is spoken of in this country is really shocking. I have heard things said of the Deity too disgusting, too horrible even to think of. Hay has a sketch called "Little Breeches," said Little Breeches being a dirty, tobacco-chewing, precociously sinful little wretch, whose father had gone West. This little rascal was lost in a snow-storm, and found in a sheep-fold. The question then was, in the fine and frenzied language of our poet, "How did he get thar?" And the poetic answer was "Angels," as the child could never have walked in that storm. But this is the moral which our poet draws from those fearfully illogical deductions:—

> "And I think that saving a little child,
> And bringing him to his own,
> Is a darned sight better business
> Than loafing around the throne."

. . . .

I read the *Sunday Herald* of this day. They call themselves the "Hercules of Religion." They contend that they are equal to all the pulpits of America. Having no particular religion themselves, they teach religion to all the world, but their theological "platform" seems to be no more than the abolition of the new-fangled notions of sacraments, dogmas, "fire and brimstone," &c., and the establishment of a common brotherhood by all pious persons. "They have the gratification to know they have thus far succeeded beyond their expectations in quickening the pulse of grace in various communities, in infusing new and enlarged ideas into pulpits, and in spurring the laggard professionally religious Press all over the country to livelier work under the banner of their chosen and halo-crowned Leader." But its estimate of itself is in this very paper put forward in a more extravagant, and therefore more ludicrous manner. "The religion of the *Herald*, nowadays at all events, is like its treatment of all worldly and world-wide movements, measures and matters—as boundless as earth, and as illimitable as God's goodness. Nothing is greater than the *Herald's* comprehensive grasp, nor grander than its journalistic conception. It continues to be the foremost paper in the world."

This is one of the things that vexes me most in America— the self-sufficiency of men proclaiming themselves and their institutions to be the grandest in the *whole world*.

But we must not look for consistency in the *New York Herald*. All must admit it is a paper cleverly conducted, that is to say, it relaxes no effort in procuring news from all the world to satisfy the curiosity of its readers; expense is no consideration ;—it seems to have correspondents in every great country on the face of the earth. But it takes care to tell you so, over and over again ; and in the *New York Herald*, the *Herald* reporter or correspondent is spoken of as if he were high-priest of the Delphic Oracle, a being to be honoured, respected, feared by all; he is one whose "open sesame" unbars the gates of palaces and admits the Great Irresistible into the saloons of ministers, the closets of kings, and boudoirs of empresses, who impart to him the inmost secrets of their souls as if he were a Nepomunce of silence, instead of being a mere professional blab. The *Herald* embraces no peculiar phase of theological opinion, and enlisting itself under the banner of no special church or creed, professes to give a "fair show" to all. But what is this but to say there is no need of any special form of worship, or that God may be worshipped any way. The most that the *Herald* will admit as its theological platform is the existence of God, and the immortality of the soul, and because it maintains these doctrines, it inflates itself into the dimensions of a colossal censor, and is terribly vexed if any one dares to preach against either of them. And yet I have read letters to the *Herald* trying to disprove the immortality of the soul, and the *Herald* has said never a word in reply.

The *Herald* regards itself as the great moral teacher of New York, and probably of America, and constantly gives itself credit for keeping preachers of all churches within proper orthodox bounds by its approval or castigation of their tenets. And there are some people who gravely assert that a vast deal of moral good is effected amongst its readers by the Monday morning *resumé* of the previous Sunday's sermons. But in its reviews of these sermons there is an air of lightness, of badinage, of scoffing calculated to weaken an indifferent reader's respect for great dogmas. For example, the doctrine of eternal punishment is laughed at by the *Herald*, which alludes to that state as "perpetual roasting," "eternal basting," "everlasting brimstone," etc., etc. Other doctrines are treated with like levity. But it is amusing to witness the airs of the *Herald* when speaking of religion—it seems to regard itself as having a special mission from heaven to teach the truth, while it is well known that most of its religious articles are written by men who have no religion at all. Since this Boulsby business came to light, it has sent its reporters into all kinds of dens. The Paul Prys of the Press have been interviewing the inmates of those hells, and the edifying conversations are duly published every morning in the *Herald*, so that with all this guilt and shame, and those murders and hangings, explosions and collisions, one grows shocked and bewildered, and begins to regard mankind and the world as a spectacle of unmitigated horror and woe. While the *Herald* gives all these horrors to the world, it introduces them as a clown might introduce a fellow-clown in a circus. I have already alluded to its vulgar proclivity to alliterative headings. Surely when dealing with a horrible story of guilt and shame the editor might spare his brains the worry of finding out alliterations, and his readers the *bizarre* effect of reading them. But the *Herald* is the *Herald*, and so we have "Rosenzweig's Rascality," and the "Terrible Tale," "the Trunk Tragedy," "the Boulsby Butchery," and, best of all, the "Hudson River Railroad: Harrowing, Revolting Record."

One other fault in the *New York Herald*, and I have done. It always presumes the guilt of a man accused of crime—it hangs him first and tries him after. Rosenzweig, though not yet brought to trial, is condemned by the Great Oracle—he is guilty, and justice will be frustrated if he is not sacrificed. This is freedom of the Press with a vengeance. Give me the Press which respects the majesty of the law, and which honourably subscribes to that glorious principle which the law inculcates—that every man is presumed to be innocent until he is found guilty.

September 12*th*.—I have never left this village* since the 30th of August, save for a carriage ride. I have been very ill all the time; so much so that coupling the fact with the consideration that I have been more or less unwell all through the summer, I have resolved on sailing for Europe on the 11th of next month by the Cunard s.s. "Java." It is needless to go into all my reasons for forming this resolution—it is formed, and there's an end of it.

Having thus, for the last fortnight, had plenty of time for observation on my hands, it is a pity I had not a wider range for my speculations than an obscure village, but such as the village is, let me describe the life of an ordinary resident therein—that ordinary resident being ourselves. Our house is a very pretty one—"frame," of course, like all its neighbours, standing on the outskirts of the village, railed off from the road on two sides, for it is at a junction of two roads, and surrounded by flower-beds, now in full bloom. The house is three storeys high is painted white, with green blinds; has a "stoop"— a piazza and gallery projecting from the first floor. The gallery and piazza are united by pillars around which creepers grow in profusion. The roof is invisible, and a balustrade running all round on the top gives the whole a square appearance. It is, as I have said, a very pretty house, and it is pleasant to sit in a rocking chair on the piazza and read the paper to one's self, or chat with a

---

* Huntington, L. I.

friend, as the case may be. We rise early, breakfast about eight, get the post and "paper" at 10.30, dine when we please, drive out, and spend the rest as we may. It is hard to keep up a conversation where materials are so few. We have no intercourse with the villagers, and consequently, no sympathy. We hear of some forthcoming clam-bake, but not having any interest in it, can get no further than the fact that it is about to take place. The weather is, as everywhere else, the staple topic, the great resource when all fails. It is always very hot, or rather cool, or going to rain, or we are about to have a "storm," which means *any* change for the worse.

There is a great scarcity of birds here. No matin song of thrush or blackbird salutes the drowsy ear, and warns us to rise. "This gloomy shore skylark never warbles over." At evening, when the sun sets, there is scarcely any twilight. We sometimes sit and "cool off," after the heat of the day, on the "stoop," with, and sometimes without, company. Sitting on the "stoop" is a favourite enjoyment amongst Americans. Here no bird's song is heard, and yet the air is filled with sound. I should rather say with sounds, for it is a most extraordinary melody. In one discordant strain are heard the croaking of the toad, the shrill cry of the cricket, not your little "cricket on the hearth," but a loud, tremulous piping sound, harsh as the grating of a file against steel, the eternal whizzing of the locust, and the unceasing croak of the "katy-did." This latter creature, an insect, so called because the sound it makes (by its wings, I am told) is very like that of a human being crying, "Katy did," and sometimes "Katy didn't." While all this weird concert is going on, the atmosphere is lit up by the star-like gleam of

z

fire-flies, which is very beautiful, and in the cloudless azure overhead the galaxy and the ursa major, unaltered in their everlasting brightness and beauty, sometimes delude me into the idea that I am gazing on my own native sky. Just as the sun sets one pretty sight is seen—it is that of the charming little humming-bird, tiny as a butterfly, and yet a bird, flying through the garden from flower to flower, and poking his long bill gently yet effectively into the bowl of sweets which he knows so well how to find. He is not afraid of you; he comes quite close, and sometimes, but not always, you hear the little humming sound from which he derives his name.

. . . . . .

Nothing can surpass the neatness of Americans, especially American ladies. In dress they are not more extravagant or fashionable than the ladies at home, but they are always neat, their children are particularly well dressed, and it is refreshing to see a crowd of boys and girls going to or coming from school, so elegantly dressed, and brought up to notions of neatness from their very infancy. And here I may remark that the Americans appear to be extremely fond of their children. This is evinced not only in this matter of dress, but in the care which parents take of their young ones. Go where you please, in steamboat or train, and you see the children with their parents, sometimes in arms, but oftener more mature. Parents seem as if they could not enjoy a day's pleasure except in the society of their children.

And yet why do so many children turn out badly in this country? For two reasons, as it appears to me. First, because of this very care and love which they receive from their parents—an unwise love, which overlooks faults, and gives the will too much license ; secondly, on account of the system of education from which the religious element is carefully excluded. It is manifest that where, for example, geography is taught, and religion is not, the child knows far more about the former science than he does of the latter.

The neatness of Americans is very remarkable in their houses. You never see a dirty house anywhere. Be it ever so poor it is cleanly and orderly—in the country the farmer's house is a model of neatness. The style is pretty, the walls are freshly painted, the flower garden blooms in fruit, while within the carpet and hangings and pictures look bright and cheerful. Many of our Irish people who live here have learned those habits of neatness and conformed to them. What a pity they do not learn them at home! Of how many pleasures do they deprive themselves by not adopting the simple means which Nature has placed in their hands for being happy! The very cultivation of flowers, the very science of good cooking, would tend much to enlarge the sphere of their enjoyment. Their habits are greatly improved by their transfer to this country—at home they seem doomed to eternal stagnation.

October 1st.—Left Huntington at 7 a.m., accompanied by Charles Underwood O'Connell, 20 miles to say Mass. Have done this every second Sunday since I came here. What a long journey, quite across Long Island, from sound to sea, and such a strange road, so unlike what we see in Ireland. The weather, always delightful, was peculiarly so to-day. We drive through the village where no one is yet astir, but a few smoke wreaths gracefully curl into the lazy air, and seems loth to dwindle into non-existence. We creep up the hill and pass by the Episcopal Church, which is made of wood, and painted white from the base to the apex of the spire. Then out into the country, along a good road, with good houses at each side; houses, as usual here, made like the church, of wood, with the closed blinds painted green, and with the balcony above, and the piazza below, and plenteous flowers around. No human being is visible. Our road lies for about five miles through a dense wood; it is so narrow that the wheels brush constantly against the brushwood on either side. The eye wanders through the tall and silent trees, and the vision is limited within a few yards by the density of the plantation—the plantation of Nature, by the way, for human foot may have pierced this solitude, but human hand has never sown a seed in this ungenial soil. And why plant trees, O man, when Nature spreads them around in such lavish profusion? As we pass through this valley and find ourselves shut in from human view on every side, we cannot help thinking what a lurking place this were for the highwayman. But robbery here is unheard of, though black men abound who are generally ready for this kind of thing. When we catch glimpses of light we see the mosquitoes in thousands swarming around us, and they never quit us the whole way. Our handkerchiefs are constantly brushing them away, a laborious and almost fruitless task, for they swarm and swarm, and although thousands are killed or repelled, fresh thousands rush to the encounter, and drink your blood, and poison what they do not drink, in spite of you.

Out of the woods we find ourselves again in the free air, but now our way lies through other miles upon miles of scrub oak, which extends at each side as far as the eye can see like a vast ocean, dense, close, solid, and through all the way, whether in wood or thicket no bird song is heard, and few specimens of the feathered tribe display their plumage.

At length after three hours driving we arrive at the little church, where about 200 Irish people are assembled, wonderfully neat and well dressed, with about 50 waggons—for all are farmers and have waggons—not common carts, but spring vehicles and a "team," and all have to come long distances, as far as eight or ten miles. Mass is only every second Sunday. I hear confessions, say Mass, and preach. We start on the homeward journey and reach Huntington at 4 o'clock.

October 2nd.—I leave Huntington to-day for New York. The girls are very sad. No wonder; they were lonely for Father Crowley, and the presence of an old and sincere friend reconciles them somewhat to his absence. Then they do not know who is to take my place, and so they are lonely and sad. But life is made up of meetings and partings.

APPENDIX.

FUGITIVE PIECES
IN
VERSE AND PROSE.

Dunmanway Town.

Air: "The Groves of Blarney."

ALL ye who hear me, I pray draw near me,
    And kindly cheer me while I sing for you,
In strains melodious, sweet and sonorous,
    A song harmonious and most strictly true.
My subject splendid and in it blended,
    Are themes attended with most high renown
In sweet-sounding phrases and poetic mazes
    I sing the praises of Dunmanway Town.

Mid mountains hoary and famed in story,
    Great Carbery's glory Dunmanway lies,
With the Bandon flowing, its charms bestowing,
    Which in Mount Noen does take its rise.
And there a lake is, where the duck and drake is,
    And the crane can take his sweet feast of frogs,
But when night comes round it, the spirits surround it,
    Since there was drownded Sir Richard Cox.

Then quite adjacent, both clane and dacent,
    With high railings facin' it, does the chapel stand,
With the cross high o'er it, and a lawn before it,
    You'd almost adore it, 'tis so mighty grand.
In Cork or Cloyne ye never saw any
    Man like Father Doheny, he can't be found,
'Tis by him we benefits, for out of that head of his,
    He raised that edifice up from the ground.

'Tis there in Shrovetimes, those famous love times,
    The maidens oft-times they do repair,*
With cheeks like roses, not to mind their noses,
    And artificial posies set in their hair.
On every Tuesday, their nate and spruce day,
    In new cloth boots they assemble there,
From mountains wandering, and through vales meandering
    They come philandering from far and near.

The lovely lasses, as a bouchal passes,
    Through pigs and asses, they look so sly,
While Dhonal Cruaig or Paddy Buaig,
    And ould Nell Twohig† make the match hardby.
A few nights after, midst mirth and laughter,
    Each sooty rafter looks bright with joy,
While the lovely maiden like Eve in Eden,
    With smiles is wedding her darling boy.

Black turf spontaneous, from distant ages,
    Grows quite contagious unto the town,
Likewise the *giush*‡ is growing most beauteous,
    And quite profusious much farther down.
'Tis mighty plazing to see them blazing,
    And the natives feasting with a happy smile,
With their sons and daughters on the kids they slaughters,
    And huge beef quarters so juvenile.

---

* On the Tuesdays immediately preceding Shrove-Tuesday, pig fairs are held in Dunmanway, at which, in addition to the sale of grunters, a good deal of business is done in matrimonial speculations.

† Names of celebrated local match-makers.

‡ *Giush* is the Irish word for "bog-wood."

Were I Tyrtæus or Polyphemus,
    Or Prout, whose name is spread through the *Globe*,
In sweet effusions more soft and studious,
    Dunmanway's beauties I would enrobe.
Old Mother Nature, the jealous creature,
    Gave to them, each one, most high renown,
But did I inherit their poetic sperrit,
    You'd get your merit, Dunmanway Town.

The Cork Cathedral Bells.

[Written on the occasion of erecting a Peal of Bells in St. Mary's Cathedral, Cork.]

I.

WHAT joyous chimes, so new and sweet,
    Ring out upon the winter air?
See people pause in crowded street,
    And peasants form their thanks in prayer;
The solemn day—the promised hour,
    The smiling face of Nature tells
That now at length from yonder tower
    Peal forth the Cork Cathedral Bells.

II.

Three hundred years have come and gone
    Since last we heard those sacred chimes;
But patient Faith kept burning on,
    Expectant of more gracious times,

And heaven's voice the tempest stays;
　　Once more the Christian bosom swells,
And Cork pours forth responsive praise
　　To-day from her Cathedral Bells.

III.

Three hundred years of night and gloom,
　　Enlightened statesmen, was your meed
Of justice to a land whose doom
　　Was to preserve her cherished creed.
Vain all your arts to quench a flame
　　Which God's Almighty breath compels.
Peal forth a pæan to His Name,
　　Once more, ye Cork Cathedral Bells.

IV.

Ring out—the Lee, whose source Finbar
　　Hath blessèd, stops upon its way
To hear those melodies which are
　　By his successor waked to-day—
To hear those mellow numbers fall,
　　Weaving in air their solemn spells,
After oppression's iron thrall,
　　To hear the Cork Cathedral Bells.

I'm Left Alone.

[Written on the death of an intimate friend, a Fellow Student in College.]

I.

I'm left alone! I'm left alone!
  And sorrows now betide me,
And drearily the hours have flown
  Since thou wert here beside me.
My heart is lone! My heart is lone!
  And dark'ning clouds surround it,
Because thy sunny smiles are gone,
  That late were beaming round it.

II.

I'm left alone! I'm left alone!
  Should friendship thus deceive me?
Her sweets I scarce can call my own,
  Ere those I cherish leave me.
Tho' charming was the wreath of love
  She wove for us together,
'Twere better far she never wove
  A wreath so soon to wither.

III.

I'm left alone! I'm left alone!
  No more are round me ringing
That merry laugh, and mellow tone,
  Of music once too winning—

Yet, still each loved and well-known sound
    Within my bosom lingers,
On soft and sadden'd key attuned
    By mem'ry's fairy fingers.

IV.

I'm left alone ! I'm left alone !
    Each morn brings thee before me.
And when the last day-beam has flown,
    Thy image still hangs o'er me.
I'm compassed round with happy smiles ;
    For me they've sadness only :
My heart no alien joy beguiles,
    For I, alas ! am lonely.

V.

I'm left alone ! I'm left alone !
    But shall it be for ever ?
No—there's a sphere where souls live on,
    To be dissunder'd never.
There free for love, and love alone,
    No sorrows shall betide me ;
And Heaven to me shall sweeter be,
    When thou art there beside me.

The Young Jdea.

In childhood's days I had a feeling
Around my soul for ever stealing,
As 'twere a secret, bright revealing,
    That I should never die :

Though youth and age around me faded,
By dark disease and sorrow shaded,
Yet I was ever well persuaded
    Grim Death would pass me by.

But soon came Reason's light out-gleaming
My blissful childhood's starlike dreaming,
And showed me with her moon-bright beaming,
    Alas! another doom—
She seemed to say serenely, slowly :—
" Away, my child, that thought unholy,
And wake to Truth, however lowly ;
    Thou'rt destined for the tomb."

And yet, amid my spirit's sighing,
An angel voice was ever crying :—
" Within is something never dying
    That meets no earthly goal ; "
When thro' the clouds with light surprising,
High o'er my doubting and surmising,
Religion's sunburst proudly rising
    Revealed—it was my soul.

She pointed to the skies above her,
Saying :—" Would'st thou be Religion's lover,
And I will to thy soul discover,
    The regions of the Blest ;
Let earth take back what earth has given,
And when the chains of life are riven,
Come share with me and mine in Heaven,
    Eternal peace and rest."

A feeling strangely sweet came o'er me;
I felt, while stood that form before me,
As if celestial pinions bore me
    Away beyond the sky;
And since that hour Earth seems a prison,
Where shines no ray of real bliss in,
And where I ever calmly listen
    For Fate to whisper—" Die!"

KINSALE, *May 22nd*, 1856.

What wouldn't I Smash for Your Sake.

(A new song, dedicated to John M'Auliffe, Esq., New York, by the Author.)

OH! Molly, my darling bewitcher,
  Before I retire from the scene,
Here's your health in a full-flowing pitcher
  Of genuine Irish potheen.
And here are the stick and the hand, dear,
  A neck or a noddle to break,
Oh! give me the word of command, dear,
  What wouldn't I smash for your sake?

When roaming alone o'er the prairie,
  Far, far, from sweet Ballinaclash,
I envied the boys of Tipperary,
  Who had skulls full and plenty to smash.
But, twirling my darling shillelagh,
  That I cut in the ould Irish brake,
I thought of sweet Moll, and cried gaily,
  "What wouldn't I smash for her sake?"

But soon, dear, I took to despairing,
    And grieving we ever should part,
For I feared that the boys of ould Erin
    Might steal from the exile your heart.
And, therefore, one fine summer's morning
    My road o'er the waters I take,
To give all your lovers fair warning,
    What wouldn't I smash for your sake?

I've traversed the sweet groves of Blarney,
    Where grows the shillelagh in style,
I've seen the proud lakes of Killarney,
    Where nature so sweetly doth smile.
But dearer than ash, oak, or holly,
    And sweeter than mountain or lake,
Was one glance in the bright eyes of Molly—
    What wouldn't I smash for her sake?

And now, dear, alas! I'm returning,
    To traverse the prairie once more;
My bosom with love, dear, is burning,
    Farewell, darling Molly asthore.
But one day, if I don't fall in battle,
    In the land of the shamrock I'll take
The hand of sweet Molly, and rattle
    "What wouldn't I smash for her sake?"

CORK, *September 12th*, 1863.

Hope and Inisfail.

On a lonely rock, beside the sea,
   Sat one of Earth's fair daughters,
And her eyes were gazing wistfully
   Over the waste of waters;
And by her side an ancient crown,
   Stript of its pearly dower,
Bespoke a queen without a throne,
   Bereft of queenly power.

Betwixt a rainbow and the sea
   Uprose a charming vision,
The fairest sylph she seemed to be
   E'er sent from realms elysian;
Who, as she neared the rock-bound shore,
   Ere winds or waves could keep her,
In sweetest tones e'er heard before,
   Addressed the wondering weeper :—

"Daughter of Earth, why weepest thou?
   Why mourn thus sad and lonely?
Why seek this bold rock's beetling brow,
   Where sea-birds habit only?
What is thy name, and what thy race,
   And what thy doleful story?
Is it a tale of dark disgrace
   Or of extinguished glory?

"Why gaze thus mournfully o'er the deep?
  What is't thy soul distresses?
Mayhap thy shipwrecked children sleep
  Within its dark recesses.
Though sad to-day, thy bosom ope;
  Speak frankly, child of sorrow,
For I am the consoler, Hope,
  Who brings the gladsome morrow."

"Bright messenger of Heav'n, hail!"
  Replied the beauteous mourner;
"Hast never heard of Inisfail,
  Or how the Fates have shorn her?
Of all that man's rapacious greed
  E'er deemed a priceless booty,
Of Freedom, land, wealth, blood and breed,
  And almost all her beauty?

"A tyrant once came o'er the sea—
  A tyrant grim and gory;
Ah! well-a-day, 'twas then for me
  Began this doleful story.
Smitten by these two fatal charms,
  The Saxon robber wooed me;
My children rose in hostile arms,
  He in their blood imbrued me.

"And prompted by the lust of gold,
  The monster, cold and cruel,
Wrenched from my crown its wealth untold,
  Each sparkling pearl and jewel;

Some emerald gems remain alone,—
  Alas! I little need them,—
The brightest gem of all is gone,
  The priceless pearl of Freedom.

"And seven long hundred years have flown
  Since o'er the seas he hied him,
And even the wealth of my poor crown
  Glitters at home beside him.
I grudge him not his bauble prize;
  Poor gems, I little heed them.
Save one whose loss bedews those eyes,
  That peerless pearl of Freedom.

"I've sent my children, many a year,
  To win me back my treasure;
The tyrant laughs with wanton jeer,
  And gains them to his pleasure.
He gives them office, rank, and gold,
  And bribes them to submission,
Till they forget, or lightly hold,
  Their Mother's lost condition.

"You ask why mournfully I gaze
  Over the waste of water:
Who knows there may come brighter days
  For Earth's most tearful daughter.
Eastward the tyrant's stronghold lies;
  Some genius yet may lead him
Backward beneath yon azure skies,
  To pay me back my Freedom."

"Fond, foolish child of Earth!" cried Hope,
  "Thou little know'st the tyrant,
Or to his mercy's narrow scope
  Thou wert not thus aspirant.
Ere thou thy Freedom could'st regain
  By such poor mild resources,
He'd gash asunder every vein
  Through which his life-blood courses.

"What was't ungemmed thy crown? the sword!
  Aye, hear it, Earth's lone daughter;
And by the sword must be restored
  Thy wealth beyond the water.
For never yet beneath the sun,
  However rant or rave men,
Was Freedom to a nation won
  But by the blood of brave men.

"Mark how the still unvanquished Pole
  Bleeds for his dear Sarmatia;
Remember Tell while ages roll,
  How well he freed Helvetia.
Beneath the despot's iron goad
  Gaul languished long unhappy,
Till brave men's blood in torrents flowed,
  And drowned the line of Capet.

"Thy children bleed in foreign lands,
  For others' freedom fighting;
Would they but lift their vengeful hands
  Their mother's wrongs in righting,
Ah! then the gloom would pass away
  That shrouds the Past's dark story,

And in the light of Freedom's day
   Rise Inisfail to glory.

"Why only weep for giant ills?
   Rise! leave this lonely station;
Go! sound the clarion o'er thy hills,
   And wake a slumbering nation.
Quick! summon all thy children brave,
   And onward bravely lead them;
Thus only, on both land and wave,
   Can'st thou win back thy Freedom!"

A Legend of the Shannon.

On Shannon's fair majestic tide
   The moon in queenly splendour,
Looks down in her meridian pride
   While vassal stars attend her,
Light zephyrs dancing o'er the wave
   Scarce break its peaceful slumbers,
While Echo from each rock and cave
   Sings forth her magic numbers.

But why doth yon frail shallop bear
   Across the rippling water,
At such an hour, Teresa fair,
   De Burgo's only daughter?
Why flee's she thus, alone and free,
   From home and kindred speeding?
Why seeing sigh, yet sigh to see
   Portumna's towers receding?

Ah! sure 'tis love alone can teach
  A maiden thus to wander,
Yes, see! upon the moonlit beach,
  A youth awaits her yonder.
With bounding heart and eager glance
  He views Clanricard's daughter,
Like some aerial being dance
  Across the rippling water.

The brave O'Carroll!—he for years
  Had dared the Saxon power,
And taught the force of Irish spears
  On battlefield and tower,
Till one sad day saw fall his best
  And bravest kerns around him;
Insatiate for revenge, the next
  'Mid Burgo's clansmen found him.

'Twas then Teresa's soft blue eye
  First wrought its magic power;
Teresa's love now bids them fly
  For aye from yonder tower.
"Now hie thee, love!" O'Carroll cried,
  "By yon fair moon I swear thee,
Far, far away from Shannon's tide
  This faithful steed shall bear thee."

"For this I braved thy father's wrath,
  He swore the kern should shun thee,
But I had plighted thee my troth,
  And I had died or won thee.

Now hie;" but hark! Teresa fair—
   What peril now had found her?
Oh see! 'mid shrieks of wild despair
   The waters close around her!

As to the serpent's witching eye
   The victim bird is borne;
Quick as from out the warring sky
   The lightning flash is torn—
So dashed into the dark, cold wave
   Teresa's frantic lover,
But while he stretched his hand to save
   The tide rolled calm above her.

Though time hath since flowed fast away,
   The Shannon rolls as ever,
And oft upon a moonlit bay
   That hems the noble river,
The midnight wanderer has espied
   A steed, while o'er the water
The tiny bark is seen to glide
   That wafted Burgo's daughter.

A Beautiful Translation.

[We direct the attention of our readers to a translation of the German poet Bürger's celebrated ballad, "Lenore," at the hands of the Rev. M. B. Buckley, of Cork, which appears in our columns to-day. Amongst the numerous translations of this immortal *chef d'œuvre*, we doubt if any so forcibly expresses the meaning, or so artistically fashions forth the beauty of the original, as this. In one respect, at least, it differs from them all, and that is its strict fidelity to Bürger's metre. It is refreshing, in this hard, practical age, to find that a man, burdened as Father Buckley is, with the cares of an arduous mission, can snatch a few moments, now and then, to wander himself, and conduct others, through the pleasant paths of literature. But, even in his moments of pleasure, the priest is not forgetful of his sublime vocation, viz.:—to inculcate lessons of virtue, for "Lenore," embodies one of the noblest morals ever preached to Christian man.]—*American Paper*.

Lenore.

[From the German of Gottfried August Bürger.]

LENORA sighed, one early morn,
   From troublous dreams awaking :—
"Oh! Wilhelm, wilt thou ne'er return,
   Thy love so long forsaking?"
With Frederick's army to the war
Had Wilhelm gone to Prague afar;
And never sent, that distance,
A token of existence.

The king, and eke his royal queen,
   A love for war disclaiming,
Forget at length their hateful spleen,
   A welcome peace proclaiming:
And home the host, with trump and drum,
And flute, and fife, and bugle come,
Green leaves their brows adorning
That merry sunbright morning.

Then far and wide, in swelling tide,
　　Through high and by-way spreading,
Flocked young and old, to view the pride
　　Of heroes homeward treading.
"Now, God be blest!" cried wife and child,
"Oh, welcome!" shouted bride half-wild;
But, ah! no soldier wore a
Sweet smile for lorn Lenora.

Then low and high, with speech and eye,
　　She questioned of her lover;
But not a trace of Wilhelm's face,
　　Or fate, could she discover.
And when at length the march was o'er,
Her raven hair she wildly tore,
And on the earth, with passion,
She sat in maniac fashion.

Her mother cried, with gesture wild,
　　And heart with grief o'erladen :—
"Oh, God! have pity on my child!"
　　And clasped the frantic maiden.
"Oh, mother—mother, all is o'er;
Now life for me hath charms no more;
Oh! speak not of God's pity—
Alas! what kindness did He?"

"Have mercy, God!" the mother cried,
　　"Strike not, but pity, rather.
What Thou hast willed hath best betide—
　　My child say one Our Father."

"Oh! mother, mother, idle dreams!
God hates thy child too well, it seems;
Sure prayer avails one never
When hope is past for ever!"

"From God alone, if we repent,
   A Father's love we borrow,
My child, receive the Sacrament,
   'Twill soothe thy pain and sorrow!"
"Oh! mother, mother, speak not so,
No sacrament can soothe my woe!
What sacrament can waken
The dead whom God had taken?"

"Thy lover, child, hath sure trepanned
   Thy heart with love o'erladen,
And traitorously ta'en the hand
   Of some Hungarian maiden.
Then teach thy bosom to forget—
He'll reap the curse of treason yet,
When soul and body sunder
His vows will wake Heav'n's thunder!"

"Oh! mother, mother, woeful day!
   He's gone, and I'm forlorn,
Come, death, and snatch my soul away—
   Oh, would I ne'er were born!
Out, out, my lamp of life and light!
Out, out, in gloom and endless night!
Oh, speak not of God's pity!
Alas! what kindness did he?"

"Oh, God! Thy vengeful scourge withhold
    From her who raves before Thee,
She knows not what she says, then hold
    Her guiltless, I implore Thee!
Ah, child, forget those griefs of clay!
Think, think on God, and yet one day
To thy soul will be given
Th' eternal Spouse of Heaven!"

"Oh, mother what is heaven's bliss?
    And what to lose salvation?
With Wilhelm is eternal peace!
    Without him is—damnation!
Out, out, my lamp of life and light!
Out, out, in gloom and endless night!
Since Wilhelm's gone and vanished
All joys from earth are banished!"

Thus rolled the tide of dark despair
    Through lost Lenora's bosom,
Thus did she rage 'gainst God, and there
    Blasphemingly accuse Him!
Her breast she beat, her hands she wrung,
Till night o'er earth her mantle flung,
Till in the heaven's far height
Shone out the silver starlight.

And then, without was heard the stamp
    Of horse hoofs, sudden ceasing;
And then a horseman's martial tramp
    In dreadsome sound increasing.

The door is reached—the tinkling bell
Sounds through the darkness like a spell—
Then through the hall there fluttered
A voice, as 'twere one uttered—

"Up, up, fond child—my lost Lenore!
    Art waking, love, or sleeping?
Would'st thou on Wilhelm gaze once more?
    Art laughing, love, or weeping?"
"Ah, Wilhelm, thou, so late at night!
Alas! I've watched and wept outright,
Sad were my wails and bitter,
But say, how rid'st thou hither?"

"I took to horse at early night
    And rode from far Bohemia.
Come let us speed our true-love flight,
    Quick, quick, sweetheart, why dream you?"
"Ah! Wilhelm, now that danger's past,
And coldly sweeps the midnight blast,
Why hurry thus and haste thee?
Let thy Lenore embrace thee!"

"Psha! let the blasts of heaven bestride
    The valley and the highland,
Back to Bohemian plains we ride,
    This is no longer my land.
Come! quickly dress, and spring behind:
We needs must travel as the wind
A hundred miles away, love,
And thou'lt be mine to-day, love."

"A hundred miles, and wed to-day,"
  Replies Lenora, doubtful.
"Thou sure must err, my gallant gay,
  Eleven has rung out full."
"Behold, the moon shines bright," cries he,
"We and the dead ride speedily.
Ere midnight's hour I vouch, love,
Thou'lt reach thy bridal couch, love."

"Tell me, where is thy chamber small?
  Where may our bridal bed be?"
"Far, far from here, lone, cool and all
  Tranquil as where the dead be!"
"Hast room for me?" "For thee and me,
Come don thy garb right speedily,
The wedding guests are waiting,
The chamber doors are grating."

Quick did she dress, and quickly bound
  Upon the charger gallant,
Her lily hands she flung around
  Her lover, leal and valiant;
And, sweeping wild as winter's blast,
Away, away, far, far and fast,
They ride with wings of lightning,
The road with hoof-sparks bright'ning.

Before her eyes the landscape flies,
  The scene shifts quickly round her;
Meadows and green can scarce be seen,
  Hollow the bridges thunder.

"Dost tremble, love? the moon shines bright
Hurrah! the dead can ride aright—
Dost fear the dead, Lenora?"
"Oh! speak not, I implore you!"

But hark! what means that doleful wail?
   Why croaks the bodeful raven?
The death-bell tolls—the death-song rolls:—
   "Let's put the dead the grave in!"
And then a spectre-band draws near,
And bear a coffin on a bier,
Lamenting through the hedges,
Like croaking frogs in sedges;

"With sigh and groan, at dead of night,
   Inter the corse all pallid;
Now cometh home my bonnie bride
   Unto her bridal pallet—
Come, Chaunter, swell the wedding-hymn
Be Hymen's joy thy tuneful theme;
Come, Priest, and speak the blessing,
My sweet bride needs caressing!"

The dirge is o'er—now halts the bier,
   Obedient to the speaker—
Now distant noises reach the ear,
   Quick comes a horse, and quicker,
And now is heard the tramp, tramp, tramp,
As heavily the steel doth stamp;
Rider and steed, like lightning,
The road with hoof-sparks bright'ning.

Now right and left, and left and right,
    Fly mountains, lakes, and valleys,
Past whirl in most confused flight
    Streets, lanes, and squares and alleys;
" Dost tremble, love? the moon shines bright,
Hurrah, the dead can ride aright—
Dost fear the dead, Lenora?"
" Oh! speak not, I implore you!"

Now, lo! upon a scaffold high
    With supple feet and plastic,
Half visible in moonshine fly
    A band of elves fantastic,
" Ha! merry elves, come hither, pray,
Know you not 'tis our bridal day?
With your fantastic treading
You'll grace our gladsome wedding."

Behind the pair the elfins rush,
    As fear or fancy brought them,
Whirring as wind whirrs through the bush
    When leaves are sere in autumn,
While sweeping wildly to the blast;
Away, away, fly far and fast,
Rider and steed, like lightning,
The road with hoof-sparks bright'ning.

The moon doth like a ghost appear,
    Through seas of azure driven,
While higher up the stars career
    Across the arch of heaven.

"Dost tremble, love? the moon shines bright—
Hurrah! the dead can ride aright:
Dost fear the dead, Lenora?"
"Oh! speak not, I implore you!"

"Hark, hark! methinks the cock doth crow—
　　The sands of night are wasted;
Soon will the breath of morning blow—
　　We spirits dare not taste it!
Alight! 'tis o'er! our weary ride—
The bridal-chamber opens wide.
Ha! ha! the dead ride fast, love,
We've reached the end at last, love."

Before the iron gate now stands
　　The steed, with bridle hanging;
A gentle touch from viewless hands
　　Opes wide the portals clanging;
Asunder quick the portals fly,
Now o'er dark graves the travellers hie,
While ghastly in the moonshine
The stones o'er many a tomb shine.

Hark! trembling, hark! a wonder dread,
　　To start each slumbering feeling!
The rider's garb falls shred by shred,
　　A spectral form revealing!
His head, a hairless, skinless skull,
Grim, ghastly, gaunt, and horrible,
An hour-glass and a sickle
Equip the goblin fickle.

High pranced and snorted wild the steed,
  While blue flames skimmered o'er him;
Then lo! the ground yawned wide beneath,
  And from the vision bore him.
A howling cry, a serpent's hiss
From moonlit sky and dark abyss!
Lenora raved with horror,
For death, grim death, cried for her.

Then danced beneath the pale cold moon
  The elfin-band till morning,
All singing, to a sad quaint tune,
  Those solemn words of warning:—
" Be patient, though thy heart should break;
Bear all for the Great Chastener's sake.
Peace to your clay, Lenora—
May God be mild before you!"

Flax.

[Written in 1864, when Flax culture was revived in the South of Ireland, and a large Factory erected in Cork under the auspices of the late Mr. Maguire.]

Sound a pæan to the flax,
  Seeds of flax!
What a harvest doth it promise of fine linen to our backs!
  Let us scatter, scatter, scatter,
    From Rathlin to Cape Clear,
  If we'd richer be and fatter,
  Come, the flax-seed let us scatter
    In the spring-time of the year:

Sow in time, time, time,
In the merry vernal prime,
Come drain the swelling sacks and exhaust the heavy
  packs
Of the flax, flax, flax flax,
Flax, flax, flax!
Then hurrah for the scattering of the flax!

See the beauty of the flax!
Growing flax!
In the smiling days of summer-time how pretty doth it
  wax!
In the corners and the nooks,
By the bogs and by the brooks;
Greenest of the green,
Gently it is seen
Waving to and fro:
How it smiles
And beguiles
The leisure-time of labour,
As you saunter with your neighbour
Down the furzy old boreen,
While the setting sun is seen
Pursuing golden tracks just behind the mountains' backs.
Oh! there's not a crop we grow
Fit to sow,
Pull, or mow,
But the merry smiling flax,
Yes, the flax, flax, flax, flax,
Flax, flax, flax!
Then hurrah! boys, hurrah! for the flax!

Hear the music of the flax,
    Mills of flax!
Where the clangour of machinery of peace and plenty smacks.
    Hear the merry voices ringing
    Of the men and boys and women;
    See the merry eager clutching
      And the dexterous unsheaving;
    Hear the melody of scutching,
      And the spinning and the weaving
        Of the flax!
Hear the sounding of the pounding
    And the scientific whacks,
    As the O's and Mac's,
    The Jennies and the Jacks,
    Never dreaming to relax,
      Work the flax!
Oh! merry sight to see, in those halls of industry,
    The son of Erin's isle,
    With the jocund genial smile
    And the merry repartee,
    Oblivious of the tax
    Which their pocket never lacks,
Working ever at the flax
With the energy of blacks,
Singing flax, flax, flax, flax,
    Flax, flax, flax!
Then hurrah! boys, hurrah! for the flax!

Oh! the future of the flax,
    Glorious flax!

When old Erin from her ashes, 'spite of smashes and draw-
    backs,
        Like the phœnix shall arise
            After seven hundred years,
        From her melancholy eyes
            Brushing off the silent tears,
        And in holiday apparel,
            Robed in linen of her own—
        A *Te Deum* she shall carol
            In the place of ullagone !
When that happy time befalls,
        Should some minstrel take the lyre,
            From the walls
            Of Tara's ancient halls,
            And the fire
            Of his poesy inspire
            His merry roundelay,
        Let us pray,
    As his memory recalls
    All the great ones of the past,
Who have lived and died for Erin, struggling onward to the last,
        One name, at least, may not
        By the minstrel be forgot ;
        But as his visions glow
            In the light of heaven's fire,
        May his noblest anthem flow
            To the memory of—MAGUIRE !
For we were, indeed, at zero, until he arose the hero of the
    flax, flax, flax, flax,
            Flax, flax, flax,
        Until he arose the hero of the flax !

APPENDIX.

  Come scatter, then, the flax,
   Saviour Flax!
Annuller of evictions, of the crow-bar and the axe!
   In the bog and in the mireland—
   Through the length and breadth of Ireland;
   Let us scatter, scatter, scatter,
   On the lower land and higher land,
   The seedlings of the flax.
    Sow in time, time, time,
    In the merry vernal prime;
Come drain the swelling sacks, and exhaust the heavy
 packs, of the flax, flax, flax, flax,
    Flax, flax, flax,
   Then hurrah for the scattering of the flax!

           FLAXMAN.

LOAM LODGE, 8*th Feb.*, 1864.

An Irish Acrostic for '68.

A is an Army 'tis ours to repel,
B is a Bigotry breathing of hell,
C is the Church of the Saxon and Stranger,
D is the Dizzy Dog *not* of the manger,
E is Education demanded, denied,
F are the Famines that flow as the tide,
G is the Gibbet well superintended,
H is the Habeas Corpus suspended,
I are Informers, by Government backed,
J is a prejudiced Jury well packed,
K are the Keoghs that dispense us the Law,
L is the Landlord, a needy Bashaw,
M are the Martyrs for whom Erin grieves,
N is the Nothing that Ireland receives,
O is the Orangemen sighing for slaughter,
P is a Parliament—over the water,
Q is the Queen of Balmoral and Wight,
R is the Rope, the great giver of Right,
S is the Scorpion that sits at the helm,
T is the Tory-crew ruling the realm,
U is a Union by infamy planned,
V is Venality stalking the land,
W are the Whigs, "bloody, brutal and base,"
X is an Excellent change in the case,
Y is Young Ireland in Fame's highest niche,
Z's the New Zealander on London Bridge!

The Last Rose of Summer.

'Tis the last rose of summer,
  Left blooming alone,
All her lovely companions
  Are faded and gone!
No flow'r of her kindred,
  No rosebud is nigh,
To reflect back her blushes,
  Or give sigh for sigh.

I'll not leave thee, thou lone one,
  To pine on the stem,
Since the lovely are sleeping,
  Go, sleep thou with them;
Thus kindly I scatter
  Thy leaves on the bed,
Where thy mates of the garden
  Lie scentless and dead.

So soon may I follow,
  When friendships decay,
And from love's shining circle
  The gems drop away!
When true hearts lie withered,
  And fond ones are flown,
Oh! who would inhabit
  This bleak world alone?

Ecce ultima rosa
  Florescit æstatis,
Nec rubet ex omnibus
  Una cognatis!
In hortu, heu! sola
  Suspirans marcescit,
Nam flos qui confleret,
  Jam diu discessit.

Non sinam te miseram,
  Sic deperire,
Sed volo cum sociis
  Te condormire;
Sic clemens do folia
  Supra rosetum,
Perierunt sodales
  Et gusta tu lœtum.

Sic peream, caris
  Cum fuerim orbatus
Nec orbis Amoris,
  Fulgebit gemmatus!
In mundo horrendo,
  Quis ultro maneret
Si simul amatis
  Carisque egeret.

Fill the Bumper Fair.

Fill the bumper fair
   Ev'ry drop we sprinkle
O'er the brow of care
   Smooths away a wrinkle,
Wit's electric flame
   Ne'er so swiftly passes,
As when thro' the flame
   It shoots from brimming glasses.

    Fill the bumper fair,
      Ev'ry drop we sprinkle
    O'er the brow of care
      Smooths away a wrinkle.

Sages can, they say,
   Grasp the lightning's pinions,
And bring down its ray
   From the starr'd dominions.
So we sages sit,
   And 'mid bumpers bright'ning,
From the heaven of wit
   Draw down all its lightning.

Would'st thou know what first
   Made our souls inherit
This ennobling thirst
   For wine's celestial spirit?
It chanced upon one day,
   When, as bards inform us,
Prometheus stole away
   The loving fire that warms us.

Pocula replete,
   Frons enim rugosa,
Curæ, potu læti,
   Vini fit formosa.
Calicis ex ore,
   Alte si potares,
Alus lepore,
   Facile præstares.

    Pocula replete,
      Frons enim rogosa,
    Curæ, potu læti,
      Vini fit formosa.

Cælo de profundo,
   Sapientes vere,
Jovis summi mundo,
   Ignem detulêre,
Sapientiores,
   Nos, ut debacchamur,
Cælo de leporis,
   Fulgura furamur

Velles scire quare,
   Pellimur confestim,
Vini sic amare,
   Spiritum celestem?
Vates Prometheum,
   Scimus cecinisse
Ignem æthereum,
   Olim rapuisse.

The careless youth, when up
  To glory's fount aspiring,
Took nor urn nor cup
  To hide the pilfered fire in.
But oh! his joy, when round
  The halls of heaven spying,
Among the stars he found
  A bowl of Bacchus lying.
	Fertur autem illum,
	  Nulla cum adstaret,
	Urna quâ scintillam,
	  Rutilam celaret.
	Jovis inter aulas,
	  Circum se spexisse,
	Ibique Bacchi mollis,
	  Crateram reperisse.

Some drops were in that bowl,
  Remains of last night's pleasure,
With which the sparks of soul
  Mix'd their burning treasure.
Hence the goblet's show'r
  Hath such spells to win us,
Hence its mighty power
  O'er the flame within us.
	Fœcibus cum meri,
	  Funditur scintilla,
	Quœque cum crateræ,
	  Coruscaret stilla.
	Virtus inde vino,
	  Hincque dum vivamus,
	Igne hoc divino
	  Semper ardeamus.

Fill the bumper fair,
    Ev'ry drop we sprinkle
  O'er the brow of care
    Smooths away a wrinkle.
	Pocula replete,
	    Frons enim rugosa,
	  Curæ potu læti,
	    Vini fit formosa.

The Old Irish Jig.

Oh! my blessing be on you old Erin,
    My own land of frolic and fun;
For all sorts of mirth and "divarsion"
    Your like isn't under the sun.
Bohemia may talk of its polka,
    And Spain of its waltzes grow big—
Och! sure they are nothing but limping,
    Compared with our own Irish Jig.

CHORUS—

Then a fig for your new-fashioned waltzes,
    Imported from Spain and from France,
And a fig for the thing called the polka,
    Our own Irish Jig is the dance.

I heard how this jig came in fashion,
    And believe that the story is true,
By Adam and Eve 'twas invented,
    The reason was—partners were few.
Although they could both dance the polka,
    Eve thought it was not over chaste,
She preferred our jig to be dancing,
    And, 'faith, I approve of her taste.

The light hearted daughters of Erin,
    Like the wild mountain deer that can bound,
'Their feet never touch the green island,
    But music is struck from the ground.

Tripudium Hibernicum.

HIBERNIA, sis benedicta!
    Jucunda enim insula es:
Gratiori non occurrit viator
    Quocunque dirigitur pes.
Bohemia de Polka se jactet—
    Hispania jactet et se—
Hibernica solum chorea
    Delectat tripudium, me.

CHORUS—

Hinc Gallicæ, ergo, choreæ!
    Hispanæ, valete et vos!
Valete, Bohemia, vestræ!
    Oblectat, tripudium nos.

Tripudii fama inceptum
    Adami ingenio dat,
Hevæque, nam in paradiso
    Consortium non fuit sat—
Potuerunt et Polka saltare,
    Sed Heva non gaudens in re
Tripudium magis dilexit
    Et bene dilexit, nonne?

Puellæ venustæ nostrates
    Ceu cervæ resiliunt, et

Non possunt attingere terram
    Quin musicæ sonitum det.

And oft in their hills and green valleys,	Et sæpe in colli seu valle
The old jig they dance with such grace,	Saltantibus, sicut est mos,
That even the daisies they tread on,	Præ gaudio sese pandentes
Look up with delight in their face.	Subrident et gramen et flos.
This old Irish jig, too, was danced	Tripudio quondam nostrorum
By the kings and the great men of yore,	Regum fuit deditum cor,
King O'Toole himself could well foot it	O'Toolius Rex id amabat,
To a tune they called " Rory O'Moore."	Sonantibus Rory O'Moore
And oft in the great halls of Tara,	Temorensibus quoque in aulis
Our famous king Brian Boru,	Saltabat Brianus Boru,
He danced an old jig with his nobles,	Nobilium stante coronâ
And played his old harp to it, too.	Suæ citharæ sonitu.
And sure when Herodias' daughter	Herodem vix unquam placatum
Was dancing in King Herod's sight,	Movere Herodias scit ;
His heart, that for years had been frozen,	Tyranni cor diu gelatum
Was thawed with pure love and delight.	Saltante pupâ liquefit.
And oft and a hundred times over	At nisi tripudium saltasset—
I heard Father Flanagan tell	Audivi a parocho rem—
'Twas our own Irish jig that she footed	Cor regis scelesti movendi
That pleased the old villain so well.	Omnino abjiceret spem.

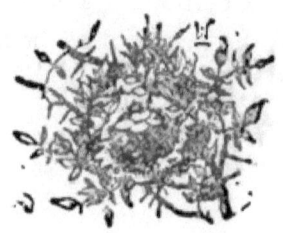

FACETIÆ.

A BOWL OF BISHOP.

It is no use striving to *cope* with a bishop, for he is sure to carry everything by *mitre-right*. He is the most imperious of men, because he *gives orders* the moment he finds anyone fit to receive them. Bishops, in old times, were given to *powdering*, now they are content to make *canons;* though he may decry the use of wine, we are credibly informed that he has many *reserved cases* of his own. A bishop, though having *very bad sight*, may have a very good *see*. Though he could not become a bishop without "Nolo," yet he holds *no low* position in the Church; dwelling in a *palace*, and oftentimes sitting on a throne, he frequently gives away a *crown*, and yet, at other times, could not raise a *sovereign*. Though averse to prize-fighting, he makes his living by the *Ring*. However he may denounce the vocation of Calcraft, no man is a better hand at *suspension* than he. Like the cholera, he makes a periodical *visitation*, but while the cholera *weakens* all the firm, he *confirms* not only all the *weak*, but all the year round. He may not *translate* a foreign language, but he may himself be *translated* to foreign parts. He may not lend you money, but he'll tell you when and how it is *Lent*. Not over indulgent to himself, he grants *indulgence*, nay even *license* to others, especially to those who wish to lead a *fast* life. He may not have *toast* for breakfast, but he often gets a surfeit of *toasting* after dinner. He is ever hospitable, particularly to young clergymen; indeed he no sooner gives a priest an *entrée* into his diocese, than he helps him to a *remove*. He may be a *handsome* man, but he must be *ordinary*. Sometimes, though quiet and subdued in his disposition, he is often to the end of his life an *Arch*-bishop. Performing *rights* for others, he is content with *dues* for himself. The bishop is the *head* of his own chapter, which reminds us that he is the *tale* of this.

DEATH OF A DISTINGUISHED GRINDER.

This morning I lost by death one of my very oldest and most cherished friends. I made his acquaintance some thirty golden years ago, and from that moment to the hour of his demise we lived and loved together. I cannot boast of having properly appreciated or requited his friendship, for the manifestation of that tender feeling was altogether one-sided—he lived and laboured for me, while I did very little to promote his comfort or convenience. I could only admire and commend his devotion on every occasion that offered; in truth, it may be said, he was ever in my mouth. But he did not stand in need of me, being perfectly independent in his own resources, possessing a considerable interest in his native soil, and having, moreover, a large and profitable connection with the gum trade. He is a person of a very modest and retiring disposition, living in a quiet row, where he was known only to his immediate neighbours. The natural sweetness of his disposition was never for a moment marred, though creatures of extreme acidity of temperament frequently passed his way. When I was preparing for college he was invaluable to me as a grinder, for he was exceedingly well up in that profession, and imparted his services with right good will, as if he had a personal interest in the matter. And yet, with all his natural talents, that modesty of character to which I have alluded would never permit him to be drawn out, even in moments of his greatest excitement, which were not rare, as he was very nervous by nature. I am indebted to him for many wise saws, but his pet one was, "My boy, I would fain keep a guard upon your tongue." Towards his latter end he contributed largely by his energy and zeal to promote the interests of a local corporation, which grew and expanded beneath his fostering care, and which now with unfeigned sorrow deplores his loss. He had a *penchant* for neatness, and even to the last morning of his life brushed up with all the air of a gallant. A short time before his departure he was to all appearance in his usual good health, having breakfasted heartily on spiced beef and the etceteras. Resting after the meal in his easy chair, he suddenly dropped off and expired. A coroner's inquest was held, and the verdict had well nigh been "acci*dental* death," until it was ascertained that the deceased had been for some time suffering from a decay of the constitution, which, acting on a nervous temperament, caused him to indulge during his latter days in loose habits of living. He leaves no issue, having disappeared root and branch. It may be said in truth that he leaves a void which cannot be easily filled up. His neighbours regret his demise exceedingly, for he was to them a constant prop and support, and they look forward with considerable apprehension to their own not remote decease, which will no doubt be greatly accelerated by his lamentable removal. He was interred with all the honours, and sleeps in the hopes of a glorious resurrection, his occupation being gone, and never to be resumed, even in a future world ; for who on earth could imagine what would be the functions in heaven of such a thing as—

A JAW-TOOTH?

www.ingramcontent.com/pod-product-compliance
Lightning Source LLC
Chambersburg PA
CBHW032021220426
43664CB00006B/320